JUDAISM MUSICAL AND UNMUSICAL

JUDAISM MUSICAL AND UNMUSICAL

Michael P. Steinberg

THE UNIVERSITY OF CHICAGO PRESS

CHICAGO AND LONDON

MICHAEL P. STEINBERG is director of the Cogut Center for the Humanities, Barnaby Conrad and Mary Critchfield Keeney Professor of History, and professor of music at Brown University. His most recent book is *Listening to Reason: Culture, Subjectivity, and Nineteenth-Century Music.*

The University of Chicago Press, Chicago 60637
The University of Chicago Press, Ltd., London
© 2007 by The University of Chicago
All rights reserved. Published 2007
Printed in the United States of America

16 15 14 13 12 11 10 09 08 07   1 2 3 4 5

ISBN-13: 978-0-226-77194-6   (cloth)
ISBN-13: 978-0-226-77195-3   (paper)
ISBN-10: 0-226-77194-6   (cloth)
ISBN-10: 0-226-77195-4   (paper)

Earlier versions of several chapters in this book were previously published, as follows. Chapter 2, as "The Family Romances of Sigmund Freud," in *Metropole Wien: Texturen der Moderne*, ed. Roman Horak, Wolfgang Maderthaner, and Siegfried Mattl, 2: 107–23 (Vienna: Universitatsverlag, 2000). Chapter 3, as "Broken Vessels: Aestheticism and Modernity in Henry James and Walter Benjamin," in *Rediscovering History: Culture, Politics, and the Psyche*, ed. Michael S. Roth, 202–23 (Stanford: Stanford University Press, 1994). Chapter 4, as "The Collector as Allegorist: Goods, Gods, and the Objects of History," in *Walter Benjamin and the Demands of History*, ed. Michael P. Steinberg, 88–118 (Ithaca: Cornell University Press, 1996). Chapter 5, as "Reading Charlotte Saloman: History, Memory, Modernism," in *Reading Charlotte Saloman*, ed. Michael P. Steinberg and Monica Bohm-Duchen, 1–20 (Ithaca: Cornell University Press, 2006). Chapter 7, as "Leonard Bernstein in Wien oder: Das Judentum durch die Musik," in *Quasi una Fantasia: Juden und dei Musikstadt Wien*, ed. Leon Botstein and Werner Hanak, 169–78 (Vienna: Wolke Verlag, 2003).

Library of Congress Cataloging-in-Publication Data

Steinberg, Michael P.
    Judaism musical and unmusical / Michael P. Steinberg.
        p.   cm.
    Includes bibliographical references and index.
    ISBN-13: 978-0-226-77194-6 (cloth : alk. paper)
    ISBN-13: 978-0-226-77195-3 (pbk. : alk. paper)
    ISBN-10: 0-226-77194-6 (cloth : alk. paper)
    ISBN-10: 0-226-77195-4 (pbk. : alk. paper)
        1. Jews—Europe, Central—Civilization. 2. Jews—Europe, Central—Identity.
    I. Title.
DS135.E83S73 2007
305.892'4043—dc22

                                                                2007035062

For Suzanne

CONTENTS

ILLUSTRATIONS

There is a Jewish freethinker's saying about Paris—*wie Gott in Frankreich*. Meaning that even God took his holidays in France. Why? Because the French are atheists and among them God himself could be carefree, a *flâneur*, like any tourist.
—Saul Bellow, *Ravelstein*[1]

What is Jewish in Mahler does not participate directly in the folk element, but speaks through all its mediations as an intellectual voice, something non-sensuous yet perceptible in the totality. This, admittedly, abolishes the distinction between the recognition of this aspect of Mahler and the philosophical interpretation of music in general.
—Theodor Adorno, *Mahler*[2]

This is a study of modernity and Jewish self-consciousness. The term self-consciousness resonates ambiguously in English, referring at once to self-knowledge and self-doubt—the two components, one might argue, of interpretation. In keeping with much recent writing on Jewish history and culture, the approach here finds accuracy and reality in a pattern of contiguous Judaisms rather than in a single, encompassing Judaism whose principle of coherence must perforce depend on criteria of exclusion. Judaism's encounter with modernity is a complicating and above all a self-complicating affair. It involves an encounter with time and space, with the legacies, residues, and inadequacies of history, and with the world at large in its endless variations. In all these spheres, which themselves intertwine, it encounters infinite variation. It commits increasingly to secular time and worldliness rather than to sacred time and a messianic understanding of history.[3]

Inhabiting the modern—a term, like all the others used here, which requires constant definition—means inhabiting two of its major arteries: secularity and aesthetics. These forms of self-conscious experience are to be understood as primary categories and not as epiphenomena, displacements, or symptoms of loss. They require rigorous and constant definition and analysis but no apologies.

"Modernity" I understand as a post-Romantic reconsideration of the Enlightenment, as a ratification of the latter's drive to emancipation combined with a revision of its proclamation of the new, the transparent, the ahistorical. Modernity works, in the shadow of the past, toward what Freud called repetition with difference. The more accountable it remains to the pressures of repetition, the more competent it becomes to enact difference, to achieve emancipation, which in turn amounts always to an emancipation from the past. The word "modernity" is Baudelaire's; his usage—in the 1859 essay "The Painter of Modern Life"—and the term's legacy presuppose an aesthetic dimension of life and of the critical understanding of life. Modernity encompasses an aesthetic of (modern) life. The border between "modernity" and "modernism" is therefore somewhat blurred from the start. Whereas modernism tends subsequently to refer to more or less discrete movements defined within realms of art, modernity for Baudelaire and his most incisive readers—Walter Benjamin first among them—retains an aesthetic dimension of life that partners an emancipatory and otherwise political focus. As a view of modern life and indeed a demand for modern life, a will to the modern, "modernity" insists on an aesthetic component that refuses to be overtaken by aestheticism, in another word the ideology or autonomy of the aesthetic. In its most generous combinations of the emancipatory and the aesthetic, modernism offers a politically reasonable possibility of an existential norm too often appropriated by the politically illegitimate and the reactionary: namely, authenticity. Authenticity and its locutionary partner sincerity (as Lionel Trilling paired them up some decades ago) thus have and keep a place in modernity that is critically and politically viable. For Trilling, sincerity and authenticity are closely related, each embracing the value of the honest soul, a figure he associates with Jane Austen. But if sincerity remains mostly a function of utterance, authenticity accrues, for Trilling, as a "sentiment of being"—including the being of the unconscious—and as a sentiment of art. These values derive mostly from Jean-Jacques Rousseau, for whom the juxtaposition of being and art is equal to—and equally vexed as—that of life and theater. Thus Trilling:

> A synonym for the sentiment of being is that "strength" which, Schiller tells us, "man brought with him from the state of savagery" and which

he finds it so difficult to preserve in a highly developed culture. The sentiment of being is the sentiment of being strong.[4]

As a way of inhabiting and analyzing the world, modernity revisits two basic Enlightenment discourses on politics and art. The first addresses the relationship between authority and freedom. The second addresses that between form and pleasure. As a friendly revision of the claim of Enlightenment, the modernism of "repetition with difference" retains a close, dialectical relationship with the past. This same characteristic defines, in my usage, the term "secularity," which I use as distinct from the more generic historians' word "secularization." Secularization implies a linear and total process with a goal, and that goal is either the emancipation from the sacred combined with a victorious rationality if the process is a normative one, or the loss of meaning and morality and the decay of culture if the process is a negative one.

Secularity incorporates a theory of history: an interpretation of the meaning of the past along with a reinterpretation of the past itself. It involves a taking of distance from the past together with a critical preservation of its enduring meaning. Secularity must not be confused with cultural loss or with "assimilation," a category that has thankfully lost much of its authority in modern Jewish historiography. (Not much is gained, however, by "acculturation," its default replacement.) Neither "assimilation" nor "acculturation" approaches the existential and epistemic grasp of secularity, which strives to harness history and particularity in the making of a viable modern life. In a passage I will cite again in chapter 6, Arnaldo Momigliano identified secularity's character (and his own scholarly as well as existential attachment to it) when he wrote: "I am not collecting facts for academic purposes when I try to understand what moved the Jews to refuse assimilation to surrounding civilizations." Although he continues, "I could choose to give an answer to this question in religious and moral terms," he chooses instead "to clarify my ideas on this matter in historical terms."[5]

Modernity, secularity, aesthetics. With these categories, and in the ways I want simultaneously to historicize and theorize them here, the nineteenth century reclaimed the Enlightenment through the lenses of Romanticism. In central Europe, Romanticism follows continuously from the Enlightenment, combining aesthetics and temporality with reason and freedom. German Romanticism divides into a long, emancipatory phase and a second, conservative phase, in which mystery and authority resurge. The later life of Goethe (1749–1832) becomes the carrier, calendar, and metaphor of Romanticism's emancipatory youth. Goethe's legacy and the Enlightenment-Romantic continuum are best characterized according to the principle of *Bildung*, or self-imaging. The engine of *Bildung* is thoroughly modern. It loves history but rejects origins; it is aesthetically constituted but ethically demanding. It therefore rejects aestheticism as well. For these reasons, it becomes the "secular religion," the ideology, perhaps even the fetish of German Jews, for whom Goethe remains the culture hero par excellence.[6] The idea and ideology of *Bildung* carry Romanticism westward, through Mme. de Staël to France and through Samuel Taylor Coleridge and his readers, foremost among them John Stuart Mill, to Britain. Mill possessed early fluency in French (as well as, more famously, in Latin and Greek); he learned German privately during a decade, the 1820s, when only two scholars at Oxford University were able to read it.[7]

This book focuses on Central Europe, a category in need as well of ongoing definition. It is a famously rubbery category. It is often assumed to encompass German Europe only. The term *Mitteleuropa* in fact served this nationalizing purpose for over a century.[8] Alternatively, the idea of central Europe functions more attractively as a transnational and translinguistic indicator, stretching latitudinally to include Hungary and parts of the Slavic world; occasionally it stretches to the south and includes northern Italy (most specifically the regions under Austrian control between 1797 and 1867). The idea of central Europe, unlike *Mitteleuropa*, allows the Italianness of Trieste, for example, to reside alongside its inherited and lingering Austrianness. In the post-Cold War era, the Central European University, located in Budapest, flags perhaps most clearly the renewal of central Europe as a transnational idea.

Geography remains a basic indicator, allowing for cultural and political complications to come forward. Though central Europe's internal political boundaries are brittle and volatile, its cultural and linguistic inhabitations are fluid and multiple. Its physical and cultural topographies encourage participation in as well as identification with multiple cultures and languages. Education partners multilinguality, and the multilingual and multicultural mind often wonders which language to call home. Most of the people addressed in what follows spoke many languages, sometimes by choice, sometimes by necessity, and often by both. Multilinguality and its relations to deeply constituted multivalent subjectivities are topics just beginning to be engaged seriously.[9]

The discussions here focus mostly on German Europe but include Italy in one chapter as well as England, France, and the United States in parts of others. At the same time, they highlight the cosmopolitan character and reach of the figures and discourses in play. Central Europe engaged and transformed all these places. The well-known identification of Jews with Central Europe as well as with the Enlightenment and the modern fits with the valorization of the multicultural. European Jewish modernity, from the Enlightenment on, chose a multicultural option, arguing for the deterritorialization of culture in general more than for the deterritorialization of their particular culture alone.[10]

Of course Jewish culture was not cosmopolitan or global by intention alone; consistently subject to anti-Judaism and anti-Semitism, it was forced, after 1933, to emigrate in order to survive. Cosmopolitanism, in exile, served resilience. Diasporas and multiculturalisms of choice sometimes blended with those of necessity. The forced migrations of the twentieth century increasingly dislodged culture, memory, and lived experience from the assumption of native ground. Thus, Hungarian Jews spoke and/or learned German as a preferred language of cosmopolitanism; German Jews spoke and/or learned French for the same reason; many of these same Hungarians or Germans then learned Spanish and English, in these cases most often by necessity. Accordingly, New York also became a part of central Europe, as any habitué of many of its neighborhoods and much of its cultural life can detect still today, despite the waning of the émigré generations.[11] Indeed, serious studies of European, Asian, and Latin American cultures in the late twentieth and early twenty-first centuries must be diasporic and global in both genealogy and reach, and they must certainly not remain satisfied with the geographical borders of the metropolitan powers, which inherit nineteenth-century ingatherings of languages and nation states. If, to be blunt, the Jews and Jewish culture formed a dimension of German culture, then German culture may itself be judged to be richer in New York in the middle third of the twentieth century than in Germany.

The word "Judaism" in my title is an uneasy fit. It functions as a challenge, a gamble, an aggressive question posed to myself and to the reader. I am choosing here the strongest term by which to refer to a historical inheritance, but one whose remaking and reinterpreting is a modern demand. I do not refer here strictly to the structures and claims of a lasting religion, to its claim of a sacred covenant sustained in ahistoricity and immutability from the revelation of the laws at Sinai to the coming of the Messiah. Neither do I refer to the displacement of this principle of totality and immutability onto the claims of a quasi or explicitly national entity: the Jewish people; the nation of Israel, whether before 1948 or since. Rather, I refer to the evolving, diverse, yet referentially coherent experiential world that the German language names *Judentum*.

It is poignant that this most generous term should exist only in German.

An Anglophone rendering of its sense and its implications might more accurately be "Jewishness," "Jewish culture," "Jewish experience." The rigor and subtlety of one recent study of Jewish late antiquity, Shaye Cohen's *The Beginnings of Jewishness*, exemplify the viability of the first term.[12] Cohen consistently reminds that Jewishness is a "variable not a constant." He is not concerned (as one might argue that I should not be either) about the potential weakness of a noun that is itself reclaimed from an adjective. To my ear, however, all the categories save "Judaism" carry a certain timidity, a hunching of the back in the shadow of the doctrinaire *ism* of the master category. I am therefore risking the term "Judaism" because I do not cede marginality to the subject positions I analyze. On the contrary, the fundamental and central place of these subject positions vis-à-vis secular modernity and Jewish inheritance forms both the historical and polemical core of the book. "Jewishness" sounds to me like an apology, a subcategory. Judaism, on the one hand, stands for a tradition of law, language, text, interpretation, and practice of an overwhelming richness and complication, more massive and more profound than what might pass in the contemporary world as an emblem of Jewish culture. True, Torah is more than a bagel, to put the proposition somewhat vulgarly. On the other hand, the bagel may always turn out to be the Proustian madeleine, the skeleton key of memory and history. In this respect, Judaism itself might well be understood as a subcategory of Jewish culture or Jewish experience, if such culture and experience understand the tradition to be contingent on and a dimension of the world. The modern and secular discourses I look at here find their places and their responsibilities, I contend, alongside or in response to religious tradition, to historical particularity, and to the world at large. The modern world is increasingly varied and complex, and modern Jews secularize as they choose to take it on without exclusion, as they distance themselves from the willed pariah status of their ancestors. Modernity wants particularity without isolation from the past or from the world at large. Modernism, by the same token, resides always in a repulsion-attraction dialectic with history.

In a recent essay called "Defining Judaism," Michael Satlow grapples with the same terminological and typological problem, showing how recalcitrant even those scholars who have argued for plurality have been in abandoning some degree of essentializing unity. In seeking a non-essentializing principle that might render the traditions, practices, and histories that fall under "Judaism" coherent, Satlow himself validates, finally, the Wittgensteinian metaphor of the family resemblance. This trope seems to me historically legitimate, so long as the notion of "family" that it works with is complex—constructed, contestable, and fluid. A family resemblance must sustain all the pressures of a family reunion.[13]

In this sense I take as a valid and helpful precedent of my own terminological map the choice to translate into English the title of Momigliano's posthumously published Italian collection of essays *Pagine Ebraiche* as *Essays on Ancient and Modern Judaism*.[14] The second, "modern" part of the collection includes an essay called "The Jews of Italy," as well as portraits of Felice Momigliano, Jacob Bernays, Gershom Scholem, Walter Benjamin, and an analysis of the value and flaws of Max Weber's "definition of Judaism as a pariah religion." In other words, the referential world gathered under the rubric "Judaism" is quite similar to the vexed, secularized central European world that I engage in this book. In both cases, complex and contingent subjectivities form and reform themselves according to ways of knowing and self-knowing forged in the Enlightenment and reforged by modernism, in which knowing overtakes being, epistemology displaces ontology. You don't always know who you are, but you are what you know.

The concerns and arguments explored here have accrued over many years. The book's more recent motivation and polemic, however, I can date precisely. They involve a juncture in the unfortunate U.S. presidential campaign of 2000. It becomes steadily clearer that this grim affair amounted to a potentially lasting assault on American democracy. Though it was clear in 2000 how much of an assault on American democracy and decency the Republican campaign and eventual coup d'etat was, no one could have predicted the extent of the political, cultural, and material assault on the world that would accumulate through two terms of the Bush administration.

The 2000 campaign was sustained by Republican violence on the one side and by Democratic martyrology on the other—two different capitulations to the politics of cultural hatred. In one of the season's unexpected moves, Democratic candidate Al Gore selected Joseph Lieberman as his running mate, apparently bringing the "Jewish question" into presidential politics. As my longtime colleagues Laurence Moore and Isaac Kramnick wrote then, however, the Lieberman factor had less to do with Judaism or with the conquest of anti-Semitism in American politics than it had to do with the celebration of a generic, "unassailable, unembarrassed religiosity" as a legitimate and indeed required aspect of American political discourse. Thus the introduction of the "Jewish question" functioned in fact as a summons and satisfaction of the popular, conservative craving for God-talk and for a moralism definable through religion alone.[15] For the neoconservative columnist Charles Krauthammer, writing in *Time* magazine in August 2000, the Lieberman factor posed its most interesting challenge in fact not to Christians but to Jews, specifically to the figure Krauthammer insidiously called the "nominal Jew"—an alleged synonym for the secular Jew. For too long, Krauthammer asserted, American Judaism had been represented by the non-religious—read, in the new code, the non-moral. Thus the virtue of Lieberman's symbolic position affirmed the trinity of morality, religion, and, in his case, Judaism, against the triad of decadence, secularism, and the colonization of religion by immorality and of American *Judentum* by such figures as Woody Allen and Philip Roth.[16]

Such reaction, in my view, assaults the emancipatory potential of the modern. Modernity emancipates by interrogating past absolutes, by making the marginal central. Modernity, as Baudelaire wrote in 1859, is one side of art, the other of which is the eternal and the absolute. In the argument I pursue here, I seek to recombine the marginal and central through an appeal to historical realities, veracities, and complications that have tended to be erased by simpler narratives. Several spheres are in play. The first is the problem of "what is Jewish." The second is the question of what is musical.

What is musical? What is unmusical? Why are such questions important to cultural analysis? Why privilege music, as this book does, in tracing the aesthetic dimension of modernity? Why privilege the musical and the unmusical as metaphors of cultural and critical adequacy?

Music's place in the chapters that follow is both literal and metaphorical. I consider musical works and experiences to be central to the construction of modern European modernity and subjectivity. Because of rather than despite its internal critique of representation, the intelligence of music provides a worthy partner to what Thomas Crow has recently called the intelligence of (visual) art.[17] Such is the argument of my recent book *Listening to Reason: Culture, Subjectivity, and Nineteenth-century Music.*[18] I ask there why music, in its inability (for some), refusal (for others) to signify, to articulate, to represent, became paradoxically a preferred language of inner life in the long nineteenth century from Mozart to Mahler. I argue that music's sincerity and authenticity as a language of subjectivity accrued precisely in conjunction with its suspicion of representation, and its suspicion of the predominantly visual world in which representation is so privileged. The critique of representation is also the critique of modes of old-regime power, of a baroque universe in which the sovereign functions as the earthly representative of divine power and authority. Baroque power displays itself theatrically, through visual pageantry on stages and in pictures. This is representation from above, and thus a political dynamic contrary to the representation from below that we associate with parliamentary or other forms of representative government. The critique of representation can occur within visual media, to be sure. That very agenda is central to modernism. But the rejection of the image or the relative dislodging of the authority of the image and the visual in comparison with other senses and modes of knowledge, such as sound, speech, and music, forms another and perhaps less explored aspect of modernist politics and aesthetics and of the critique of old-regime power and form. Yet because of its incongruity with words as well as other signifying practices, music as a pattern of meaning remains conventionally, and on conventional grounds, underengaged by cultural analysts.

Musicality as a metaphor, in addition, forms another bridge between the literally musical worlds and others. To be musical, to recognize the aesthetic and cultural importance of music, is to recognize the presence of meaning in a non-signifying practice. This is a significant complication. It implies that music's distance from signification and representation is self-aware, and perhaps self-conscious, in the dual meaning this term has in English. Self-consciousness in English means self-aware, self-possessed: what *selbstbewusst* means for Hegel. More idiomatically, it means self-doubting. Thus the resistance to representation and articulation also carries an anxiety about these things. What is musical may also be anxious about its own musicality. In some contexts, the unmusical may be the opposite of the musical; in others, it may be a dimension of the musical, a resistance to the loss of self-consciousness (in both senses of the word).

The modernist "degree zero" of this problem is Arnold Schoenberg's opera *Moses und Aron*, left unfinished in 1933. The opposition of Moses against Aaron is that of truth versus idolatry, of idea versus style, in Schoenberg's own jargon. The character of Aaron and his musical style fuse idolatry with representation. Thus the problem of the image and its prohibition—the *Bilderverbot* often (and often too glibly) associated with Judaism—involves the fusion of representation and absolute, divine power. Pictures are not the problem; pictures with power are. In an idiom marked as seductive and false, Aaron sings in a mellifluous lyricism redolent of operatic tradition, while Moses restricts himself to *Sprechstimme*, to speech patterns placed on designated pitch values. Moses's music—like Schoenberg's, it would not be inaccurate to say—is hypermusical and, to the ear, deliberately unmusical, at least with regard to the more standard sound patterns which opera audiences are likely to have in their ears and which, even if they don't, they hear from the voice of Aaron. When the power of music builds golden calves, truth-in-music refuses music.

In the construction of modernity and its debates about religion and secularity, the metaphor of unmusicality rings most resonant from Max Weber's well-known depiction of himself as "unmusical" in matters of religion. It is not easy to know just how Mosaic this remark was meant to sound, in other words what the mixture is between disdain for religion and a fear of some incompetence in its presence. Thus the founder of the sociology of religion was not a participant himself in religious practice: *ich bin religiös unmusikalisch*, he remarked, I am unmusical in matters of religion, a position later echoed (with the requisite citation) by Jürgen Habermas. Weber's remark is about religion and specifically about the deeply felt awkwardness of his own existential response to it. Habermas's adherence to it reflects the suspicion of the self-conscious (in both senses) German generation of intellectuals after 1945, who fear any form of repetition of what Freud called the oceanic in 1930, in a clear indictment of fascist political seduction.[19] Weber's sentiment and its importance to his intellectual program parallels Freud's and brings to mind as well the more personally fearful resistance to ritual participation of Aby Warburg, who found the mysteries of religious experience in the Hopi serpent ritual (which he did not himself witness) but refused, phobically, to attend his father's funeral and participate in ritual—to recite the Kaddish, or mourning prayer, as the eldest son would be called upon to do.[20]

Freud's diagnosis of religion as a collective neurosis can be placed alongside his professed aversion to music. But we must do so carefully, as recently scholarship has argued that this aversion was much more professed than experienced.[21]

It is Weber's metaphor of unmusicality that has a life of its own. The remark—coming as it does from the founder of the sociology of music as well as the sociology of religion—extends instinctively into questions of music and musicality as well. (Such is not the case for Habermas, with his self-confessed aesthetic allergy.) In Weber's formal work, music evolves historically as a carrier of the general process of "rationalization."[22] Rationalization, a value-neutral term, denotes the historical development of systematic human reason and exchange: language, ritual, economy, etc. Weber's sociology of music stands therefore on the same ambiguous ground as his other sociological models. Is rationalized culture plural or singular; does rationalization occur differently in varied world settings, or is there a single history of rationalization moving inexorably—à la Hegel but then past him—to Weber's own fast-paced and melancholic fin de siècle? It would follow, then, that Weber's own sociologization of music is not in play in his casual remark about his own unmusicality. Indeed, musicality, in the remark itself, figures as the antidote to the rationalized. Musicality, in the metaphor, carries both fact and value; the values it carries are those of sensation (the literal meaning of the "aesthetic"), life, and a performative (in Austin's sense of the word) authenticity. What is musical may have literally to do with music, but it might not. Musicality as a metaphor may function on its own as a critique of rationalization. Rationalization and its critique are normatively ambivalent for Weber, like their close analogues in the typology of the modern, namely disenchantment and reenchantment.

Weber's self-characterization as unmusical did not imply a desire to be more musical in matters of religion. Like Arnold Schoenberg's character Moses, he presumably chose not to enter into a world of melody and sensuality. Moses's religion is a religion of truth, law, and social governance and not a religion of enchantment. Schoenberg's Moses, like Spinoza's, is thus a secular Jew. In question is not belief in God—one cannot imagine Moses without God or Spinoza as an atheist—but rather the exclusion of divine authority as the basis of social legitimacy. The counter-position, Aaron's position as expressed in his melodic singing, can be the world of ideology and idolatry. Faced with this alternative, unmusicality comes into relief less as an inability than as a deliberate disavowal. The question then remains as to whether music and musicality can sustain critique and self-critique. If music can become a language of critique, of critical and self-critical subjectivity, then musicality becomes a kind of ideal, the combination of an aesthetic and analytical discourse and sense of life. In that ideal, the unmusical remains present and essentially, but as a mode of knowing critique, not as a simple absence of the aesthetic. Blunt tone-deafness is also a phenomenon of the musical universe. As a political metaphor, it signals a potentially unhindered barbarism: the failure to hear, the disavowal of other voices and, ultimately, of the voices of the self.

⁂

This book's first chapter was written initially as the keynote address to the symposium "Jewish Identities: An Interdisciplinary Exploration," organized by Lisa Silverman and Marcus Pyka in Vienna in May 2003. This highly rewarding experience cast me—to my amusement and anxiety—in the part of the (relatively) senior scholar for the first time in my career. Being older was no fun; my reward came from the recognition of the profound and rigorous interest in the question of Jewish identity as analytical problem on the part of European and American scholars much younger than myself. Among the Austrians I recognized a new generation of rigorous thinkers about an issue that had gained urgency and public exposure through the Jörg Haider crisis of 1999–2000 as it had not through the Waldheim affair of 1986 and after.

The rigor of these scholars' interest in the "'what is Jewish' question," it seemed to me, involved the overcoming of a cultural exoticism on the part of the (mostly non-Jewish) Europeans, an overcoming at the same time of the temptations to fetishization and its occasional byproduct, namely philo-Semitism. The rigor of the (mostly Jewish) Americans, on the other side, required the transcendence of a certain familiarity and of the dangers (dare I say it) of a certain cultural narcissism. The American Judaism that I know from my childhood and adulthood—from its institutions and its training of children—is routinely guilty, I would assert, of a new intellectual and political provincialism produced by the complacent embrace of "identity" in a safe society (at least for the inhabitation of Jewish identity). Taboos on intermarriage (as indeed, in their most absurd guise, on so-called "interdating"!) and the insistence on an unexamined and uncritical loyalty to Israel form perhaps the primary elements of that embrace. At the same time, the marriage of identity and assimilation is showing signs of stress in American society, with high rates of intermarriage and thus the alleged threat of cultural disappearance hailed as severe symptoms. Rather than responding with viable offers of education about the cultural past and its realities, American Judaism has responded with desperate measures which alienate the most critically aware among the young people it claims to want to keep within the fold. One successful author and speaker, often invited to a congregation I know well, advocates that parents literally pay money to their teenage children against the commitment not to date non-Jewish peers. Thus the polemical dimension of my talk in Vienna and the version of it that opens this book address the present as well as the past. My general position—namely, that the discourse of "identity" does no good for the analysis or appreciation of Jewish history, coherence, or continuity, as it does no good in and for the contemporary world—generated a lively discussion in Vienna, where the issue's stakes are high, as I have occasion to discuss in chapter 1.

Chapters 2, 3, and 4 are revised for their present context from earlier work that seemed to me to contain both the seed and the need of further development. Chapter 2 began as a paper delivered, also in Vienna, to a conference held in 1996 on modernism and urbanism in Austria. Chapters 3 and 4 bring together two essays on Walter Benjamin, a thinker for whom the burdens of secularity—or disenchantment, to use Weber's term—were both heavy and productive. Benjamin himself, against his devotees, cannot be identified with the historical phenomena he engaged so seriously: Messianism, Marxism, and language itself. These concerns and his position relative to them are continuously separate, independent variables that communicate across gaps opened by modernity's whirlwinds, as if Michelangelo's image of the fingers of God and Adam had been caught photographically at the instant prior to their violent separation rather than at the instant of their connection. Thus Benjamin himself resembles the angel of history most often associated with his work via Paul Klee's haunting image. In this respect as well, he belongs in the company of the other figures engaged in this book.

For Charlotte Salomon, a figure who, like Benjamin, did not survive the Nazi persecution and murder of European Jews, the burden of inheritance was mixed: biographically and emotionally overwhelming, but often light and even comical in its capacity for aesthetic reproduction, satire, and, indeed, "working through," Salomon's work is unclassifiable, and for this reason among others, overwhelming.

Unclassifiability also informs the work of Arnaldo Momigliano, though the tone and presence could not be more different. Momigliano, whose depth and agility of learning and whose command of the history of learning have no equal in my frame of reference, is the one figure engaged here whom I knew personally, as my teacher at the University of Chicago. An exile from Italy for the almost fifty years between Mussolini's racial laws of 1938 and his own death in 1987, Momigliano made his principal career in England and the United States but retained an affiliation with the University of Pisa and carried always and only an Italian passport. My first seminar with him devoted a full academic quarter to Max Weber's *Ancient Judaism.* My conjecture above concerning Weber's possible critique of his own model of rationalization finds consistent corroboration in Momigliano's work. For Momigliano, the historian's work seeks the specific, the non-systematizable. Momigliano's lifelong interest in religion as an object of historical analysis combined increasingly, as G. W. Bowersock has written, with an interest in the category of the person, understood as an existential term as well as in an anthropological sense.[23] In the examination of other scholars' work, Momigliano also sought out the personal angles of scholarship, even the eccentric ones. "He was interested in their families," Bowersock wrote, "their marriages, and their drinking habits." But the source of the anthropological discourse of "the person," Marcel Mauss, Momigliano found, in Bowersock's words again, "conspicuously wanting": "He took pains to point out that Mauss was a Jew," and he confessed that "as an Italian, he felt uncomfortable with the French *moi.*" Chapter 6 explores Momigliano's personal as well as historiographical epistemology with respect to the question "what is Jewish." Momigliano's insistence on the sharpest respect for the contexts and vagaries of subjectivities make it hard to say whether his historiography is more science or more art. With some mischief, then, but with less irony that one might assume, I invoke Aby Warburg's bibliocentric "law of the good neighbor" in placing the chapter on Momigliano between those on the artists Salomon and Bernstein.

With an uncanny if undercritical sense of modernity's pulse and troubles, Leonard Bernstein named his *Second Symphony* "The Age of Anxiety" (1948, after W. H. Auden). For Bernstein, the most anomalous figure in the book—in part for his American birth—the burden of history was nonetheless perhaps altogether too light. The result was a sentimentality enabled by a surfeit of sensual genius combined with a poverty of analytical judgment. I first wrote this chapter on Bernstein "on assignment," so to speak, invited to contribute a catalogue essay on Jews in the Viennese musical world after 1945 in conjunction with the exhibition *Quasi una fantasia: Juden in der Musikstadt Wien* produced by the Jewish Museum Vienna in 2003. (The exhibition traveled subsequently to New York's Yeshiva University Museum in 2004.) At first I found the assignment impossible: how to turn absence into presence, to historicize a vacuum? Vienna, "city without Jews," was simultaneously a culture that had exorcised its own cosmopolitanism, its own sense of multiplicity and complication. As it turned out, the focus on Bernstein and his strange fate as a local hero in Vienna in the 1960s provided an unexpected entry into the symbolic return of Jewish culture and "Jewish music" to Vienna, alongside the question of the delusions attached to such a claim of return—whether made by the institutions and spokespersons of Vienna, by Bernstein, or by any historian.

The modesty of the Jewish Museum Vienna, its housing in the so-called Palais Eskeles in the inner city's narrow Dorotheergasse, its restricted exhibition spaces and sparse permanent collection, its housing of a serious bookstore—is contradicted theatrically by the grandeur of the Jewish Museum Berlin. The irony is poignant. Vienna, a city identified with the baroque and therefore with the stage and with the ideology of the world-as-stage, combines museology with the critique of this very ideology. Berlin, inheritor of both the anti-theatricality of its civic and Protestant past and the urban theatricality of the Second and Third Empires *(Reichs)*, combines public history with overwhelmingly theatrical architecture, performance, and ritualization. The Jewish Museum Berlin and its powerful intervention in the culture and politics of memory form the topic of my last chapter. This museum's grandeur is itself multifaceted and possibly self-contradictory. Daniel Libeskind's building is a dramatic act of mourning, memory, and music, expressed in metal and geometry. The historical panorama that fills it is, perhaps, just as large, but as conventional as the building is experimental, as prosaic as the building is sanctimonious. My analysis stresses these ambivalences with respect to the museum's architectural, intellectual, and historiographical success. Libeskind's commission for the rebuilding of the World Trade Center site explicitly brings to the United States the questions of mourning and commemoration, as they have so far related to his formal and descriptive discourses in a European, post-Holocaust context. As such, they encounter the discursive forcefield of what I would call the "new sacredness," which has come, through the 1990s, to inhabit much American academic discourse. At the same time, my skepticism with regard to new sacrednesses notwithstanding, I would suggest that the very presence of an institution such as the Jewish Museum Berlin, and of its Viennese counterpart as well, testifies to the public and financial commitment to the kind of mental work that the German language calls *Vergangenheitsbewältigung:* mastery over the past.[24] To a point, as my short discussion of Freud in chapter 1 will argue, I consider this principle basic to historical work and knowledge: whether personal or general, scholarly or popular, disseminated in print or in other media such as, for example, museum installations.

Clearly, German, Austrian, and Italian responsibilities to the modern past carry specific urgencies. Though public discourse in central Europe may shoulder that burden with mixed success, the proliferation in recent years of sites and other initiatives of memory and history (again, with mixed records of success) shows how seriously states and civil society have begun the task of working through the burdens of the past. Italy remains a puzzling exception here, as its engagement with its fascist past remains stalled in comparison to Germany's, and ever more so in recent, Berlusconi-defined years. A deep sense of history is a long recognized dimension of central European culture, for good and for ill. But among those patterns that form the intricate web of central European culture, this sense of history can often function as a measure of public discourse and public health, and that often in sharp contrast to the discourses emanating from less historically minded and politically more condescending parts of the world.

❦

To an extent, this book's genealogy implies the structure of its acknowledgments as well. Dialogue, exchange, the invitations of friends and the kindness of strangers are the enablers of thinking and scholarship, as they are of culture in general. I am most grateful to teachers, colleagues, and students in settings that really "get" what this book is after, specifically Chicago, Princeton, Cornell, Brown, and Bard; Vienna's Internationales Forschungszentrum Kulturwissenschaften (IFK), the University of Amsterdam's School of Cultural Analysis (ASCA); the American Academy in Berlin. A sabbatical year from Cornell in 2003–2004, combined with a fellowship from the John Simon Guggenheim Memorial Foundation and the Berlin Prize of the American Academy, Berlin, offered the time, place, and collegiality that removed some impediments and excuses from the book's completion but in fact also added others (Berlin has three opera houses . . .). This same combination of inspiration and distraction was repeated in my move to Brown in 2005, where my new colleagues in History, Music, and Judaic Studies have engaged this project in ways that really have made me feel at home.

Working with Susan Bielstein and the University of Chicago Press has also been a kind of homecoming for me. Like the other home in which I grew up, the University of Chicago seems to demand and to reward most. As a child in an émigré family redolent of cosmopolitanism, wisdom, anxiety, and generosity, I learned to trust most those who asked the most of me, and learned often that most was being asked when I was being recognized for who I really was. I have been repeatedly blessed with the same austere luxury in both my professional and personal life. It's a lesson not lost in recording my gratitude to my parents, my children, my friends, and above all to my spouse Suzanne, who "converts everything to knowledge," and to whom I dedicate this book with love.

CHAPTER ONE

The House and the World

On Jewish Experience
and the Critique of Identity

I

In July 2000, by his own account, Edward Said—University Professor of English and Comparative Literature at Columbia University—was invited to give the annual Freud Lecture at the Freud Institute and Museum in Vienna. The proposed date was May 2001. By his own account again, he "promptly accepted, having written about Freud and for many years been a great admirer of his work and life."[1] Several weeks before receiving the invitation, Said had visited southern Lebanon with family members, where, in a much debated and much disputed incident, he was photographed at the site of an abandoned Israeli border post, throwing a stone. The incident was widely reported as a gesture of symbolic or indeed real participation in the actions of *Intifada*, though most of this reporting accumulated after the onset of the so-called second or Al Aqsa intifada in September 2000, several months following this incident.[2] Said's own account of the event does not completely clarify its intention or its meaning. He writes: "During our 10-minute stop I was photographed there without my knowledge pitching a tiny pebble in competition with some of the younger men present, none of whom of course had any particular target in sight." In the same piece, however, Said also describes his action as "having thrown a stone (an act rightly characterized as protected speech)." Presumably, pebble pitching requires no such protection.

Among the multiple repudiations and, indeed, hostile campaigns, professional and personal, that ensued, the invitation to lecture at the Freud Museum in Vienna was withdrawn. The withdrawn invitation became part of the controversy; an article in the *New York Times* in March 2001 included a statement from the Freud Institute's chairman, W. Schulein, to the effect that Said's presence might offend Viennese Jews in the aggravated context of Jörg Haider's prominence and the recent entry of his Freedom Party into the government.

At this point the London Freud Museum stepped into the fray, inviting Said to present his lecture there. He did so, giving the lecture he had written for Vienna, entitled "Freud and the Non-European." Subsequently published as a small book, this piece is largely a reading of Freud's last work, *Moses and Monotheism*.[3] The circumstantial ironies of both event and text are rich. Freud wrote Parts 1 and 2 and the first pages of Part 3 of *Moses and Monotheism* in Vienna in 1937 and early 1938. He continued in June 1938 in London, almost certainly writing in the study of the house that is now the Freud Museum in Maresfield Gardens. Thus Said's "Freud and the Non-European" repeats *Moses and Monotheism*'s path of exile from Vienna to London.

Within and in many ways contingent on this circumstantial shell, however, resides Said's reading of Freud. In this reading, the category of the non-European occupies a structure and position parallel to the non-Jew. For the Freud that Said interprets (not only correctly, I would dare to suggest, but brilliantly), European culture and Jewish culture exist and exist centrally and overwhelmingly as bearers of consciousness, inheritance, and subject position. These existences are material and palpable, but reside below the threshold of articulation. This is the same kind of vexed presence that Said recognizes in music. Like Theodor Adorno, to whom he paid increasing attention in his later work, Said found in music a rigorous engagement with cultural reality and cultural argument, always informed by a high degree of self-consciousness, indeed by an anxiety, about the possibilities of legitimate articulation. The integrity of such categories as the European, the Jewish, and indeed the musical exists precisely in the borderlessness between them and their formal opposites, namely the non-European, the non-Jewish, the nonmusical. In this position Said finds Freud's radicality as a cultural thinker.

"Freud," Said writes, "had his own ideas about non-European outsiders, most notably Moses and Hannibal. Both were Semites of course, and both (especially Hannibal) were heroes for Freud because of their audacity, persistence, and courage" (15). He cites "Freud's implicit refusal, in the end, to erect an insurmountable barrier between non-European primitives and civilization," and he locates "the severity of Freud's argument" in the principle of *Nachträglichkeit*, the return of the primitive, the return of the repressed, which winds up being unexpectedly similar to Aby Warburg's unexpectedly subversive principle of the survival through European history of the ancient and the pagan—of which more later.

"Freud's view of Moses as both insider and outsider is extraordinarily interesting and challenging," Said writes (16). He understands Freud's last text as an example of *Spätwerk,* in the company of Beethoven's final and "bristlingly difficult works," apparently composed for himself,

> with scant attention to frequent and often ungainly repetition, or regard for elegant economy of prose and exposition. . . . Everything about the treatise suggests not resolution and reconciliation . . . but, rather, more complexity and a willingness to let irreconcilable elements of the work remain as they are: episodic, fragmentary, unfinished (i.e. unpolished). . . . Like Beethoven's late works, Freud's *Spätwerk* is obsessed with returning not just to the problem of Moses's identity—which of course, is at the core of the treatise—but to the very elements of identity itself, as if that issue so crucial to psychoanalysis, the very heart of the science, could be returned to in the way that Beethoven's late work returns to such basics as tonality and rhythm. (28–29)

As if the issue of identity could be returned to—this is Said's most trenchant and, at this point, most cryptic, proposition.

In contrast to many of his most sympathetic interpreters (to say nothing of his hostile ones), Freud does not reach conclusions about what is historically Jewish because, as Said argues, "the actual Jewishness that derives from Moses is a far from open-and-shut matter, and is in fact extremely problematic." Said describes Freud's position as "deliberately antinomian," invoking a category he (I would assume) knows to resonate from the contexts of anti-rabbinicism, kabbalism, mysticism, heresy, and—in a more secular context—the position of the pariah, as Hannah Arendt deployed the term to refer to a Jewish voice that speaks through barriers of exclusion and self-exclusion both from the Gentile world and from official Judaism. Here Said recalls the hubristic opening of *Moses and Monotheism,* in which Freud claims that in his account of the historical Moses he will "deny a people the man whom it praises as the greatest of its sons," and that he will do so in the interest of truth and with a heavy heart as "one belonging to that people." The point here, of course, is that Freud's Moses is "outed" and "othered" as an Egyptian, as the leading inheritor of the monotheistic revolution of Akhnaton. But in fact Freud does not take Moses away from the Jews; rather, he takes identity and the myth of origin (Moses's origin, Judaism's origin) away from Moses and thereby also away from the Jews.

For Said, Freud's othering of Moses is contradicted, at least to a point, by his wish to preserve the fundamentally European identity of the Jews, a

position Said ascribes to Freud's desire "protectively to huddle the Jews inside, so to speak, the sheltering realm of the European" in a period of raging
anti-Semitism, itself founded on an exclusion of Jewry from the category
of the European. But here I think Said's position is ultimately less radical
than Freud's, less willing to disavow the very idea of identity, the very idea
of a boundary. For Said, the European ideology of twentieth-century Jewry
becomes identical to the Zionism that excludes "non-Europeans," i.e. non-
Jews, from Palestine. Said's anti-Zionist stance, which he is obviously not
taking for the first time here, would in fact be strengthened in the context
of this particular argument were he to point out of that the Eurocentrism
of early Zionism pertained in fact to Theodor Herzl's version, which succeeded first in neutralizing the binational Zionism of Bernard Lazare and
the *Brit Shalom* movement, but has been displaced in recent years by a
politics of Jewish inclusion focusing on African and Middle Eastern Jews
in absolute distinction from non-Jews from the same regions. As a form of
nationalism, and consistent with the governing principle of all nationalisms
whereby inclusion is contingent on exclusion, contemporary Zionism has
clearly adjusted its earlier Eurocentrism. Freud's time and generation may
have foreclosed on a sensitivity to the politics of Eurocentrism that someone
like Frantz Fanon would call so passionately into question a generation later.
Europeanness, however, like Jewishness, sits potentially on all points of
the political spectrum. The European ideas of Metternich and Cecil Rhodes
may stand for central and colonial authority both within and beyond the European continent; the Europeanness of cosmopolitanism and international
cooperation stands as a challenge to the centralized power of nations and
nationalism. The structure of Jewishness is similarly complex. European
Judaism—in the sense of *Judentum*, or Jewish culture—is closely linked
to cosmopolitanism; Zionism is without doubt a representative of modern
nationalism. Nationalism signifies in conflicting ways—as legitimate self-
constitution, as a stamp of legitimacy on power and violence. Thus, the
state of Israel is understood on one side as a bearer of European cosmopolitanism, on the other as European colonialism. The overwhelming presence
of historical and political contingency impugns the veracity of any alleged
sameness, or identity, as a handle on these categories.

Said distinguishes, finally between *identity* and *Identity*. Freud's Judaism, like Freud's Moses, preserves identity in the sense of a cultural continuity, coherence, and solidarity but disavows the incorporation of that
identity "into one, and only one, Identity." This kind of distinction is in fact
quite common. At most of the discussions, conferences, and symposia on
questions of Jewish identity in which I have participated, the consensus has

been to avoid the advocacy of a specific historical, religious, or other notion of identity, but to obey a basically Eriksonian sympathy with—and desire for—a notion of identity as a lived authenticity, whence the desire to keep in play a vocabulary of identity—now made kinder and gentler in the guises of the multiple, the ever evolving, the diasporic, the negotiated, the performative. But the problem, to my ear, is that the word identity simply explodes if its definitional assertion of sameness is abandoned. Sameness, that is, not only coherence, continuity, or communication, or indeed for that matter adherence, solidarity, or citizenship. In other words, the vocabulary of identity carries a lexical implication of sameness; it posits, or claims to posit, an identity between two entities. The ideological structure of a proposition such as "Fritz is a German" lodges in its inherent desire performatively to transform an attribute or characteristic into an identity, in other words to transform an "A = B" proposition into an "A = A" proposition. If its nationalism is working, then "Fritz is a German" carries the claim of "A = A" and not "A = B." But for the cultural analyst, as indeed for the psychoanalyst, an "A = B" formulation cannot be changed into an "A = A" equation without a certain violence. The word identity and its usage thus activate the risk of a measure of both analytical and political laziness, if not violence, at the very least. The sameness invoked by the vocabulary of identity asserts a sameness between individuals and collectives, past and present, self and other, and indeed between layers of the self-knowing and self-deceiving self.

Said concludes "Freud and the Non-European" with a stunningly generous statement of hope about the ultimate resolvability of the conflict between Jews and Palestinians (note that he says Jews, not Israelis, a choice both understandable and questionable). He stakes his optimism on the example of Freud's "unresolved sense of identity," a condition that he, like Freud, perceives to be "more general in the non-European world than [Freud] suspected" (55). Although the characterization of "Freud's unresolved sense of identity" is certainly generous and in no obvious way wrong, it clouds the radicality of the fact that Freud never relied on a principle of identity of any kind, in any field, from the clinical to the speculative, the therapeutic to the anthropological, the psychological to the so-called metapsychological. Identity, like "memory," is a term of desire redolent of our own time, our own fin de siècle. Both give way, in Freud's lexicon, to the language of subjectivity, culture, history, and knowledge.

Freud's radicality on this issue opens up a reading of *Moses and Monotheism* that is likewise consistent not only with Said's reading but with his own overall political posture in relation to Judaism. From this angle, *Moses and Monotheism* emerges not as an intellectual rape of Judaism and its sense of identity, which would require Moses to be in some strong sense a Jew, i.e. of Jewish origin, but rather a valedictory gift to European Jews and Judaism at a desperate moment. Freud's account of Moses opens the possibility of his Jewishness by constitution and not by origin. (The classificatory category of "constitution," used by Heinrich Graetz in his *Structure of Jewish History*, strikes me as highly productive for its emphasis on legality and historicity.)[4] Freud's Moses thereby gives to the Jews—and now I refer to the European Jews at the moment of their most desperate danger—the understanding of contemporary Jewishness that is in fact a Jewishness of constitution—of subjectivity, history, culture, and knowledge, and precisely not the mechanistic regression to origins which in its most horrible form is the argument of the Nuremberg Laws. Freud can therefore be understood to say to his fellow Jews what his hero Goethe famously said—a citation Freud highlighted in another context:

Was du ererbt von deinen Vätern hast,
Erwirb es, um es zu besitzen.
What you inherit from your fathers,
Earn it, in order to possess it.[5]

Freud's position on this thought, crucial to the Oedipal conflict which he invents, at once honors and revises it, arguing that for sons and fathers as for culture and history, the past is never overcome or replaced, but engaged and confronted, with the happiest result being a combination of internalization and repetition on the one side, and autonomy, dignity, and peace on the other. The knowledge that mediates between the two sides is knowledge of history, the knowledge allowed to and capable of organizing the relations of past and present, other and self. The historical consciousness that feeds the healthy ego on the other side of the Oedipal conflict might be summarized according to the motto "Make it/history your own, in order to manage it." Oedipal resolution (or, rather, more modestly, functional resolution), works as a kind of *Vergangenheitsbewältigung*, which in turn functions always as generational or intergenerational work. In this sense, Freud's *Moses* (the text now, not the man) is indeed antinomian, but it commands that key, double aggression that takes on both Jewish and anti-Semitic ideology, the laws of the rabbis and the laws of Nuremberg.

If Freud's *Moses* is thus readable as a gift to the Jews, Said's lecture is understandable in the same light. The delivery of his lecture on Freud in Vienna, as originally planned, would have been a gift to public discourse in Austria, to the discussion of Judaism in Austria, precisely because the politics of Jewish identity is of urgent concern there, possibly more so than it is in England, the host country of Said's exiled Freud lecture.

2

The historiography of modern Jewish life in central Europe has paid scant attention to regional differences and comparative dimensions. The spectrum of north and south, Protestant and Catholic, Prussia and Austria is particularly unattended. Thus, "the Jews of Germany" and "the Jews of Austria" are instinctively separated into discrete scholarly spheres, perhaps correctly so, but that separation usually pays insufficient attention to its own analytical motivations and, more importantly, insufficient attention to the ramifications of those differences with respect to internal Jewish consistency. It is crucial, in my judgment, that the majority culture of the German north is largely Protestant; that of the south, largely Catholic. Historical experience in general must be understood in the context of these facts. So must the sub-categories of such experience—intellectual, political, religious; Jewish, Protestant, Catholic. That the Jews of Prussia engaged with a Protestant world remains fundamental not only for dialogue with the outer world but for the inner constitution of Jewish subjectivities, individual as well as collective.

The northern Enlightenment, Moses Mendelssohn's Enlightenment, is thus both dialogically and internally consistent with a Protestant ideational and discursive world, a world of words, texts, and the suspicion of visuality and regimes of representation. The word carries authority over the image in this culture. Mendelssohn's friend and interlocutor G. E. Lessing argued this case in aesthetic terms alone in his treatise *Laocoön: An Essay on the Limits of Painting and Poetry* (1766). With reference to the classical sculptural group depicting the murder of the Trojan priest by serpents unleashed by the pro-Greek god Neptune, Lessing argues that the poet, in this case Virgil, can use words and their sequential, temporal unfolding *(Nacheinander)* to depict violence and bodily pain with a sense of reality. The sculptor, however, who must present the full story in a single, synchronic flash *(Nebeneinander)*, must mediate the depiction so as not to render it obscene. Look to words for reality, Lessing argues, rather than to pictures, a position perhaps more redolent of cultural context than of formal authority.[6]

Lessing is identified most closely with the city of Hamburg, where he both founded and theorized (as his *Hamburger Dramaturgie* [1767–68]) a new theater. This was a theater of the word, as distinct from a theater of the image, which he identified with the Catholic world. The German Enlightenment and its main voices worked with words.

How Lessing's aesthetics relate to his lifelong campaign for Jewish dignity (the motivations of which remain unknown) remains an open question.[7] The Jewish Enlightenment in the northern German world was largely conceived in dialogue, with the Mendelssohn-Lessing dialogue and friendship serving as its center and example. The dignity of argument produced the partnership and indeed the symbiosis of philosophical enlightenment and political emancipation. The relative absence of anything that might be called a Jewish Enlightenment in Austria is at least partially interpretable, on the other hand, in terms of Jewish-Catholic incompatibility on these issues. The absence of a Jewish-Austrian Enlightenment results in an increase of pressure, for the formation of Jewish modernity, on the liberal and modernist generations after 1859, the year in which military defeat in Italy led the young emperor Franz Josef to capitulate to those liberals campaigning for a parliament. Austrian modernism, Jewish and non-Jewish alike, thus evolves with little reference to an Enlightenment foundation. The history of Austrian Jewish modernism runs through two, perhaps three generations; the history of German Jewish Enlightenment and modernism courses through at least double that number.

It is perhaps this increased pressure on the generations of Austrian modernism that has produced two substantial errors in the interpretations of its Jewish dimensions. I will call these Gombrich's error (i.e., the claim that Austrian modernism has nothing to do with the Jews) and Beller's error (i.e., the claim that Austrian modernism has only to do with the Jews). Gombrich's undervaluation and Beller's overvaluation of Jews and Jewish culture in the production of Austrian modernism both result from a certain kind of essentialism or, indeed, identitarianism in their discussions of culture itself. Both positions turn their backs on the multiplicities and contingencies of the modern: Jewish-Protestant in the north; Jewish-Catholic (a more vexed relationship) in the south.[8]

The differences between the cultures and multicultures of northern and southern central Europe intensify if we track its continuities to the constitution of émigré culture following 1933 (for Germany) and 1938 (for Austria). History requires such an extension, as central European culture traveled with the émigrés. It is well known that the intellectual and university cultures of Great Britain and the United States were profoundly affected—in the case of the United States, decisively transformed—by émigré scholarship. In this context I would risk the speculation that in those fields where reference to specific genealogies of discourse is relevant, i.e., in the social and human sciences, the conscious reference to Germany exceeds and outlasts that to Austria. This hypothesis would need much more testing than

I can provide here. But the intellectual legacies of German philosophy and political theory, to name two fields, resonate powerfully and with conscious reference to their German genealogies. This intellectual style differs pointedly, to cite the most obvious counterexample, from the way that psychoanalysis after Freud becomes British and American in its articulations and disseminations.

3

In October 1943, in New York, half way through her eighteen-year trajectory as a stateless person but already as a master of idiomatic, polemical English, Hannah Arendt composed a withering review of a popular memoir written by a fellow émigré thinker. The book was *Die Welt von Gestern, The World of Yesterday*; the author: Stefan Zweig, born in Vienna in 1881 and recently a suicide in his place of exile—Petropolis, Brazil. The famous biographer and storyteller had attracted significant attention in the double *Liebestod* he staged along with his second wife. That attention peaked with the publication of his suicide note, in which he declared his inability to live outside the bounds of his native language.

Arendt, who could so easily have sympathized with Zweig's predicament, turned on him instead with surging venom. Arendt's own bilinguality was a function of both linguistic and emotional prowess. She held onto German as she mastered English. After all, she told a German interviewer in 1964, it was not the language that went crazy.[9] Zweig's attachment to his native language was, for Arendt, a symptom of his regressive sentimentality, the emotion that governed his sense of the world in general. Zweig, she wrote, had never understood the world he lived in, and moreover he showed no understanding for the past he now brought to life, in *The World of Yesterday*, with heightened nostalgia. He confused political dignity with personal and social privilege; such had been his own undoing. In his writing, he confused the aesthetic and aestheticizing claims of Habsburg Vienna with social and political reality. He took his models from the stage and thought that the world of the Burgtheater carried a revival of democratic Athens: the rebirth of the polis that had once produced the art of tragedy, the polis that in fact lodged at the core of Arendt's own normative political philosophy. But the theatrical world of fin-de-siècle Vienna that Zweig compared to Athens, Arendt asserted, was in fact its opposite. It was—and here is her most devastating punchline—Hollywood. Zweig, wrote Arendt, "overlooked the fact that the Athenians attended the theatre for the sake of the play, its mythological content and the grandeur of its language, through which they hoped to become the masters of their passions and moulders of their national destiny. The Viennese went to the theatre exclusively for the actors. . . . The star system, as the cinema later perfected it, was completely forecast in Vienna. What was in the making there was not a classical renaissance but Hollywood."[10] All *Schein*, she would have said were she still writing as a German philosopher, and no *Sein*.

Not that Arendt was hostile to the theatrical. In fact, the political sphere she strove throughout her career to defend and restore depended on the performative abilities of its participant speakers. But Arendt's theatricality is that of the speech act and not of the stage in a literal sense, where—*pace* performance studies—original utterances and originary deeds are not primarily at stake. Arendt vs. Zweig thus amounts to a strong distinction (if not necessarily a clean opposition) between reason and representation, action and acting, performativity and theatricality.

Arendt vs. Zweig also replays the cultural enmity of Berlin vs. Vienna, a dimension of central European culture that travels far and wide into the émigré experience and remains too regularly overlooked in all of its venues by American scholars of central Europe. Berlin vs. Vienna inherits the chasms between Protestantism and Catholicism, between the word and the stage, an attitude carried with special urgency when carried by the Jews: the Protestant Jews, we might call them, in their disdain for the Catholic Jews. (A reminder: these cultural recipes have nothing to do with "assimilation," but with intricate patterns of learned, lived multicultural experience as well as ideology.)

Hannah Arendt was an émigré from Prussia. In a famous exchange from 1963 with her fellow Berliner Gershom Scholem, a severe rift emerges between these two cultural *semblables* whose temperaments would seem much closer than those of a Berliner and a Viennese. Arendt and Scholem knew each other personally, but certainly not well, through meetings in Germany and in Paris (the latter in 1935), and through their mutual interest in Walter Benjamin. They differed increasingly and bitterly over their understandings of Jewish identity, modernity, and Zionism. That divide emerged with the publication of Arendt's 1944 essay "Zionism Reconsidered" and Scholem's response in a personal letter of January 1946. Arendt wrote in the aftermath of the meeting of the American branch of the World Zionist Organization in October 1944, and specifically of their unanimous call for a "free and democratic Jewish commonwealth . . . [which] shall embrace the whole of Palestine." [11] Arendt judged this turn of events an accommodation with "extremists" and "a deadly blow to those Jewish parties in Palestine itself that have tirelessly preached the necessity of an understanding between the Arab and the Jewish peoples." She understood this turn as an extreme nationalism, aggravated by injustices in Palestine and "the terrible catastrophes in Europe."

Scholem told Arendt that her essay had disappointed and embittered him.[12] "I am a nationalist," he asserted, who believes "in what can be called, in human terms, the 'eternity' of anti-Semitism." As he does not "give a rap about the problem of the state," he declares himself ready to vote either for partition or for a binational (Jewish-Arab) state, an assertion borne out by his long-lived accommodationist position. Scholem concluded by citing Martin Buber (a thinker for whom he had expressed only contempt as a younger man), and expressing the hope for Arendt's redemption and "return."

This split over the very legitimacy of nationalism deepened as a result of the better known and more public rift between Arendt and Sholem, in the wake of the publication of Arendt's book *Eichmann in Jerusalem: A Report on the Banality of Evil.* Now, in a letter in June 1963, Scholem invoked the principle of "*Ahabath Israel:* 'Love of the Jewish people . . .' In you, dear Hannah, as in so many intellectuals who came from the German Left, I find little trace of this." Arendt responded, a month later:

> I am not one of the "intellectuals who came from the German Left." . . . If I can be said to "have come from anywhere," it was from the tradition of German philosophy. I have always regarded my Jewishness as one of the indisputable factual data of my life, and have never had the wish to change or disclaim facts of this kind. There is such a thing as a basic gratitude for everything that is as it is; for what has been given and was not, could not be made. . . .
>
> To come to the point: let me begin, going on from what I have just stated, with what you call "love of the Jewish people." . . . You are quite right—I am not moved by any "love" of this sort, and for two reasons: I have never in my life "loved" any people or collective—neither the German people, nor the French, nor the American, nor the working class or anything of that sort. I indeed love only my friends and the only kind of love I know of and believe in is the love of persons. Secondly, this "love of the Jews" would appear to me, since I am myself Jewish, as something rather suspect. I cannot love myself or anything which I know is part and parcel of my own person.

Scholem embraces the meaning and value of identity within and beyond Judaism and Zionism, while Arendt disavows them. The position that Arendt works out in these remarks should be understood as a political one,

indeed as the basic orientation of a liberal political philosophy which remains suspicious, above all, of *Weltanschauungen* or other totalizing constructions. Arendt mentions the category of *Weltanschauung* in her correspondence with Scholem, using nationalism and imperialism as examples.
Along with anti-Semitism, these are the historical constellations through
which she organized her massive *Origins of Totalitarianism* (1951). In this
political orientation and specifically in its formulation through issues pertaining to Judaism—historical and her own—Arendt's thinking shows substantial affinity with Freud's, a thinker in whom she had no interest. Indeed,
Arendt had so little interest in Freud that she felt no compunction to account
for her lack of interest. Her philosophical training and her political concerns
kept their distance from the life of the mind according to psychoanalysis.
Here she remained part of a disciplinary as well as a north German fraternity that included her friend Hans Jonas and her antagonist Leo Strauss. The
ethic of responsibility that they brought to bear on the political world and
subsequently on political philosophy had no truck with the unconscious,
individual or cultural, no room for the possibility that the subject of freedom
(to indulge in a Hegelian spin) might not be a master in his own house (to
cite an Oedipal cliché). But in Arendt's case the parallels with Freud are ultimately more significant than the differences, and they account, in my view,
to a great extent for the generosity of her thinking, in marked comparison
to that of Leo Strauss. Freud also rejected, explicitly, the notion of a *Weltanschauung;* for him as well, history was too massive to be bridled by ideology.
Ideology instrumentalizes the past—event, phenomenon, or text.

   Leo Strauss has been canonized by his American followers as an antihis-
toricist, a position he no doubt claimed but also one that he argued and analyzed with much more subtlety, anxiety, and inconsistency than his legacy
allows. For his followers, the point was precisely to instrumentalize the
past, to find a teaching, a use-value, in canonic thinkers of the past. Thus
the past becomes a library, to be consulted by modern thinkers who have
been liberated from its grasp. There is no allowance for *Nachträglichkeit.*
Strauss himself, always more interesting, more complicated, and more self-
admittedly conflicted than his followers, did not hesitate to historicize his
own intellectual formation in the context of German arguments and anxieties of the 1920s. Thus, in his 1962 preface to the English-language edition of
Spinoza's Critique of Religion, a work that began as his dissertation in 1925–
28, Strauss discussed the intellectual world that generated his own thinking
as it did that of Arendt and Scholem. Much *Nachträglichkeit* informed the
youthful work, as the older Strauss recollects forthrightly.

   "The author," Strauss wrote in 1962, "was a young Jew born and raised in Germany who found himself in the grip of the theologico-political predicament."[13] This predicament was defined by Carl Schmitt and Franz Rosenzweig. These figures were the prophets of young Weimar intellectuals, and recognized as such by many, including Walter Benjamin. Schmitt and Rosenzweig both pursued the resacralization of Western thinking away from the weakness of secularization, rationalization, and other faces of modernity. In recalling their power, Strauss simultaneously works through and acts out, symptomatically, their recurrent effect on him. He immediately calls the Weimar Republic weak: the "sorry spectacle of justice without a sword"—a Schmittian position if ever there was one. The first edition, in 1930, had been dedicated to Franz Rosenzweig, who had died in 1929. Strauss recalls him in 1962 as the major critic, along with his own teacher Hermann Cohen, of Spinoza's critique of religion, in other words of Spinoza's theory of secularity. Spinoza had been the hero of German Jewish secularity since the early 1780s, when F. H. Jacobi "outed" G. E. Lessing as a Spinozan.[14] Strauss's abiding loyalty to Rosenzweig and his "new thinking," however, depends less on the resacralization of the world than it does on its dehistoricization. For Rosenzweig, asserts Strauss, "the Jewish people is the ahistorical people."[15] Revelation trumps history, but antihistoricism may be good enough on its own.

What Rosenzweig "meant," writes Strauss, is that "Cohen was a more profound thinker than Spinoza because unlike Spinoza he did not take for granted the philosophic detachment or freedom from the tradition of his own people; that detachment is 'unnatural,' not primary, but the outcome of a liberation from the primary attachment, of an alienation, a break, a betrayal."[16] Written in 1962, these words may in fact have been written—consciously or not—against Hannah Arendt. They echo the terms of Gershom Scholem's attack on the author of *Eichmann in Jerusalem*, cited above.

For Arendt and Freud, the "givenness" of the past insures its *Nachträglichkeit* and its intractability. Thus for Freud as for Arendt, history constitutes a materiality that must be worked through as the cost of subjectivity. History and culture fill what is articulated as the unconscious for Freud, the givenness of the world for Arendt.

That said, it should be noted that the single mention of Freud in Elisabeth Young-Bruehl's intellectual biography of Hannah Arendt concerns the ironic conferral of the 1967 Sigmund Freud Prize by the Deutsche Akademie für Sprache und Dichtung.[17] The award was for excellence in German prose, and it pleased her immensely, just as Freud's 1930 Goethe Prize had been his favorite honor. In Arendt's case, however, as she wrote to the society's general secretary, German style had withstood exile for over thirty years: "It wasn't the German language that went crazy."[18] In the letters to Scholem,

cited above, she persisted, to his clear annoyance, in addressing him as Gerhard, not Gershom, and in one such letter, with the same mischief, she
praised the émigré scholar Kurt Blumenfeld for refusing to change his name
in Israeli immigration, to the outrage, at the time, of David Ben-Gurion. The
attachments are not to Germany, certainly not to nationalism, but to the
past and its presence, or rather its presentness.

Two years before she went to Jerusalem to cover the Eichmann trial for
the *New Yorker*, Arendt had accepted the Lessing Prize of (and in) the Free
City of Hamburg. The published version of her address on that occasion, "On
Humanity in Dark Times," emerges as a double allegory, in which Lessing
stands for Arendt and the troubled Enlightenment for the multiply more
troubled twentieth century. Through this allegorical investment, Arendt
develops with unique clarity and force her lexicon of the worldly, the political, and their individual enactments through the experience of friendship.
"The world lies between people," she asserts, thus attaching worldly values
directly to politics and paving the way for the definition of friendship itself as a political commitment.[19] Lessing's theory and practice of friendship,
which he enacted personally in his well-known friendship with Moses Mendelssohn and which he argued allegorically by portraying Mendelssohn as
Nathan the Wise, marked him as "a completely political person." Lessing's
politics, and Arendt's, insist "that truth can exist only where it is human-
ized by discourse."[20]

The commitment to the world and the worldly stands apart from being at home in the world, "[f]or Lessing never felt at home in the world as
it then existed and probably never wanted to, and still after his own fashion he always remained committed to it."[21] The "dark times" that give the
essay its title (as well as the collection into which it was placed) Arendt
characterizes as periods in which "the public realm has been obscured," in
which survival and self-interest form the limits of political commitment,
and the world itself is understood as "only a façade behind which people
could conceal themselves." Bonds of humanity are then recovered through
friendship: "Lessing considered friendship—which is as selective as compassion is egalitarian—to be the central phenomenon in which alone true
humanity can prove itself."[22] The selectivity involved in friendship, its differentiation from compassion, marks the presence of the world—the outside world, without areas or categories of exclusion—as a third entity in the
dual or dialogical structure of friendship. Here Arendt posits Lessing against
Rousseau, for whom fraternity and compassion were values in themselves,
markers of a community and communitarianism that would override an
insistence on ethics as a condition for friendship. And here, contrary to the

reader's assumption or expectation that Arendt will connect both compassion *(Mitleid)* and Rousseau to a Christian context, she in fact turns to the Jews for a political and historical example: "Humanity in the form of fraternity invariably appears historically among persecuted peoples and enslaved groups; and in eighteenth-century Europe it must have been quite natural to detect it among the Jews, who then were newcomers in literary circles. This kind of humanity is the great privilege of pariah peoples." Here Arendt inhabits her most controversial and most critical position, her critique of the favoring of house over world: "And worldlessness, alas, is always a form of barbarism."[23] In this context, Lessing prized friendship over love; "he wanted to be the friend of many men, but no man's brother."[24]

The politics of friendship is a literal enterprise for Arendt as for Lessing; friendship exists in the dialogue between two persons who share a commitment to the world. But the same commitment informs thinking itself as a form of political commitment. Arendt thus cites "Lessing's famous *Selbstdenken,*" thinking for oneself, as a component in this worldly nexus: "For Lessing, thought does not arise out of the individual and is not the manifestation of a self. Rather, the individual—whom Lessing would say was created for action, not ratiocination—elects such thought because he discovers in thinking another mode of moving in the world in freedom."[25]

In a fascinating recent study called *The Survival of Images: Art Historians, Psychoanalysis, and the Ancients,* Louis Rose examines the play of depths and surfaces, movement and stasis, that informs both of these fin-de-siècle intellectual practices and that marks them both as cultural sciences. His two leading subjects of analysis are Freud and Aby Warburg (1866–1929), founder of the Hamburg-based Kulturwissenschaftliche Bibliothek, the cornerstone of the Warburg Institute, which has been based in London since 1933. Warburg had also—like Arendt—no interest in Freud. Yet the affinities run deep for him as well.

For Warburg, the survival of the ancients in Renaissance and neoclassical art involves the survival of Dionysian paganism more than Apollonian order, the presence, in fact, of cultural and psychological demons. In Horst Bredekamp's summary, "for Freud, like Warburg, the individual faces daily the task of distancing, of freeing oneself from blindly projecting one's own instinctive motives onto the surroundings and thereby in a magical or neurotic way confusing the ego with the world."[26] Modernity, for Warburg, is traceable precisely as the production of distance from the pagan, the primitive, and the demonic; the making of what Warburg called _Denkraum_. Warburg, like Freud, regretted his generation's and his historical moment's removal from Lessing's Enlightenment; Warburg's _Denkraum_ can be understood as a synonym of Lessing's _Selbstdenken_, as understood by Hannah Arendt.

The three sources of Warburg's exposure to the pagan primitive and its demons accrued at once through existential and scholarly experience, and on the scholarly side more through anthropology and psychology than through art history as it was understood and practiced at the time. As an amateur anthropologist in the mid-1890s, Warburg spent a period of several months among the Hopi Indians of the American southwest. In 1907 he wrote to the director of the Smithsonian Institution in Washington, D.C., that the theory of the Renaissance he had since formulated owed everything to his experience with the Hopi, specifically the ritual of dancing with serpents, i.e. dancing with demons. The essay he ultimately wrote on the subject was delivered in 1923 to an invited audience at Ludwig Binswanger's Kreuzlingen Sanatorium, where Warburg had been a mental patient for four years. Throughout this process, it was clear to Warburg that the play of demons and distance applied to his own person just as much as to his mode and objects of scholarly analysis. Among the American Indians Warburg experienced paganism as a ritual drama; at the end of his life, on a return visit to Rome, he experienced it as a popular carnival in the form of fascist exuberance. He happened to be in Rome on the day the Concordat between Mussolini and the Vatican was signed; he described the carnival in the streets as the return of paganism to Rome.[27] The third source, and the one that terrified him the most, involved the rituals of Judaism. On the death of his father in 1910, he refused to attend the funeral or participate in the recitation of the Kaddish, writing to his brother:

> The whole celebration acquires, in a natural and subjectively absolutely justified manner, the character of a demonstration for the faithful Jews. I do not wish to disturb this. I am after all in the eyes of others an unreliable customer, but in my eyes a political opponent of clerical elementary schools such as the Talmud Torah School, and above all I am a "Cherem" through my mixed marriage and as the father of non-denomenational children whom I shall never lead to Judaism. . . . The Mourner's Kaddish is a matter for the eldest son; it signifies an external act, but at this public memorial service demonstrates acceptance of the moral inheritance. I will not make myself guilty of such hypocrisy. No one is entitled to demand this of me.[28]

A diary entry several days later equated explicitly the participation in ritual prayer with the experience of being attacked by demons.[29] Psychologically more fragile than most, as he well knew, Warburg's subjectivity remains symptomatic of the modern insistence on *Denkraum* as a bargaining chip, so to speak, in the negotiation of cultural inheritance. In Warburg's case, Jewish inheritance was fundamental and terrifying to him because it represents the invalidation of a principle of identity. The problem was not that this cultural inheritance meant too little but rather that it meant too much. The violence of cultural inheritance, in Freudian terms, lies in its capacity to overstimulate the ego; thus, paradoxically, the survival of the ancient is aggravated by that condition of modernity which also involves overstimulation, what Walter Benjamin called shock.

I am myself of the "school" that understands Freud's thinking to be historically constituted and context-contingent, the school of the cultural historians and cultural analysts rather than that of the biologists, who would disavow the cultural contexts or structure of Freud's arguments. The school, perhaps, of Carl Schorske, Peter Gay, Michael Roth, and Louis Rose as against that of Frank Sulloway. But among the historians there is an equally strong divide, which I would articulate as Schorske vs. Gay. For Schorske (and for Roth, Rose, and myself), the cultural, political, and ideological referential world to which Freud responds and rebels is decidedly Austrian, Viennese, post-liberal, neo-baroque. It is the Viennese cosmos which Freud persisted in inhabiting throughout his life, a persistence, indeed an addiction, that he often commented on. For Gay, Freud is a post-Enlightenment and German thinker, for whom Berlin is as relevant as Vienna. The centrality to Freud of the Vienna as I have described it involves, in my own work, the duality of a regime of ideology and a regime of representation, whose power and authority are to be penetrated through the counteroffensive of analysis. Manifest content thus cedes its power to the latent at the same time, at least in dreams, that vision and images cede their authority to text. Warburg pursued a similar agenda. It is at once a Protestantizing and a Judaicizing agenda, this drive to text, to emancipation through the word.

What is latent, what is unconscious, carries too much meaning to be permitted to cross the barrier into the conscious or the manifest without disguise and distortion. Its content is historical violence. Psychoanalysis posits a paradoxical duality of the overmeaningful and the underarticulate. This underarticulation, indeed the suspicion of articulation, functions as well as a critique of ideology. In the context of the baroque regimes of representation, it functions as well as a critique of representation.

4

Cultural integrity can be understood as a materiality of experience that has
no clear boundaries. This argument also approximates the question of what
is musical. In 2002, Edward Said and Daniel Barenboim published a series
of conversations, essays, and political interventions under the title *Parallels
and Paradoxes: Explorations in Music and Society.*[30] The friendship between
the two figures was by then a decade old; the first conversation recorded in
the book took place as part of a Columbia University conference on Wagner
in October 1995, which I had attended. I recall being quite underwhelmed
at the time, especially by Barenboim's refusal to engage the question, as
posed repeatedly and entreatingly by Said, of Wagner and politics, of Wagner
and anti-Semitism, beyond the usual and suspect pieties upholding the autonomy and apoliticality of art. In 1999, in the city of Weimar, on the 250th
anniversary of Goethe's birth and the year of Weimar's designation as a European cultural capital, Said and Barenboim inaugurated the West-Eastern
Divan Workshop, a summer institute for young Israeli, Palestinian, as well
as other Arab musicians who meet annually to form an orchestra as a fount
of literal as well as symbolic cooperation. Weimar is the city of Goethe; it
is also, as Said stresses, adjacent to the death camp Buchenwald, by explicit
Nazi design. In the same year, as Said later wrote for the London-based Ara-
bic language newspaper *Al-Hayat,* Barenboim became the first Israeli musi-
cian to perform on the West Bank, in his case at Bir Zeit University.[31] *Parallels and Paradoxes* is dedicated to the young musicians of this project. The
sophistication of Barenboim's discourse in the published text is, to my ear,
quite remarkable. He and Said clearly had many conversations, about music
and the world, about Israel and Palestine, and indeed about the nineteenth
century and its modes of art. Here is Barenboim:

> This is the difference between the eighteenth and nineteenth centuries. It
> is a great paradox that music can really have its greatest force of intensity
> and expression if it is isolated from the rest of the universe. The actual
> element of isolating music from the rest of the universe is extremely
> important because, in a way, it is the creation of a sound universe. If a
> listener is able and willing to attach himself, as it were, to the first note
> in a performance and really stay attached, without any wavering of con-
> centration, to the end, he has actually lived through a whole universe,
> whether it is a short work of Chopin or a huge symphony of Bruckner.
> On the one hand, music exists in isolation and, on the other, it mirrors
> or often anticipates social development.[32]

The pun, likely unintended, in the words "sound universe" is an appealing one, expressing both a universe of sound as well as a universe that is sound, i.e., that stands as a viable parallel universe, with a similar degree of complexity to the worldly one. On May 9, 2004 Daniel Barenboim addressed members of the Knesset in Jerusalem as a recipient of the Wolf Prize. Named for Ricardo Wolf, the Hanover-born inventor who emigrated to Cuba and served as Cuban ambassador to Israel from 1961 until the severing of diplomatic ties in 1973, the Wolf Prizes recognize achievements that "promote science and art for the benefit of mankind." Announcing that he would devote the prize monies to projects in music education in Israel and Ramallah, Barenboim asserted the divide between the principles of the Israeli Declaration of Independence and the present-day occupation. He posed the question: "Can the State of Israel allow itself an unrealistic dream of an ideological end to the conflict instead of pursuing a pragmatic, humanitarian one based on social justice?"

Edward Said takes a symmetrical position in his article for *Al-Hayat*, cited above. The article focuses on the controversy generated by Barenboim's performance of the prelude to Wagner's *Tristan und Isolde* at a concert of the Berlin Staatskapelle at the Israel Festival in July 2001. Barenboim thus broke the taboo against the playing of Wagner in Israel. For Said, the question of Wagner in Israel presents a test-case for a dialogue with a cultural "other." He writes:

> The irrational condemnation and the blanket denunciation of complex phenomena such as Wagner is indiscriminate and finally unacceptable, just as for Arabs, it has been a foolish and wasteful policy for so many years to use phrases like "the Zionist entity" and completely refuse to understand and analyze Israel and the Israelis on the grounds that their existence must be denied because they caused the Palestinian *nakba*.[33]

"Wagner," in Said's reference, refers to a cultural object, in other words to a group of works, a canon of art. For some listeners, these works may carry intolerable associations, as the music was not only championed by Nazi ideology but broadcast in the death camps. Barenboim's position on this issue is clear: no one should be compelled to listen to the music. In this respect, Said's demand of his fellow Palestinians is categorically different from and more stringent than his—or Barenboim's—demand of the Israeli musical public. Barenboim's often repeated position that no one should be forced to listen to Wagner is based on the obvious fact that one cannot offend an object. Said demands that subjects be listened to.

In an interview with *Ha'aretz* magazine, Tel Aviv, Said famously referred to himself as the last Jewish intellectual.[34] The utterance is as witty and as profound as its placement. Either you get it or you don't. In a similar spirit, I would offer Daniel Barenboim the epithet of the last *Yekke*. Let me explain.

The word *Yekke*, as many readers will know, was coined by Russian and other Eastern European Jewish émigrés mostly in Israel but also in the United States to describe the cultural style of the German Jewish émigré. Many Austrians will qualify too, certainly Arnold Schoenberg, who never bothered with the myth of the Austrian as less serious, indeed less Protestant, than the Prussian. So stiff and pompous, so self-imbued with the personal responsibility of carrying high culture into the wilderness, the *Yekke* never permitted himself to take off his jacket, even in Tel Aviv, even in New York in August. He became known by his jacket, by his cloak of formality, pretense, and nostalgia for lost status. The lost status is behavioral as well as professional; the *Yekke* is therefore largely a male sobriquet. Indeed, in an aspect of émigré social history that remains underexplored, the melancholy men, the former lawyers and businessmen, had a hard time adjusting to émigré life and needs, while their wives, many of whom had never worked outside or inside the home, put prestige aside and found work as caterers, seamstresses, and housecleaners. German Jewish men and women came quickly to refer to themselves with the word *Yekke*, but when they had occasion to write it down (which happened rarely), they spelled it *Jäcke*.

Barenboim was born in Buenos Aires of Russian-born parents and grew up in Israel from his adolescence on. At age eleven his parents took him from Israel to Salzburg to meet the conductor Wilhelm Furtwängler, who became his main musical model. The point is that the *Yekke*, following Goethe's imperative as cited above, inherits and adopts a cultural style, a take on the world at once aesthetic, historical, and political. This culture of adoption and multiplicity belies a well-known, quite witty, but equally curmudgeonly warning about the conceits of German and German Jewish intellectual history, uttered in my most recent experience by Walter Laqueur, the distinguished émigré historian.[35] "There is too much German Jewish intellectual history," he advised a conference devoted to this very topic, "and it's always about the same ten people, half of whom were not German and half of whom were not Jews." Laqueur's error here is the assumption of the primacy of origins over beginnings, in Said's distinction. Daniel Barenboim, who entered the music world under the eye of Wilhelm Furtwängler, has also come to carry the legacy of Lessing and Mendelssohn.[36]

"Music is transition," Barenboim says early in *Parallels and Paradoxes;* "I am happiest when I can be at peace with the idea of fluidity." He elaborates:

> If one is active in a profession which is more than a profession, which is a way of life, as it is for us—beyond nine to five—then geographical location is less important. I'm sure that when you read Goethe, you feel, in a funny way, German, as I do when conducting Beethoven or Bruckner. This was one of the lessons of our workshop in Weimar. Precisely that it's not only possible to have multiple identities, but also, I would say, something to aspire toward. The sense of belonging to different cultures can only be enriching.[37]

The multiple subjectivity that Barenboim advocates requires cultural hospitality and political permission, as he well knows. This fragile and, for him, coveted state of being reforges the links of music and culture first combined by the three foundational generations of the Mendelssohn family.

Barenboim and Said's bond is a political friendship, at once public and private, private and published, in the tradition of Lessing and Moses Mendelssohn. A political friendship implies not only that the conversation, supported by trust and affection, addresses the political world. The friendship itself exists as a form of politics, as world politics in a microcosmic frame. Following the key distinction of Hannah Arendt's, we can differentiate precisely between friendship and brotherhood, the latter of which presumes a bond presupposed by an absorbing, coherent cultural collective. Arendt's Lessing is the most thoroughly political figure imaginable because he took friendship so seriously. On this count I would offer a friendly disagreement to Akeel Bilgrami, the editor of Said's posthumous collection *Humanism and Democratic Criticism.* In an eloquent introductory tribute, Bilgrami suggests, no doubt correctly, that "Said's intellectual legacy will be primarily political." "But," he continues, and my disagreement is with that preposition, "the present work . . . allows us to situate this legacy in the larger philosophical setting of his humanism—perhaps the only 'ism' that, with stubborn ideals, he continued to avow."[38] Where the world is at stake, there can be no category larger than the political. This is the Arendtian position. The humanistic politics that Said shares with Hannah Arendt insists on facing the world according to principles of access and justice, without exclusion.

CHAPTER TWO

The Family Romances of Sigmund Freud

I

There are many Viennese modernists and many Viennese moderni-
ties, and some of them are less obviously Viennese than others. It is
questionable whether many of the canonic figures of fin-de-siècle Viennese
modernism can be considered Viennese, as so much of their energy was di-
rected against the imperial city's dominant culture. On the other hand, as
Nietzsche suggested, there is nothing more bourgeois than disdain for the
bourgeoisie. By that logic, there may be nothing more Viennese than the
disdain for Vienna, and the combative modernists may be the most Viennese of anyone. For Karl Kraus and Gustav Mahler, this kind of identification through contradiction holds, as Kraus was always the creature of the
theatricality he attacked, the theatricality that marked the dominant culture
of the Austrian secular baroque. Mahler was drawn to it as well, within and
beyond his conversion to Catholicism in 1897. And Theodor Herzl's Zionist
program of the same decade had been preceded by two alternative strategies
for solving the problem of anti-Semitism. First, he had proposed a series of
duels between Jews and the leaders of anti-Semitism, including pan-German
league leader Georg von Schönerer, Christian Social leader (and mayor of
Vienna as of 1897) Karl Lueger, and Prince Alois von Lichtenstein. Second,
he had dreamed of a conversion pact with the Vatican, replete with a mass
conversion of Vienna's Jews in St. Stephen's Cathedral.[1]

Up to the demise of the Habsburg Empire in 1918, Austria's most crucial
act of theater remained the performance of its own imperial coherence and
unity, a role that grew more desperate as the empire's centrifugal forces of
nationalism, ethnicity, and religious, class, and political tension increased.[2]
Even the modernists, who became known for exploring their culture's fis-

sures and contradictions, were often also attracted to its life-as-theater. For
Mahler, Kraus, and many other Jewish modernists, Catholic conversion is
most reliably a sign of deep attraction to the dominant culture. Even Arnold Schoenberg, who exorcised baroque Vienna from his soul by choosing
Protestantism as his religion of object-identification and then by moving
to Berlin, never left baroque Vienna behind in an absolute way. His ultimate anti-ideological opera, *Moses und Aron*, remains after all an opera,
with more than suspicious echoes of that earlier purification opera, *Parsifal*.
Moses's final lament "O Wort, du Wort das mir fehlt!" [Oh Word, you Word
that I lack!] carries a positively Lutheran take on the Hebrew Bible. At the
same time, the line evinces no apparent irony in the inevitable theatricality
of its own gesture. Moses is a character on a stage: a position not ultimately
different, for example, from that of Hugo von Hofmannsthal's fin-de-siècle
figure of Lord Chandos, who lives at the center of a highly contrived linguistic performance which ostensibly announces the impossibility of any
sincere linguistic act.

Sigmund Freud was a lifelong inhabitant of Vienna. Late in his career he
remarked: "I have lived in Vienna all my life and have never come across
a new idea here." This wonderful remark reminds me of an anecdote from
my own university days. Apparently, the most well-liked building on my
university campus was also agreed to be the ugliest. Yet it was very popular.
Everyone wanted to be inside it because, as it was often repeated, if you were
inside it, you didn't have to look at it. Freud, by this same logic, was the only
figure in Vienna who didn't have to contend with Freud.

Freud never thought of conversion of any kind. His secularity is as fundamental as his Jewishness itself; their coexistence presents no contradiction
at all. Yet if he was a modernist in relation to Vienna, he was also one in
relation to Judaism. In this chapter I will work with a definition of modernism that relies on a key trope of Freud's: repetition with difference. I will
argue that Freud's modernism, as a form of repetition with difference, is a
modernism historically conscious and indeed historically contingent. It is
chiefly concerned with fathers and sons and the possibility of filial production, filial autonomy, and their treacherous cohabitation. But there are also
mothers in the picture, and the Austrian baroque is one of them.

In contending with Freud, are we also necessarily contending with the
culture of fin-de-siècle Vienna? A historians' debate on this question remains
in place. For Peter Gay, Freud was the heir par excellence of the German Enlightenment, and his life in Berggasse 19 had nothing whatsoever to do with
the life of the surrounding metropolis.[3] The locus classicus for the location of
Freud's project within a Viennese modernist context remains Carl Schorske's

essay "Politics and Patricide in Freud's *Interpretation of Dreams*."[4] For Schorske, the psychoanalytic project was a pursuit of an Austrian politics of resistance by other means. If I cannot bend the surfaces, Freud has Virgil remind us on the frontispiece of *The Interpretation of Dreams*, I shall move the depths: *Flectere si nequeo superos, Acheronta movebo.*

Schorske's analysis predates the theoretical expansion of the political (an argument most strongly associated with feminism) into realms beyond the formal, public practice of politics. His argument is nonetheless compatible with such an expansion. The scientific world that had rejected Freud was politically constituted; the subversive impetus of his own discourse was so as well. The world of the university was ideologically allied with the world of postliberal Austrian and Viennese politics, defending their authority against the other and the new, with anti-Semitism the new literal and symbolic language of reaction. If liberal politics had failed, the subversive new politics, including the politics of psychoanalysis, must battle not only its conquerors but also its own weaknesses. Patricide, in this vein, means the disavowal of patriarchy for its weakness rather than for its strength. Hence Schorske's many citations of Freud's dreams of the weakness of his father, Jakob Freud, in the face of anti-Semitic brutality.

Schorkse's argument receives a lovely addendum in an essay by the British psychoanalyst Darian Leader called "Freud, Music, and Working Through." Leader questions one of the basic myths about Freud, which has also served as a metaphor for his separation from his surrounding urban culture, namely, his utter apathy and disdain for music. It is, as Leader points out, in "The Moses of Michelangelo," an essay I will return to below, that Freud explains the mystery of aesthetic affect with the comment "as for instance in music, I am almost incapable of obtaining any pleasure."[5] Some of Freud's best friends were musical—or, rather, important musical figures, such as the musicologist Max Graf and the music critic of the Viennese newspaper *Die Arbeiterzeitung*, David Josef Bach. Freud referred to *Don Giovanni* as "the greatest opera there is." But Leader's interest is not in Freud's taste or distaste for music but rather in the potential similarities between musical and psychoanalytic structures and arguments. Music has in fact a larger place in Freud's world than as an element of Vienna's referential world.

I would frame the issue in the following way. Music can be heard to embody subjectivity by the way it seems to listen to and work through a past—its own past. Thus the implied first-person voices in much music of the long nineteenth century from Mozart to Mahler constitute a drive to the future as inseparable from a grounding in and a responsibility to the past. Music's resolution or arrival at a satisfying conclusion—the arrival of the work itself as well as of the performance—embodies a certain stability and cohabitation of past and future. Music and psychoanalysis evince structural similarities as historical arguments and as arguments about the relations between subjectivities and worlds, between the self and the world. Music's drama results from the difficulty of such relations.

(The course of musical and dramatic action in *Don Giovanni*, by the way, begins with a patricide—indeed, with a double narrative about the failure of patricide. Thus the overture opens with a *Schreckensfanfare*—a terror fanfare, to borrow, aptly, the popular term for the opening of the final movement of Beethoven's Ninth Symphony. It continues with an unconvincing dispatch of this terrifying, minor-mode presence with a light major-mode melody. When Don Giovanni is introduced in scene 1, he quickly kills the father of his current object of seduction. The overture's *Schreckensfanfare* is subsequently attached to the returning, avenging spirit of the murdered father, now in the guise of a statue.)

Freud, as Schorske has often pointed out, named one of his sons Oliver, after Oliver Cromwell, England's first emancipator of the Jews. But the eponym and its choice are overdetermined. Oliver Cromwell was also England's most famous patricide, as it was his revolution that overthrew the Stuart monarchy and his hand that held up the decapitated head of King Charles I to the crowd assembled at Whitehall in February 1649. Charles's crime of treason, in Cromwell's eyes, was also a crime of weakness, made manifest in particular by his attraction to the Catholic Church and its political power in Europe, to what one hundred years after the English Reformation many called "popery." The symbolism of the hero Cromwell against the traitor Charles falls into place alongside that of Hannibal against Rome and Freud against Karl Lueger, except that Freud, unlike his two role models, must find a different language for politics: *Flectere si nequeo superos, Acheronta movebo.*

Freud's Hannibal phantasy, in William McGrath's summary, "fused a militant rejection of Catholic anti-Semitism with a strongly democratic opposition to clerical, aristocratic, and monarchical power." Freud wrote of his identification with Hannibal in *The Interpretation of Dreams*, specifically of the oath he swore on the direction of his father to take vengeance against Rome (which Freud associated with the Catholic church). In the first edition, Freud erroneously substituted the name of Hannibal's brother (Hasdrubal) for the name of the father (Hamilcar). Freud later explained his own slip as an unconscious expression of the wish that he might himself have been born the son of his own half-brother Emmanuel. Emmanuel Freud lived in Manchester, and at the age of nineteen Freud spent a happy summer there.

The personal pleasures of being reunited with the playmates of his childhood combined with the admiration of a more liberal society. "Since Emmanuel's branch of the family," again in McGrath's summary, "enjoyed a substantial degree of material prosperity as well as the absence of any significant anti-Semitic pressure, Freud's wish implicitly criticized his father for his failure to provide these desirable conditions."[7] Thus did Freud' s most basic family romance acquire an Anglophilic hue.

Freud's scientific program had specific political coordinates. The question becomes to what extent the result, psychoanalysis, is defined in terms of those coordinates. It argues for universality. That universality is then situated within social and emotional relations, most specifically the Oedipus complex. The universality of the Oedipus complex has long been debated, most importantly within cultural anthropology and feminism in the context of the question of the cultural and gender-related translatability of Freud's basic argument. Even if we bracket this debate, we can still assert that all models of social relations, including Freud's, must be operationalized within specific historical and cultural contexts. The social relations in Freud's purview can therefore be said to be both Viennese and cosmopolitan; both transhistorical and specifically historical.

My focus here is the association of liberalism and filiation, and the association of Freud's thinking about liberalism and filiation with classical liberal philosophy, specifically the work of John Stuart Mill. Just as Freud's choice of the name Oliver for his own son was more a gesture of identification with the emancipating Cromwell than an identification with the father figure in Cromwell's patricidal drama—namely, Charles I—so did the recurrent interest in John Stuart Mill carry a strong identification with the son—literally and figuratively—of English liberalism.

By liberalism I mean a political philosophy and practice that values and attempts to produce human freedom. Liberty and freedom, as readers of Mill often remind us, are not the same. Liberty, in Nicholas Capaldi's ultra-neat distinction, "refers to external constraints," whereas "freedom refers to an internal condition . . . identified as autonomy."[8] Liberty can be provided; freedom must be inhabited psychologically. For Hegel, the two processes are fused. For Freud, inner freedom may constitute release from the strictures of a postliberal society, in other words of a world in which the confidence in emancipation and political freedom has been shaken. This is the predicament of "fin-de-siècle Vienna" as Carl Schorske and others have defined it, as well as the point and motivation of its comparison with the United States at the next fin de siècle.

By filiation I mean the transmission of this philosophy and practice through literal as well as metaphorical passages from fathers to sons. For Mill, the question of liberalism itself remained bound to the legacy of his father, James Mill, and of his father's close friend, Jeremy Bentham, to their doctrine of utilitarianism and their political movement known as philosophical radicalism. These ties supply many well-known and intractable conflicts.

In addition to the generational conflict there is the tension between liberalism and utilitarianism, in other words between the stress on the individual and the stress on an aggregate social measurement and social good. John Stuart Mill resolved neither tension. His philosophical maturity emerged from the reformulation of his fathers' [sic] doctrine. When that maturity emerged in its first full-fledged public (and published) guise in On Liberty (1859), it did so under the rubric of the human value Mill wanted most to preserve, the value he called "individuality." Individuality, one might argue, was John Stuart Mill's way of rescuing freedom from individualism on the one hand and from raw social utility on the other.

The idea to write On Liberty apparently came to Mill while climbing the steps of Michelangelo's Capitol in Rome in January 1855. He had visited the graves of Keats and Shelley and had attended mass at St. Peter's, where, according to his most recent biographer, "he caught sight of Pope Pius IX, whom he and many others considered the great reactionary of the nineteenth century."[9]

In a letter of October 1857 to Theodor Gomperz, Austrian philosopher, classical philologist, and later Mill's German translator, Mill wrote: "I have nearly finished an Essay on 'Liberty' which I hope to publish next winter. As the Liberty it treats of is moral and intellectual rather than political, it is not so much needed in Germany as it is here."[10] Mill clearly thought the necessary contribution in the political philosophy of liberty to have been made by James Mill and Bentham. It was to him to make the contribution in moral philosophy and psychology, following his reading of German thinkers and their main transmitter to England, Samuel Taylor Coleridge.

On Liberty carries a dedication to Wilhelm von Humboldt. Individuality was to be the meeting ground of freedom and Bildung, of political and aesthetic education and moral autonomy. Mill relied heavily on Humboldt's Limits of State Action but in fact argued that principle with more vehemence than Humboldt had. Humboldt had urged the removal of state authority from national culture, while assuming that national culture (German culture, in his purview), would continue to flourish on its own motivation. Thus for Humboldt, individuality and autonomy carried over into collective, national culture, and deserved to thrive there without further intervention.

Mill, inheriting Bentham's and James Mill's cultural universe, was not so optimistic. Humboldt, like Hegel, his colleague at the University of Berlin, which he founded in 1810, assumed an upward sweep of German national culture, guided by Prussia, buoyed by *Bildung*. Mill saw pushpin replacing poetry at an increased pace.

Contrary to the Romantic desires of many of his biographers, Mill did not reconcile German and British liberalism, Humboldt and Bentham, Coleridge and Bentham. What he did do was refuse to choose between them; he rescued the liberalism of his fathers by requiring that they refer to a criterion of inner life. The contextual point is the following: the meeting of liberalism and filiation in mid-nineteenth-century England allowed for a powerful but inadequate father's legacy to be embraced and revised by a son. Some additional discussion of Mill's writings will sketch this process. In fin-de-siècle Austria, this pattern of liberal inadequacy and filiation was not possible. Although Freud took the model from Mill, he endured a lifelong inability to apply it. The inner pressures of Jewishness do not seem to have contributed to this inhibition, as they had with the three important Mendelssohn generations (Moses, Abraham, and Felix) between 1780 and 1840 and as they would for Franz Kafka a generation after Freud. (The preeminent document in the last case is Kafka's "Letter to His Father" of 1919.) Freud's context here is the larger theater of European liberalism and its flimsy hold on Austria. The short-lived liberal hegemony in Austrian politics can be dated from 1859 (the establishment of parliament) to 1897 (the ratification of Karl Lueger as mayor of Vienna), but it can also be dated from 1859 to 1873 (economic depression and the rise of political anti-Semitism). Austria's liberal culture was for many analysts a liberal veneer, a "gelatin democracy"—*Gallert-Demokratie*, in Hermann Broch's phrase. In this context, Freud's continually evolving models of the human psyche and the metapsychology of culture operate according to the desire and inability to organize and reconcile freedom and filiation. Austria refused to allow Freud to be John Stuart Mill.

The mature thinking of *On Liberty* emerged first from Mill's determination to reconstruct utilitarian thought from its juxtaposition with the Romantic discourse of the imagination, that is , to combine and reconcile the Benthamite discourse of the body and its rights with the "Germano-Coleridgean" discourse of the spirit. It emerged second from the refusal of false reconciliation. We can trace this agenda through the essays "Bentham" (1838) and "Coleridge" (1840). Both were written as tributes to the recently deceased thinker-heroes, and both use the gesture of tribute to criticize their objects. In the first essay, Mill stresses the incompleteness of Benthamite utilitarianism by highlighting its stress of the rights of the body. The rights of the body define the principle of the maximization of pleasure and the minimization of pain. Pleasure and pain are too primitive to allow for a psychological dimension, Bentham's bodies have no souls. This lack infuriates Mill. For Mill, Bentham's political honor is spoiled by a lack of psychology and lack of concern for the inner lives of people. Bentham's weak psychology is also a weak epistemology. To use other categories, Bentham advances a world of subjects void of subjectivity. Freud's agenda and his criticism of his predecessors are deeply similar.

In the second essay, Mill advances Coleridge's doctrine of the spirit as a corrective to Benthamism, while at the same time bringing out its political ramifications—its encouragement of state control over the individual mind. In practice, Coleridge's advocacy of a "national clerisy" would mark the return of enlightened despotism. The heroes Bentham and Coleridge are turned both into enemies of individuality: Bentham by denying the psychological dimension and Coleridge by placing it under external control. As Mill's readers, we wait for the synthesis of "Bentham" and "Coleridge." It never comes. Mill's melancholic and deeply moral refusal to reconcile "Bentham" with "Coleridge" is apparently too grim to bear for many biographers, for whom Mill's Romanticism is all about reconciliation.[11] But in fact the closest thing we get to such reconciliation is the plea, in the third chapter of *On Liberty*, for "individuality." And individuality is doomed, in Mill's view, by the new hegemonic power of bourgeois surveillance and its internalization in the bourgeois psyche. "In our times," he writes, "from the highest class of society down to the lowest, everyone lives as under the eye of a hostile and dreaded censorship." Freud will call this power the superego.

The passage from the world of the Benthamite panopticon to the Foucauldian one is administered by the power of the unconscious. Individuality has thus two enemies: external power and its internalized proxy. In the word "as"—"as under the eye of a hostile and dreaded censorship"—Mill opens the space that will be filled by the unconscious.

In 1879 and 1880, during free time while in military service, Freud translated four essays of John Stuart Mill. The assignment came from Theodor Gomperz, still Mill's German-language editor and main translator, to whom Freud had been recommended by his teacher Franz Brentano.[12] This is all we hear of the episode in Peter Gay's biography.[13] Ernest Jones is a bit more forthcoming, but adds: "Three of Mill's essays were concerned with social problems: the labor question, the enfranchisement of women, and socialism. In the preface Mill said that the greatest part of these was the work of his wife. The fourth, by Mill himself, was on Grote's Plato." In 1883, says Jones, Freud wrote of Mill: "I railed at the time at his lifeless style and at not

being able to find a sentence or phrase that one could commit to memory."
(To which Jones adds a footnote: "In exculpation of Mill one should mention
that his wife is supposed to have been the main author of the book in question.") Continues Freud: "But since then I have read a philosophical work of
his which was witty, lively, and felicitously epigrammatic. He was perhaps
the man of the century who best managed to free himself from the domination of customary prejudices." Mill's flaw, Freud goes on, in a sentence that
Jones does not reproduce, was the lack of a sense of the absurd, as evidenced
by his positions on the emancipation of women and the women's question
in general. "I remember that a main argument in the piece I translated was
a married women could earn as much as her husband." Freud glibly rejects
Mill's argument for the social equality of women, assuming that women will
manage the household and therefore not be able to enter a public, earning,
sphere along with men.[14]

Jones is citing (and not citing) here a letter to Martha Bernays (written
on November 15, 1883), addressed to "mein süßes Prinzesschen," my sweet
little princess. One doubts that Mill ever addressed Harriet Taylor with such
condescending endearment. But more significant is the fact that Freud's remarks about Mill come in response to a remark that Martha had made in a
previous letter about Mill and Harriet Taylor. Now Freud asserts that Mill's
relation to his wife was inhuman—*unmenschlich*. "A woman's position,"
he concludes, "can never be other than it is; to be an adored darling in the
early years and a beloved wife in more mature years."[15]

As Freud's two general biographers, Jones and Gay set a precedent for
the short shrift given to the Freud-Mill connection. Jones seems to know
nothing about Mill, and Gay seems not to care. This silence is repeated in
the literature, including for example, in William McGrath's monograph on
Freud's early intellectual life.[16] Are the biographers right? Is there little more
to say about Mill and Freud? Or is this a case of a dog that didn't bark: an
interesting silence, one that repeats Freud's own silence about Mill without
questioning its tensions and concealments?

In chapters 2 and 3 of *Civilization and Its Discontents* (1930), Freud re-
enters the cosmos of John Stuart Mill with an attack on utilitarianism and
the pleasure principle:

> Its programme is at loggerheads with the whole world. . . . One feels in-
> clined to say that the intention that man should be 'happy' is not in-
> cluded in the plan of 'Creation.' What we call happiness in the strictest
> sense comes from the (preferably sudden) satisfaction of needs which
> have been dammed up to a high degree, and it is from its nature only

possible as an episodic phenomenon. When any situation that is desired by the pleasure principle is prolonged, it only produces a feeling of mild contentment.[17]

The pleasure principle has no capacity for duration. Since the memory of pleasure does not outlast the physical sensation, the pleasure principle also has no capacity for memory. Adding to his invective a fairly standard critique of the claims of technology, Freud with some embarrassment, even distaste, adopts the tone of the critic of "civilization":

> There is a long list that might have been added to benefits of this kind which we owe to the much despised era of scientific and technical advances. But here the voice of pessimistic criticism makes itself heard and warns us that most of these satisfactions follow the model of the 'cheap enjoyment' extolled in the anecdote—the enjoyment obtained by putting a bare leg from under the bedclothes on a cold winter night and drawing it in again. If there had been no railway to conquer distances, my child would never have left his native town and I should need no telephone to hear his voice; if traveling across the ocean by ship had not been introduced, my friend would not have embarked on his sea voyage and I should not need a cable to relieve my anxiety about him.[18]

The first citation makes it clear that Freud is attacking the utilitarianism of the fathers (James Mill, Bentham) and not that of the son, John Stuart Mill. The son demanded that a sense of lived interiority be at least encouraged if not mandated by a second-generation utilitarianism. And he earned such a position himself through his own "mental crisis" of 1826. Mill's subsequent reformulation of utilitarian thought preserves and repeats the nomenclature of the fathers while opposing it with an insistence on an enriched subjectivity. With the essay "Utilitarianism" of 1861, Mill declares at once the replacement and displacement of his father's position.

There is something of a family romance in Freud's silence with regard to Mill, an indication that his strong sympathy involves a desire, performed rhetorically in various places in his work—notably in these chapters of *Civilization and Its Discontents*—to take the voice of Mill and replace/displace the utilitarian father. The utilitarian father is easier to replace than the primal father. Freud and Mill share inadequate liberal fathers, literally as well as generationally. Freud's actual translation of Mill accompanies a translation of political theory into psychology, and both of these as forms of political action.

2

The family romance, as Freud explains it in "Der Familienroman der Neu-
rotiker" (1909), involves the fantasmatic ennobling of one's father, resulting
as it does from the pressures of the Oedipus complex.[19] The typical delusionary structure of the family romance is the assertion that I come from
something more noble than what I seem or have become: my father was a
king. Yet one of the attractions of a family romance is its liberation from a
myth of origins and authenticity: I come from something radically different from what I am, seem to be, or have become. For Freud to name his son
Oliver was to provide him with a full-fledged, readymade family romance.
Freud's own English family romance—his fraternal position with regard to
John Stuart Mill and their shared revisions of their fathers' examples—he
had to invent for himself.

Freud's most famous family romance is the argument of his final and
most mysterious book, *Moses and Monotheism*. Its argument that the man
Moses was an Egyptian prince takes the myth of autonomous origins away
from Jewish history and grounds its emergence in something radically other.
Freud writes as a son of this history, but in the course of this book he switches
his voice, as it were, and begins to write as a father. In other words, the narrative position duplicates the position given to Moses himself: the hero without a coherent origin, like Wagner's Lohengrin, who starts something radically new. Lohengrin forbids his new bride and her fellow Brabantians from
seeking any knowledge about his origins. For this reason he became the hero
of fin-de-siècle assimilated central European Jewish Wagnerites, who did not
have the social permission to impose a similar restriction.

The book's German title is *Der Mann Moses*. The text's trajectory is
complicated. Freud begun work on it in Vienna in 1934, published its first
two sections in *Imago* in 1937, and continued to work on it in exile in
London in the second half of 1938. The German text was published in Amsterdam in 1939. The English version, in a translation by Katherine Jones,
Ernest's wife, appeared—and has remained—beyond the borders, so to speak,
of the Standard Edition.

The confessional obbligato that follows the argument reminds the reader
of the traveling nature of the text. It makes clear as well that the pre-exile
and post-exile sections and voices are different. The pre-exile argument
claims to take Moses away from the Jews. It destabilizes Jewish historical paternity. The post-exile voice claims the position of a new father. In
exile, Freud is Moses—a new Moses. Here is the problem: does exile work
through the problem of an excessive identification with the superego, with

the replacement of the father? In other words, does Freud take on the voice of Moses only from the vantage point of exile, so that Freud's Moses—Freud as Moses—assumes the mantle of the father without fulfilling the mortal contract between primal father and son? Replacing the father in the primal contract requires patricide. Exile, however, may literally shift the grounds of succession adequately to provide an escape from the primal contract and from the bounds of patricide.

Civilization and Its Discontents had opened with a warning about one kind of cultural and political danger and had closed with a direr warning about another type. The first danger is the temptation of the oceanic, of the feeling of oneness with the world. In a diplomatic but decisive leave-taking of his correspondent and friend Romain Rolland, Freud argued for the protection of the "sense of self" *(Ichgefühl)* which evaporates in the wish to be swept away. This is the temptation both of religious ecstasy and of love. Freud's secularism conjoins responsibility to self and to world. He cites a line from the playwright Christian Dietrich Grabbe's character Hannibal— once again Hannibal!: "We shall not fall out of this world" (Aus dieser Welt werden wir nicht fallen). He defines the temptation of the oceanic as the temptation to negate the reality principle that marks the boundary between self and non-self:

> The adult's sense of self cannot have been the same from the beginning. It must have gone through a process of development, which cannot, of course, be demonstrated but which admits of being constructed with a fair degree of probability. An infant at the breast does not yet distinguish his ego from the external world as the source of the sensations flowing in upon him.[20]

Freud then characterizes the ego as a shrinking back of the connection with the world. He provides a kind of kabbalistic creation myth for the origins of the self, a version of the Lurianic myth of the creation of the universe from the shrinking of God.[21] Selfhood is thus associated with removal, exile, and difference, and not with essence or Being.

Freud soon shifts his attention from the infantile desire for the mother to the need for the father: "I cannot think of any need in childhood as strong as the need for a father's protection." We know the developmental narrative whereby Oedipal desire is resolved by the internalization of the father in the guise of the superego: "by means of identification he takes the unattackable authority into himself."[22] But this is where the trouble starts. In chapters 4 and 5 of *Civilization*, Freud offers, in the manner of Nietzsche and Karl Kraus, a critique of the Christian doctrine of love as the basis of social order. This, for him, spells an institutionalization of the oceanic and its discontents. But at the conclusion of *Civilization*, Freud fixes on the cultural power of the superego as the greatest present danger. "Civilization," he writes, "obtains mastery over the individual's dangerous desire for aggression by weakening and disarming it and by setting up an agency within him to watch over it, like a garrison in a conquered city." Moreover, "nothing can be hidden from the super-ego."[23]

The text *Moses and Monotheism* steers clear of the oceanic by turning away from the temptations of the body, including the temptation of aesthetic form, of images. As the bearer of law, Moses is also the bearer of a masculine, heroic Judaism. Recent readers of Freud's Moses have, I think, tended to protest too much by asserting that Freud overmasculinizes Moses to defend a masculine Judaism against the anti-Semitic argument of an essentially feminized Jewish psyche. Thus, in Eric Santner's recent reading, *Moses and Monotheism*

> does indeed construct an image of Judaism as a sort of hypermasculine, neo-Kantian religion of reason, as if Freud were arguing, in the spirit of Jewish rationalist philosophers such as Hermann Cohen, against the specter of Weininger's claim that the (masculine/Christian) point of view of Kantian critical philosophy was as foreign to the (feminized) Jewish psychic and moral constitution as was Wagner's *Parsifal* to the Jewish aesthetic sensibility. The conception of Jewish spirituality and intellectuality proffered by Freud suggests a posture of severe self-control grounded in an endless series of instinctual renunciation.[24]

My caveat with this very cogent reading is its underestimation of the political dangers faced by a discourse considered to be too renunciatory, too austere, and therefore too repressive. What is being resisted by Freud's Moses is the snare of the magnetic polarity of the oceanic and the superego, a repetition of Oedipal desire for the mother on the one hand, of excessive identification with the father on the other. To put this polarity in historical terms, it is the temptation to place oneself under the protection of baroque power, which is gendered as feminine, consoling, enveloping, but nonetheless absolute (think of Maria Theresa), or to identify with a brute patriarch.

Freud's own identification with Moses (or, rather, their textual products), shows a determination precisely not to take the voice of the father in a contract with brute patriarchy. Rather, it attempts a transition where the son can succeed the father in an orderly way, as Mill succeeded his father on terms reasonable to both—via a reformulation of the father's ideas. Now, I do not want to suggest a formula by which Freud in English exile can become John Stuart Mill, can become the father through the voice of Moses. But I do want to suggest that Freud the exile can allow himself to achieve the same kind of subjectivity that is defined in Mill's life and work by a nonviolent displacement of the father. This Freud is able to do only by inhabiting the reduced stakes involved in the act of becoming the father: the father in exile rather than *in situ*. Freud-as-Moses will be neither the primal father nor the baroque father, neither Moses the leader nor Franz Josef, protector of liberal subjects. He will be the exile. Exile will enable him to internalize the very experience of modern subjectivity *as* loss and dislocation. In Eric Santner's uncannily incisive formulation, "Freud will attempt to explain anti-Semitism as a refusal to mourn the losses and dislocations that found modern subjectivity."[25]

It would follow that anti-Semitism is better understood as a panic over Jewish modernism and secularity rather than as a panic over Jewish religion, tradition, or observance. Anti-Semitism's fundamental antimodernism cannot abide the delicate balance of past and future, the unending working through, the resilience, both fragile and determined, of a discourse of repetition with difference. On this issue anti-Semitism and anti-liberalism are fused.

Moses and Monotheism was not Freud's first treatment of the man Moses. With some irony, we can assert that, a quarter of a century earlier, Freud had treated the *image* Moses. In question is the essay of 1914, cited above, called "The Moses of Michelangelo," published anonymously in *Imago*. This Moses, of course, sits in the Church of St. Peter in Chains (San Pietro in Vincoli) in Rome, Freud's forbidden city. It is the principal figure in an unfinished ensemble for the tomb of Pope Julius II. Freud had stared at the statue on his first visit to Rome in 1901 and continued to visit it regularly on his returns to the city.

Freud opens the essay in the guise of a fin-de-siècle art historian. He cites Henry Thode and Friedrich Justi, famous pedagogues (Aby Warburg's teachers), rejecting their interpretations of Moses's seated and complicated position. This opening gambit—patricide through methodology—recalls the opening chapter of the *Interpretation of Dreams*. Before advancing his own reading of Michelangelo's Moses and the question of his seated position, Freud offers the following mannerist paragraph, which could have been written by Warburg or Benjamin:

Long before I had any opportunity of hearing about psychoanalysis, I learnt that a Russian art-connoisseur, Ivan Lermolieff, had caused a revolution in the art galleries of Europe by questioning the authorship of many pictures, showing how to distinguish copies from originals with certainty, and constructing hypothetical artists for those works whose former supposed authorship had been discredited. He achieved this by insisting that attention should be diverted from the general impression and main features of a picture, and by laying stress on the significance of minor details, of things like the drawing of the fingernails, or the lobe of an ear, of halos and such unconsidered trifles which the copyist neglects to imitate and yet which every artist executes in his own characteristic way. I was then greatly interested to learn that the Russian pseudonym concealed the identity of an Italian physician called Morelli, who died in 1891 with the rank of Senator of the Kingdom of Italy. It seems to me that this method of inquiry is closely related to the technique of psychoanalysis. It, too, is accustomed to divine secret and concealed things from despised or unnoticed features, from the rubbish heap, as it were, of our observations.[26]

So the exposer of false authorship—"Lermolieff"—was himself falsely authored: the Russian was an Italian, or, should we say, and Egyptian? "Lermolieff's" method is akin to that of psychoanalysis for its attention to apparently opaque details, as Freud says, but also for their common critique of myths of origins. It will take Freud another twenty-three years to claim false authorship of the man Moses. Now, in 1914, he reads Moses's character from the obscurer details of his sculpted body—where, for example, the index finger on the right hand presses into a lock of the flowing beard. This first detail yields a series of body positions signifying disruption: the right hand touches the beard drawn from the left side; the tables of the law are held upside down, lodged precariously under the right elbow. In Freud's first reading of Moses's position, a contemplative Moses is depicted at the moment of his disruption by the sudden awareness of the debauchery of his people in their worship of the golden calf. This is the reading of the art historians, who assert that Moses is at the point of rising and hurling the tablets at the idolaters. But then Freud corrects this initial reading and the reading of his predecessors, suggesting instead that Moses "will now remain seated and still, in his frozen wrath and in his pain mingled with contempt."[27] Michelangelo's *Moses* becomes a prefiguration of Jacques-Louis David's *Lucius Junius Brutus*, defender of the Roman Republic against his own sons.[28]

FIG. 2.1. Michelangelo, *Moses*

If Freud is right, the depiction is not the Moses of the Bible (as it will also not be in the case of the Egyptian Moses), who threw and broke the tablets of the law in a fit of rage. Rather, this Moses has become a model of patriarchy through the sublimation of violence:

> In this way, [Michelangelo] has added something new and more than human to the figure of Moses, so that the giant frame with its tremendous physical power becomes only a concrete expression of the highest mental achievement that is possible in a man, that of struggling against an inward passion for the sake of a cause to which he has devoted himself.[29]

FIG. 2.2. Jacques-Louis David, *The Lictors Bring to Brutus the Bodies of his Sons*

Tremendous physical power notwithstanding, the point hit close to home; as Ritchie Robertson has observed, Freud wrote "The Moses of Michelangelo" in 1914, "shortly after the Psycho-Analytical Congress at Munich in 1913, at which it became clear that Jung was following Adler and Stekel into what Freud saw as apostasy."[30]

3

Without doubt, *Moses and Monotheism* supports a Lamarckian inheritance of culturally acquired characteristics: "there probably exists in the mental life of the individual not only what he has experienced himself, but also what he brought with him at birth, fragments of phylogenetic origin, an archaic heritage."[31] Eric Santner thus glosses the book's final argument as one of "Jewish transference," or "the unconscious transmission of the cultural patterns and values—of essence—that make a Jew a Jew."[32]

The general question becomes whether modern subjectivity is to be defined in terms of a model of transference—of the inheritance of acquired cultural characteristics, of repetition. To formulate the question in the language of filiation: is generational inheritance a choice between patricide and obedience, or, more radically, do patricide and obedience amount inexorably to the same thing if the violent usurpation of the place of the father results in a repetition of the father's subject position? Or can an alternative to—a partial way out of—this bind of modern subjectivity be posited in the possibility that subjectivity can be achieved in *and* beyond the shadow of its cultural inheritance? Can subjectivity, always tied up with symptomaticity, nevertheless not be subsumed by it?

Early in the third chapter of *Beyond the Pleasure Principle*, Freud addresses the question of the transference neurosis in the clinical practice of psychoanalysis. The transference neurosis is induced by the analyst as a tool toward the uncovering of repressed memory. Transference is repetition; the staged, managed transference of the clinical context is designed to produce a repetition with difference, that difference being a way out of pure repetition. "Acting out" (repetition) is guided to "working through" (repetition with difference). "These reproductions," Freud writes, "which emerge with such unwished-for exactitude, always have as their subject some portion of infantile sexual life—of the Oedipus complex, that is, and its derivatives; and they are invariably acted out in the sphere of transference, of the patient's relation to the physician." Freud continues with the passage I want to highlight:

> The physician cannot as a rule spare his patient this phase of the treatment. He must get him to reexperience some portion of his forgotten life, but must see to it, on the other hand, that the patient retains some degree of aloofness, which will enable him, in spite of everything, to recognize that what appears to be reality is in fact only a reflection of a forgotten past. If this can be successfully achieved, the patient's sense of conviction is won, together with the therapeutic success that is dependent on it.[33]

Can we find in this clinical program the seed of a position on cultural inheritance which allows for—indeed insists on—the duality of symptomaticity and subjectivity? In question is the patient's "sense of conviction" with regard to his or her own experience of transferential neurosis. Can, in such a way, a sense of self merge with a sense of history, or cooperate with it, so that a functional life might exist as a kind of exile from the past?

For the Freud of *Moses and Monotheism*, the survival of subjectivity in exile is enabled by the definition of subjectivity *as* exile. The reader must then decide whether this position is to be understood as a function of personal exile and old age, in other words as a contingency and a symptom, or whether the position, in its very embrace of its own contingency and symptomaticity, catches a basic reality of modern subjectivity, enabled by the clairvoyance of Sigmund Freud in contemplation of fascism and its threat to human dignity.

Freud's relocation to London differs existentially from the dissemination of psychoanalysis itself as exile differs from diaspora. Diasporic movement involves a dimension of freedom and decision: exile with a difference. Freud's house in Maresfield Gardens—a museum open to the public since Anna Freud's death in 1983—is a house of diaspora rather than of exile. The house is filled with Freud's objects: his antiquities, his furniture, his books. It thus answers the lament of the emptied rooms of Berggasse 19 in Vienna. Located just blocks away from the British Psychoanalytic Institute, Maresfield Gardens is physically as well as symbolically linked to Freud's British legacy in the work of Anna Freud and D. W. Winnicott, among others. But, as I hope to have shown, Maresfield Gardens as a receiver of the man Freud reappropriates as well a resonant British past, lodged deep within the structure of psychoanalytic argument. At this level, the young Freud cooperated with John Stuart Mill, delivering a strong epistemology to the basic principles of English liberalism.[34]

The contentions that Freud' lifelong psychoanalytic project might be understood as a rewriting of the Enlightenment or of liberalism are well known and, I would argue, valid despite their inadequacies. More modestly, however, the same project might be understood as a lifelong work of translation. Id to Ego, image to word (in the dreamtext). In this regard, the fact that Freud's youthful work literally entailed translation, and specifically the translation of Mill into German, is as significant in genre as it is in content.

CHAPTER THREE

Broken Vessels

Aestheticism and Modernity in Henry James and Walter Benjamin

The ray of light falls from above, and the Grail glows brightest. From the dome descends a white dove and hovers over Parsifal's head. Kundry, with her gaze uplifted to Parsifal, sinks slowly lifeless to the ground. Amfortas and Gurnemanz kneel in homage before Parsifal, who waves the Grail in blessing over the worshipping Knighthood.

—Richard Wagner, stage directions for the final curtain of *Parsifal* (1882)

"But do you remember," she asked, "apropos of great gold cups, the beautiful one, that I offered you so long ago and that you wouldn't have? Just before your marriage"—she brought it back to him: "the gilded crystal bowl in the little Bloomsbury shop."

"Oh yes!"—but it took, with a slight surprise on the Prince's part, some small recollecting. "The treacherous cracked thing you wanted to palm off on me, and the little swindling Jew who understood Italian and who backed you up!"

"Don't you think too much of 'cracks' and aren't you too afraid of them? I risk the cracks," said Charlotte, "and I've often recalled the bowl and the little swindling Jew, wondering if they've parted company. He made," she said, "a great impression on me."

—Henry James, *The Golden Bowl* (1904)

The Breaking of the Bowls, of which we find exhaustive descriptions in the literature of Kabbalism, is the decisive turning point in the cosmological process. Taken as a whole, it is the cause of that inner deficiency which is inherent in everything that exists and which persists as long as the damage is not mended. For when the bowls were broken the light either diffused or flowed back to its source, or flowed downwards. The

fiendish netherworlds of evil, the influence of which crept into all stages of the cosmological process, emerged from the fragments which still retained a few sparks of the holy light—Luria speaks of just 288. In this way the good elements of the divine order came to be mixed with the vicious ones. Conversely the restoration of the ideal order, which forms the original aim of creation, is also the secret purpose of existence. Salvation means actually nothing but restitution, re-integration of the original whole, or *Tikkun* to use the Hebrew term.
—Gershom Scholem, "Isaac Luria and His School" (1941)

I

Can the art of modern life—or indeed the understanding of modern life as an art—maintain its critical verve and resist the pull of ideology? Most specifically, can it resist the pull of aestheticism? Aestheticism as an ideology involves the measure of humans according to criteria of the beauty of objects. It thus counts as an insult to subjects, in other words to human autonomy, freedom, and unpredictability. Racism, understood as an arbitrary hierarchy of bodily attributes, is thus understandable as an extreme form of aestheticism.

If modernity's critical power is understood according to Baudelaire's values of the transitory, the fugitive, and the contingent, then it must also be understood according to principles of life and time, posited against the claims of stasis or absolute status, i.e., against the attributes of either a divinity or an object.

Aestheticism's potent lie resides in the promise that totality and authenticity will be restored to a reconsecrated world, purged of the dissipating demons of modernity. Aestheticism in this sense refers to a strong discourse, not to the withdrawal into art but to its opposite: to the empowerment of aesthetic categories of harmony, form, and authenticity to return to the world the aura which religion had once provided.

The end of Wagner's last opera *Parsifal*, which he called a "play for the consecration of the stage" *(Bühnenweihfestspiel)*, claims to deliver on that claim, or at the very least to show how to do so. The governing metaphor of the Grail reinforces the enormity of the cultural claim; the cup that held the blood of Christ is resanctified along with the world it represents. The means of the restoration is the cleansing of culture of the element that spilled the blood: the Jews. The Jew or the Jews form the cultural category, group, or person which calls into question, jeopardizes, or even prevents closure, completeness, and, potentially, health in the body cultural. The power of the

ideology of aestheticism in the European fin de siècle—with resonances in
the American one as well—is thus demonstrated by the force of its resulting
exclusionary discourses. Anti-Semitism is one of these, not the only one.

This chapter has two parts. Both parts examine the shape of an effort to
develop a moral position in regard to the conundrum of modernity, aestheticism, and the cultural place of the Jews. In the first part the figure of the Jew
appears as a cultural object, in the second as a—or the—cultural subject. The
first part will address Henry James as the writer of, and moral actor in, the
novel *The Golden Bowl.* With the help of references to work of George Eliot
and Edith Wharton, I will try to define some principles in what I take to be
a moral and aesthetic fin-de-siècle English-language discourse, in which the
boundaries between the moral and aesthetic construction of modernity are
drawn. On these boundaries strides the figure and the person of the Jew. In
the second part, I will turn to the same topic, as seen from within the Jewish
intellectual culture of Walter Benjamin and Gershom Scholem during and
after the First World War, as the promise of Jewish assimilation faded.

The juxtaposition of James and Benjamin is motivated most immediately
by their shared attention to the image of the broken vessel. Both thinkers
make the metaphor itself into a vessel for the currents of modernity: the
critique of an aestheticized culture, and the central position in this critique
of Jews, Jewish figures and thinkers, and debates about Jewish identity and
assimilation. But beyond the metaphor itself, James and Benjamin provide,
I want to argue, a normative example, methodologically and morally, for the
ongoing historical discussion of the place of the Jews in the making of modern culture. They share the conviction that, where modernity is addressed,
the Jews are *in* question, but not *the* question.

The Golden Bowl, like *Parsifal* a final creative statement, confronts and
painstakingly, and painfully, undoes much of the ideological work of *Parsifal.* The physical object which controls the novel's symbolic world is not
golden but gilded, and it is cracked from the first. At the novel's climax—its
cracking point—the bowl is shattered entirely. How far was Henry James
willing to go in his acceptance of the crack and its full symbolic resonance?
How far, in other words, did he come finally to confront and accept a modernity defined in terms of fragmentation rather than totality and in terms
of life as severed from categories of art and aestheticism? This line of questioning is not new, although the terms in which I am casting it are altered.
The question has been asked by Martha Nussbaum in what strikes me as a
definitive argument for the novel as a moral philosophical investigation; I
will draw much on her work below.

My second question enters an underlying realm of the novel that, so far as I know, has not been addressed in the context of the overall discussion of the metaphor of the bowl. The cracked bowl comes from the hands of a Jew. What this fact seems to me to do to the life of the metaphor of the golden bowl is the following: the authorial, philosophical confrontation with the crack—ultimately, with modernity—involves an authorial confrontation with the question of the place of the Jews in modern culture, with anti-Semitic discourse, and—most personally for Henry James—with the moral necessity to work toward the inner nonacceptability of the kind of casual anti-Semitism that has, until this point, lived peacefully within elegant prose and accepted norms. In the preface to the New York edition of *The Golden Bowl*, James renounced authorial moral superiority and wrote of his wish to endure the same moral passages he designs for his characters. The book itself thus works toward a moral position about modernity and cultural fragmentation which doubles as the moral education of its protagonist, Maggie Verver.

In 1904 (the same year as the publication of *The Golden Bowl*), Edith Wharton published *The House of Mirth*, which included in its menagerie of fin-de-siècle New York *arrivistes* the casually anti-Semitic characterization of Simon Rosedale, who is attracted to Lily Bart but decides resolutely not to marry her when her reduced status can no longer serve his own social ambition. Wharton's introduction of Rosedale as a "plump rosy man of the blond Jewish type" is casual, but her narrative manipulates him into a position of evil that has nothing to do with his own intentions: it is Rosedale who spots Lily as she leaves the bachelor apartment of Laurence Selden, a meeting that throws Lily into the self-doubt which initiates the psychological predisposition to her social and emotional downfall.[1] Rosedale is the waiting serpent that kills innocence. As one might expect, he turns out to be the landlord of Selden's building (named "The Benedick").

I think it is fair to assert that James's novel of the same year—in contrast to Wharton's—argues for the impossibility of any casual moral position. To say that it "argues" at all is to recognize the kind of philosophical intentions that Martha Nussbaum has attributed to it. This ban on the morally casual postures inherent in the fin-de-siècle world the novel portrays must include the extirpation of anti-Semitism if the book's moral voice is to have credibility. To come away from *The Golden Bowl*, for example, with the judgment "Of course the narration exhibits a certain degree of anti-Semitism, but that was universal in James's world and one can't expect him to be an exception" contradicts and would entirely defeat the desire of every fiber of the book to identify and then inhabit a morally justifiable life. (This is not the same as a morally perfect life, as will be addressed below.) It is equally problematic to leave the novel's "Jewish question" unexamined.[2]

Although their correspondence shows no communication on the issue, it seems clear that James and Wharton took divergent paths in the crucial year of 1904—crucial in their publication history, but also, if largely circumstantially, in their shared exposure to political questions of Jews and anti-Semitism. *The Golden Bowl* was completed in the spring of 1904. During the height of the Dreyfus Affair and the scandal of Emile Zola's article "J'accuse," James had supported Zola and offered to shelter him in England. He described Zola as a hero and, upon his guilty sentence for libel in February 1898, suggested that only the guilty verdict had spared Zola from being "torn limb from limb by the howling mob in the streets."[3] The Anglophile adopted a Burkean Francophobia, but the enemy was on the right. In 1903 he wrote the essay "Emile Zola."[4] James's pro-Dreyfus and pro-Zola position caused the break of the friendship with the novelist Paul Bourget, an anti-Dreyfusard and an anti-Semite.[5] Curiously, there is no mention of the issue in the recently published James-Wharton correspondence.[6] Bourget had completed the triangular friendship that connected James and Wharton. The shattering of the golden bowl into three pieces may include in its resonances the breaking of this triangle.

Martha Nussbaum describes the world of *The Golden Bowl* as "a fallen world—a world, that is, in which innocence cannot be and is not safely preserved, a world where values and loves are so pervasively in tension with one another that there is no safe human expectation of a perfect fidelity to all throughout a life."[7] The recognition of this condition and the emerging will to negotiate it constitute the moral education of Maggie Verver. The first half of the novel explores the artificial world of her preserved innocence: the Edenic world provided by her tycoon father Adam, who lives in the white-walled purity of Eaton [Eden] Square. Maggie's initial retention of this paternal innocence across the thresholds of her marriage and motherhood heralds the emotional danger she falls into. Like Adam Verver, she is a collector. He is building a great museum; she aids in their shared practice of the "aestheticization of persons." The resulting portrait is of "the inveterate tendency of both father and daughter to assimilate people, in their imagination and deliberation, to fine *objets d'art*."[8]

Maggie Verver's moral education moves from the novel's first volume, named for her husband, "The Prince," to the second volume, "The Princess." James states in the preface to the New York edition that the "Prince, in the first half of the book, virtually sees and knows and makes out, virtually represents to himself everything that concerns us—very nearly (though he doesn't speak in the first person) after the fashion of other reporters and critics of other situations. . . . The function of the Princess, in the remainder, matches exactly with his."[9] The novel's opening pages portray the prince, a Roman in London, bent on recovering a personal style reflective of the *Imperium*. The novel's first *Imperium* is of course Roman; its current one is American. Within as well as between these imperial presences lie agendas of "capture" and "pursuit." The Roman's prey are the American father and daughter, Adam and Maggie Verver. The Prince's first name is, after all, Amerigo. His experience is thus clearer and more confident than that of the American Ververs, for whom conquest and exile are strangely mixed. His initial reported conversation with Maggie Verver reveals his place in the shared cosmos of father and daughter:

> ". . . the collection, the Museum with which he wishes to endow it, and of which he thinks more, as you know, than of anything in the world. It's the work of his life and the motive of everything he does."
>
> The young man, in his actual mood, could have smiled again—smiled delicately, as he had then smiled at her: "Has it been his motive in letting me have you?"
>
> "Yes, my dear, positively—or in a manner. . . . You're a rarity, an object of beauty, an object of price. You're not perhaps absolutely unique, but you're so curious and eminent that there are very few others like you—you belong to a class about which everything is known. You're what they call a *morceau de musée*." (49)

Maggie herself will come to feel "like a dressed doll," passed back and forth between father and husband.[10] But the strategies of the *Imperium* and the Museum differ: the Prince defines his conquests in terms of the unknown and the living; the future Princess in terms of the (allegedly) known and objectified.

Two pages later, Maggie describes her faith in the Prince as "divided . . . into watertight compartments," and then adjusts her image into "Watertight—the biggest compartment of all? Why it's the best cabin and the main deck and the engine-room and the steward's pantry! It's the ship itself—it's the whole line" (51). The author comments here on Maggie's ability to make images, and her image of her faith and herself is first that of an unsinkable vessel and then, after the adjustment, of an unbreakable one. In the subsequent encounter between the Prince and Fanny Assingham (the observer of the novel's action whom, along with her husband, Bob Assingham, Martha

Nussbaum places in the role of the Greek chorus), the image of the vessel is relied on by both, with the topic of the Prince's marriage discussed in terms of a vessel entering a port.[11]

The golden bowl of the title is first seen in the Bloomsbury antique shop by the Prince and Charlotte Stant. Stant herself is the crack in the fragile alliance of the Ververs and the Prince. She marries Adam Verver but then resumes an affair with the Prince, who had been her lover. The erotic charge between Stant and the Prince is palpable as they go about their ostensible search for a wedding present for himself and Maggie Verver. They see the dealer's inventory in terms of historical debris: "A few commemorative medals of neat outline but dull reference; a classic monument or two, things of the first years of the century; things consular, Napoleonic, temples, obelisks, arches, tinily re-embodied, completed the discreet cluster. . . . It was impossible they shouldn't, after a little while, tacitly agree as to the absurdity of carrying to Maggie a token from such a stock" (115). The dealer's inventory offers a panorama of history that can be described by us as Benjaminian: history as ruin, perceived in terms of dissipated and severed objects. This is the opposite view of culture and history from that of the still-confident American collectors, the Ververs, for whom objects of history are gathered by the authority with the power to represent history anew as a totality, indeed one constituted and empowered by its commodification.

As the Prince and Charlotte converse in Italian about the forbiddenness of their outing (ostensibly so that Maggie will not know of the wedding present they intend to choose), the antique dealer is revealed as conversant in Italian and as an eavesdropper. "With ceremony," he presents the couple with "My Golden Bowl." The dealer is truthful but mysterious: the bowl is gilded crystal, he says, but the work of "some very fine old worker and by some beautiful old process. . . . Call it a lost art . . . say also of a lost time" (119). The price (five pounds) is low. Charlotte is "evidently taken"; but by this time the Prince "had lost patience." Outside the store, the Prince says he saw the crack in the bowl, which he regards not as evidence of its worthlessness but as a bad omen for his happiness and his safety. Charlotte's reply: "Thank goodness then that if there be a crack we know it? But if we may perish by cracks in things that we don't know—! . . . We can never then give each other anything." This kind of observation gives Charlotte a special moral attraction to some readers as the only character in the novel who "will take great risks with flaws" (123).[12]

Notwithstanding James's authorial remark about the book's first part belonging to the Prince, the acquisitional impulses of Adam Verver and of Charlotte Stant—for things, and by way of the collecting of things, for

each other—gain in the attention of author and reader. Adam Verver un-
dertakes his own collecting expedition, in Brighton, with two objects in
view: "It served him at present to satisfy himself about Charlotte Stant
and an extraordinary set of oriental tiles of which he had lately got wind,
to which a provoking legend was attached, and as to which he had made
out contentedly that further news was to be obtained from a certain Mr.
Gutermann-Seuss of Brighton" (179). Another *objet d'art* of mysterious origins and Jewish provenance. By this point in the novel, everyone has gone
collecting except Maggie, and Charlotte has been exposed to both of the
book's Jewish antiquarians. Again we have a casually anti-Semitic introduction; Gutermann-Seuss is "a remarkably genial, a positively lustrous
young man" who receives "the great American collector" in his home, in
the company of "his progeny—eleven in all, as he confessed without a sigh,
eleven little brown clear faces, yet with such impersonal old eyes astride
of such impersonal old noses." The room is completed by "fat ear-ringed
aunts and the glossy cockneyfied, familiar uncles, inimitable of accent and
assumption, and of an attitude of cruder intention than that of the head of
the firm" (180). On the one hand, the company duplicates, in the narrator's
perspective, the Damascene tiles Verver has come to buy, as well as the parallel small objects in the Bloomsbury shop: the Jewish family as displaced
historical detritus. On the other hand, however, as Martha Nussbaum has
pointed out, the sprawling and cheerful Gutermann-Seuss family "contrasts,
ultimately, with the sexual failure of Adam with Charlotte," as Charlotte
seems to sense. When Adam and Charlotte are conducted to the room with
the "treasure," "the rest of the tribe, unanimously faltering, dropped out of
the scene." Unlike Bloomsbury, however, this is the real thing; and, unlike
the Prince, Adam Verver knows how to buy. The tiles "lay there at last in
their full harmony and their venerable splendor." Again Nussbaum: "This
image of harmony and totality gives Adam the idea of marrying Charlotte, so
as to complete the aesthetic harmony of his own life."[13] The intimacy of the
witnessed transaction bonds Adam and Charlotte, as does her acceptance of
the "mysteric rite of old Jewry"—her description, we are told, of the "heavy
cake and port wine" offered by Gutermann-Seuss in celebration of his sale
(192). On the subject of the Prince's betrothal we heard about vessels in port;
here we are told that Adam is thinking of burning ships—a reference to the
Brighton coast but also, perhaps, to the eventual failure of his new marriage
to be consummated.

The recollection of the Bloomsbury antique shop, quoted in the epigraph
above, occurs shortly after the consummation of the doubly adulterous union
of Charlotte and the Prince. The process of Maggie Verver's negotiation first

of the knowledge of the affair and then of her strategy for handling it "all depends on the bowl," which she had purchased for her father but has since placed on the mantle so that it might confront the gaze of her husband (440, 437). Her knowledge of the bowl's connection to the Prince and Charlotte came from "the so distinctly remarkable incident of her interview at home with the little Bloomsbury shopman" (479). The dealer had felt contrite for not telling Maggie of the crack:

> Left alone after the transaction with the knowledge that his visitor de-signed the object bought of him as a birthday gift to her father—for Mag-gie confessed freely to having chattered to him almost as to a friend—the vendor of the golden bowl had acted on a scruple rare enough in vendors of any class and almost unprecedented in the thrifty children of Israel. He hadn't liked what he had done and what he had above all made such a "good thing" of having done; at the thought of his purchaser's good faith and charming presence, opposed to that flaw in her acquisition which would make it verily, as an offering to a loved parent, a thing of sinister meaning and evil effect, he had known conscientious, he had known superstitious visitings, he had given away to a whim all the more re-markable to his own commercial mind, no doubt, from its never having troubled him in other connexions. . . . He had wished ever so seriously to return her a part of her money, and she had wholly declined to receive it. . . . His having led her to act in ignorance was what he should have been ashamed of; and if she would pardon, gracious lady as she was, all the liberties he had taken, she might make of the bowl any use in life but that one. (479–80)

The dealer had then spotted photographs of the Prince and Charlotte and re-vealed to Maggie that they had been in his shop and had looked at the bowl: "He himself, the little man had confessed, wouldn't have minded—about *them.*" I'll speculate below as to how the relationship between Maggie and the dealer seems to be symbolically constituted.

When Maggie reveals all this to Fanny Assingham, the latter smashes the bowl. Her motives are unclear, but she apparently fails to realize that Mag-gie has arrived at the point where she recognizes the bowl's truth—and lives with it—as residing in the cracks, not in the aesthetic claim of the *objet d'art*. When Maggie picks up the pieces, we are told that "she could carry but two of the fragments at once" (451). If these fragments are people, then the comment possibly refers to her strategy of reclaiming the Prince, re-exiling her father back to America, and ignoring Charlotte entirely.

The Bloomsbury antique dealer is certainly burdened with heavier stereotyping than Simon Rosedale. He speaks Italian and is able to eavesdrop on his customers, presumably with the goal of adjusting whatever business subterfuge may be necessary. To the Prince, he is a Jewish swindler attempting to sell faulty merchandise. To Charlotte, he is a "Jewish swindler": I think we can infer the quotation marks in her tone, for two reasons. First, she is quoting the Prince's characterization, just spoken. But she also has a different vantage point on the crack. For Charlotte, the crack holds an element of the bowl's authenticity. But her sense of authenticity is invested in moral wisdom rather than in aesthetic perfection. She thus can be said to stand at a crossroads in the moral structure of James's characterizations. The third and final discussion of the antique dealer is governed by Maggie Verver, who in this respect achieves the moral stance acceptable to James, and, presumably, to the reader. Maggie buys the bowl and learns from the dealer that Charlotte and the Prince had spent time looking at it. For Maggie, then, the dealer becomes literally the source of the truth and of knowledge about the adulterous relationship.

The dealer, in this configuration, is the other father, the other Adam, the other first man, the truthteller who confirms the falseness of the formal, aesthetic composite of the four people. His particular discomfort at the prospect of the cracked bowl being offered to Maggie's father shows a sympathy with fatherhood in general and with regard to Maggie as daughter in particular. His prior injunction to Charlotte Stant—"Call it a lost art"—resonates here as well. The mystical tone here may well be, on the surface, the tone of the salesman, but it merges as much more than that in the light of the later episode with Maggie. The dealer's voice takes on a divine aspect, both in the assumption of the godly prerogative of naming, and in the naming of an art that is lost. In identifying the category of lost art, he also identifies the categories of aestheticism and of the fallen world of the novel. The claim of the restoration of the "lost art" is in reality the ideological claim of aestheticism.

For Maggie, more decisively than for Charlotte, the crack in the bowl has direct heuristic power; from it and its source—the dealer—she learns the truth—according to the realized moral authority of the novel itself—of the split between life and art, between the negotiations with persons and, in Nussbaum's phrase, the "aestheticization of persons." In a passage that Nussbaum highlights, Maggie defends the flawed *objet d'art* and the morality of making a present of it: "The infirmity of art was the candor of affection, the grossness of pedigree the refinement of sympathy; the ugliest objects in fact as a general thing were the bravest, the tenderest mementos, and, as such, figured in glass cases apart, worthy doubtless of the home, but not worthy of the temple—dedicated to the grimacing, not to the clear-faced, gods."[14]

But is the theme of the superiority of moral realism over aesthetic perfection duplicated in the formal structure of the novel itself? Put another way, does the moral education of the novel itself, of its authorial voice, share itself in the reevaluation of the process of the aestheticization of persons? I am not so convinced as Nussbaum is of the novel's self-critical capacity with regard to its own aesthetic perfection. It is therefore reasonable to ask whether the novel itself remains guilty of the aestheticism it criticizes, and whether this condition places limits on the reach of the moral inquiry itself. James's own comment on his novel's stance, referred to above, appears in the preface to the New York edition (1909): "It's not that the muffled majesty of authorship doesn't here *ostensibly* reign; but I catch myself again shaking it off and disavowing the pretense of it while I get down into the arena and do my best to live and breathe and rub shoulders and converse with the persons engaged in the struggle that provides for the others in the circling tiers the entertainment of the great game" (20).

Henry James the novelist seems to share, in the end, Maggie's vantage point. Life and art are severed, but the meaning of this is that life cannot be made into a work of art—the trap of aestheticism. Despite his professed participation in the moral struggle of his characters, a struggle defined by the necessity of overcoming aestheticism, James does not engage the inverse of this command, namely the modernist imperative of an art that imitates life through the abnegation of holism and the rules of perfect form.

On the other hand, such a positive reading of Maggie's role and resolution at the end of the novel has been criticized for wishful thinking, of the predicament in which "many readers seem to require a heroine out of all this ambiguity, this 'milky fog,' 'white curtain,' or 'golden mist,' as the prince sees it." Thus, Robert Pippin sees Maggie as a full participant in the "great moral crash" that finally overwhelms all four protagonists. For Pippin, "she is her father's daughter and wants mostly to keep what she has," and she arranges this by engineering Charlotte's exile with a good dose of *Schadenfreude*.[15] In such a reading, Maggie resembles May Archer in Wharton's *Age of Innocence*, whose main moral high ground remains—even after her death—the contract that has sealed the sacrifice of her husband's love of another woman—more glamorous, more European, and more "fallen."

It is interesting that ambiguity and heroic resolution escape the options of women in novels of the period. Maggie Verver does not qualify, ultimately, as a modernist heroine. A similar problem affects the gendering of both structure and ending in the final work of James's predecessor and nemesis,

George Eliot. The novel in question is *Daniel Deronda* (1876), which also posits a young man of naturally aristocratic bearing between two women, Gwendolen Harleth and Mirah Lapidoth, the latter of whom is also subjected to a fearsome paternal (and fraternal) legacy. In this case, however, the legacy is defined as the political, emotional, and social question of the European Jews. And Eliot's Dickensian gimmick is the plot turn that reveals the novel's hero to be a Jew himself.

George Eliot's work was of course crucial to James's development as a novelist, and most evidently so in the work of the middle period. Leon Edel writes that "[a] great deal has been made of the resemblance of *The Portrait of a Lady* to *Daniel Deronda*."[16] Although Edel follows this comparison with a justified assertion of the autonomy of James's novel, he confirms the solidarity of the two heroines Isabel Archer and Gwendolen Harleth, as well as the two bad husbands, Osmond and Grandcourt. But Edel also reinforces the long tradition, perhaps initiated with James's own practice and perpetuated by formalist critics such as F. R. Leavis, of dividing Eliot's unwieldy novel in two, into the "Gwendolen Harleth" novel, the good novel, and the "Daniel Deronda" novel.[17] Indeed Edel goes so far as to call *The Portrait of a Lady* "a 'George Eliot novel' written by James in the way he believed she *should* have written."[18] In *Daniel Deronda*, Eliot allows the bifurcated structure of the novel itself to duplicate the modernist ambiguities and incoherences of the social tapestry it engages. This is an act of realism, courage, or recklessness which James would never allow.

The characters of Deronda and Gwendolen Harleth are drawn together by creaky coincidences of plot, and Eliot's interest did not lie in their interaction, or indeed in the interaction of the two spheres of the novel. But in an important way, that is the point. The world Deronda is drawn into, the pariah world of Mirah and her brother Mordecai and, ultimately, of his own ancestry, is a separate world, and Eliot makes it formally so. One might almost describe this novel—Eliot's last—as a work of functional modernism for the courage of its formal fragmentation.

The question becomes, then, how far did Eliot go in allowing—in insisting on—a degree of formal fragmentation that would correspond to the dual worlds she wanted to engage? Is *Daniel Deronda* itself a broken vessel, and how useful are aesthetic, formal criteria in considering the situation? For Henry James, and, I think, for Martha Nussbaum as his unsurpassed and devoted reader, aesthetic form has no essential limitations in the representation of reality. The artist has an obligation "to render reality, precisely and faithfully"; in this way Nussbaum summarizes James's combined aesthetic and ethic.[19] In the same spirit, Wayne Booth reads Nussbaum's appreciation of James in terms of the restoration of the category of beauty "to something like the breadth that it would have had in classical praise for narrative: it includes an awareness that forms are truly beautiful only when they are morally valuable."[20] If this position is not problematic—and I clearly think that it is—then Eliot's flawed novel is simply flawed. But for how long can form include the awareness of its own limitations before giving way to them, even just slightly?

Modernist practice in regard to this question tends to de-essentialize the aesthetic, the beautiful, the formal, so that no border must be defined before the point of the non-aesthetic, the non-beautiful, and the non-formal is called. This position does not imply that non-art cannot be defined in practice, on a case by case basis, but rather that its essential identity cannot be predetermined philosophically. The history of aesthetic innovation is full of anecdotes about the placement of this border, and fin-de-siècle modernism contributes the lion's share of attending examples. To invoke one: Richard Strauss was accused of writing noise, not music, for the character of Klytemnestra in *Elektra* (1909). His renowned answer: "I am placing onstage the murder of a mother by her son; what do they want, a violin concerto?" The received implication of a long-term history of an aesthetic form is the routinization of shocking innovations: the dissonances of Strauss grew comfortable, even pleasing, to the twentieth-century ears exposed to Schoenberg, just as the dissonances of Mozart—who also placed violence ruthlessly on the operatic stage—had grown pleasing to the nineteenth-century ears that couldn't, in turn, assimilate Strauss.

But once this de-essentializing move has been made, there can be no accepted borders for the aesthetic as distinct from the non- or extra-aesthetic. The distinction between the modernist and postmodernist drops out entirely here. James retains an essentialist aesthetic. Eliot, at least in the book in question, does not. A Jamesian essentialism will consider *Daniel Deronda* flawed, period. A Jamesian aesthetic cannot, it seems to me, coincide with the possibility of the radical critique of the claims of form. For James, the precise and faithful rendering of reality is still encoded into perfect form. Here I differ with Nussbaum: the Jamesian crystal is flawed because it is too perfect. The Jamesian voice, I would argue, has to be considered vulnerable to entrapment within its own aestheticism, and thus, through all its intense and intransigent work, prone to retain an affinity to the Maggie Verver of the first half of *The Golden Bowl*, who "wants, this woman, to have a flawless life."[21]

2

Midpoint in his study *Kabbalah and Criticism,* Harold Bloom describes the desire of the Kabbalah—and, a fortiori, of acts of criticism as he sees and wants them to be—to reform and re-legitimate aesthetic experience from a new vantage point, not the vantage point of the claims of Being but of the reality of exile:

> Are not the *Sefirot* ["heavenly spheres and stages"] also, and all of Kab-
> balah, an incarnation of the desire for difference, and for an end to Exile?
> *To be different, to be elsewhere,* is a superb definition of the motive for
> metaphor, for the life-affirming deep motive of all poetry.[22]

For Gershom Scholem, the scholar who restored Kabbalah and mystical traditions to Jewish history and memory, the Lurianic Kabbalah is, as Bloom asserts, itself an elaborate myth of exile. Isaac Luria's sixteenth-century com-
pilation of the interpretative tradition, which originated in twelfth-century
Provence, emanates from Palestine in the aftermath of the Spanish expulsion. The vantage point of exile returns in Scholem's life's work on Jewish
mysticism, as first conceived in Germany during the First World War and
after, and realized throughout a long career in Palestine, later Israel.

At the crux of Scholem's essay "Isaac Luria and His School," first published in 1941, comes the passage, cited in the epigraph above, about the
Lurianic myth of the breaking of the vessels. This is one of two founding
Kabbalistic myths in which the creation of the world is described in terms
of the exile of God. The deepest symbol of exile, deeper than the breaking of
the vessels, is the doctrine of *Tsimtsum:* the creation of the physical space
of the world in terms of the shrinkage and contraction of God. "According to
Luria," Scholem writes, "God was compelled to make room for the world by,
as it were, abandoning a region within Himself, a kind of mystical primordial
space from which He withdrew in order to return to it in the act of creation
and revelation."[23] *Tsimtsum* is thus a doctrine of inner exile, whereas the
breaking of the vessels describes the external exile of God. Both are myths
of the origins of evil as a realm separate from God. *Tsimtsum* describes the
creation of an autonomous space for evil; the breaking of the vessels resulted
from the "cathartic cause": the necessity of cleansing waste products and
their demonic forces from the pure substance of *Din* or "sternness."[24]

The answer to these myths of exile and fragmentation is the myth of redemption, and the doctrine of *Tikkun:* "the restitution of cosmic harmony
through the earthly medium of a mystically elevated Judaism."[25] This myth

of restoration is thus the counterpart to the myth of the breaking of the vessels. It contains, according to Scholem, "a strictly utopian impulse," as the "harmony which it reconstitutes does not at all correspond to any condition of things that has ever existed even in Paradise"—in other words, before the breaking of the vessels.[26] Its resolution occurs through Messianic agency. The problem lies in the question of the "earthly medium" which connects exile and human thought to Messianic action and cosmic restoration. The historical consequent to Lurianic Kabbalism is the phenomenon of the false Messiah in the person of Sabbatai Sevi. In Scholem's *Main Trends in Jewish Mysticism*, the chapter on Luria is followed by the chapter "Sabbatianism and Mystical Heresy," and the work to which Scholem turned on the completion of his book became his largest and most celebrated: *Sabbatai Sevi: The Mystical Messiah, 1626–1676*.[27] It seems to me that this connection is crucial to the principle of moral philosophy inherent in Scholem's work, despite, or rather because of, his consistent and modest posture as historian or "mere" chronicler of tradition. The historical passage from mystical Messianism (the myth of *Tikkun*) to the phenomenon of false Messianism resonates in Scholem's writing with an implicit moral warning against the temptation of Messianic discourse.

One can surely speculate that this fear of Messianism intensified Scholem's mistrust of Marxist discourse and fueled his sense of betrayal as his childhood friend Walter Benjamin, with whom he had first discussed his budding interest in Jewish mysticism, began to think it terms of Marxian categories in the mid-1920s. The problem of the relation of Marxism to secular Messianism is complicated—more complicated than Scholem thought it was—and will not be addressed here, short of the assertion that it was Benjamin's recognition of the problems in that association, if anything, that made him a good Marxian. Inherent in Marxian discourse, in other words, is the anti-utopianism that prevents the intellectual from anticipating and representing the future, which must first be materially constituted. Marxism as a theoretical discourse is thus a separate phenomenon from Communism either as a theory of political practice or as a practice in itself. Throughout Benjamin's career, and inherent in his Marxian turn, the key element in the connection of Communism and Messianism remains their shared identities as forbidden discourses.

It was in 1921, several years before the Marxian turn, that Benjamin wrote the two essays that most explicitly engage the themes of Messianism, which he had absorbed from his discussions with Scholem. These are the "Critique of Violence," written early in the year, and "The Task of the Translator," written between March and November. The earlier Kantian essay "On Language As Such and the Language of Man" (1916) and the "Theologico-political Fragment" (ca. 1920–21) should be included as well in this context of critical thought. These five years represent the period of Benjamin's maturation and of the attendant, intransigent Kantian position of the unavailability of absolute language, knowledge, and hence of absolute moral or political action. In opposition to the neo-Kantianism characteristic of the discourse of late Jewish assimilation—as in the work of Hermann Cohen—Benjamin arrived at the rejection of all claims to philosophical and political resolution or synthesis.

"The Task of the Translator" assimilates explicitly the Lurianic myth of the breaking of the vessels and fashions it into a Kantian metaphor for the limits of human knowledge of the world, and hence of the possibilities of linguistic and historical practice. It is a paradoxical essay. On one level, it was generated as a practical, introductory essay to Benjamin's own translations of Baudelaire's "Tableaux parisiens" from *Les Fleurs du Mal.* As such, it has several fundamental and austere things to say about the incommensurabilities of different languages and the limitations (and illusions) of the process of translating from one language into another. On another level, the very issue of translation and its necessity becomes a metaphor for the fragmentary character of the world, and Benjamin illustrates this point not with the expected image of Babel but with an allusion to the myth of the breaking of the vessels. A single language is like a shard from the broken vessel:

> Just as shards of a vessel which are to be jointed together [*um sich zusammenfügen*] must fit together one after another in the smallest details, although they need not be like one another, in the same way a translation, instead of resembling the meaning of the original, must lovingly and in detail incorporate the original's way of meaning, so that both the original and the translation are recognizable as the broken piece of a vessel, as the broken piece of a greater language. For this reason translation must in large measure refrain from wanting to communicate something.[28]

We can trace the allusion to the broken vessels to the discussions the young scholars Scholem and Benjamin had in Berlin from the summer of 1915, when they first met, to the year of Benjamin's essay, 1921. From the beginning, they discussed famous translations, especially Stefan George's Baudelaire (with which Benjamin competed), Hölderlin's Pindar, Regis's Rabelais, and Flaubert, whom Benjamin declared utterly untranslatable. Scholem translated passages from Benjamin's essay on language (1916) into Hebrew, which he read out loud to Benjamin, who joked that he wanted to hear in the "Ursprache."[29]

Benjamin's joke carried a bitter irony, as the essay of 1916, written midst of war, was a pessimistic declaration of the loss of absolute language. As such, it is not altogether dissimilar from Hugo von Hofmannsthal's 1901 "Letter of Lord Chandos," which also addressed the dilemma of the writer's loss of faith in the integrity of language. Here, the governing image is the loss of Paradise—the state of language after the Fall. He wrote: "The paradisic language of man must have been one of perfect knowledge, whereas later all knowledge is again infinitely differentiated in the multiplicity of language."[30]

Anson Rabinbach has reminded us that this imagery of the Fall carries a political reference reflective of the despair over the war.[31] Yet this connection does not imply that Benjamin saw the war as the apocalypse *tout court*. He and Scholem did not respect the war and the aims of Germany in it, and we certainly cannot equate their view of the status quo of 1914 with an image of the world before the Fall. This attitude was crucial to their friendship, as it was to their mutual mistrust of Martin Buber (of Hermann Cohen as well), who had come out in favor of the war. Indeed, their wartime dialogue took place in the atmosphere of draft-dodging.

In May 1919 Scholem decided to devote himself professionally to philosophy and Judaism (at the University of Munich) rather than to mathematics.[32] At the same time, Scholem and Benjamin both read and both disliked, for the same reasons, Ernst Bloch's *Geist der Utopie*, which proposed an explicitly Messianic conception of history in which Jewish and Christian cosmologies merged. In a letter to Benjamin, Scholem wrote that he was particularly offended by the sections "On the Jews" and "On the Form of the Unconstructable Presence." They bore the "terrible stigma of Prague," which meant the mark of Martin Buber. For Scholem, Bloch had presented a sweeping historical totality according to the rules of the philosophy of history, and he exhibited a philological incompetence that resulted in the misrepresentation of Jewish particularities.[33] Benjamin answered and expressed his "full agreement with your critique of the chapter 'The Jews.'"[34]

As 1920 progressed, Scholem "thought that Benjamin's turn to an intensive occupation with Judaism was close at hand."[35] On December 29, however, Benjamin wrote to Scholem that he could not devote himself to "Jewish matters" before his career had stabilized.[36] During a visit to Munich in the summer of 1921, Benjamin made the celebrated purchase of Paul Klee's watercolor *Angelus Novus*, and this image led Scholem to tell him of the Kabbalistic writings on the hymns of angels, to which, Scholem writes, Benjamin was very receptive.[37] Scholem does not record explicitly any discussion about the Lurianic Kabbalah and the myth of the breaking of the vessels. Until evidence to the contrary emerges, however, we can assume that Benjamin heard about the myth from Scholem. (Benjamin was in fact in contact with other Berlin Kabbalists, most notably Oskar Goldberg and his circle, whom Gary Smith refers to as *Zauberjuden,* "magic Jews." Scholem's contempt for this group was, and remained, intense enough for us to assume that the group produced little actual scholarship.)[38]

The Kantian identification of Messianism and of *Tikkun* as forbidden discourses, forbidden imperatives, was common to Benjamin and Scholem. The one difference between their views has much to do with the awkwardness in the friendship, which occurred long before Scholem was aware of it. For Scholem, this recalcitrance stood entirely apart from the political choice of Zionism. For Benjamin, it precluded that choice. Benjamin arrived at this position much earlier than Scholem ever came, apparently, to suspect; he states it in a letter to Ludwig Strauss of January 1913. The letter adopts a standard German romantic position, which posits politics as the realm of the particular. Benjamin writes: "I cannot make Zionism into my political element because politics is the choice of the lesser evil, the idea never appears in it, only the party." Zionism is thus another form of nationalism.[39]

If the early, romantic Benjamin rejected political action for its limitations and particularity, the mature Benjamin—within the First World War and after—hesitated in front of the politics of the universal, in front of political Messianism. The language essay of 1916 and the one-page "Theologico-political Fragment" also reflect this logic. The latter contains the clear assertion: "Nothing historical can relate itself on its own account to anything Messianic."[40] The 1921 "Critique of Violence" develops the position further through the distinction between mythical and divine violence.

The essay's German title, "Zur Kritik der Gewalt," illustrates the limitations of translatability. Toward a critique is implied by the first word: a formed critique would reflect a Kantian stance in relation to the object world which is as yet unachieved in the essay's relation to its object. "Gewalt" means violence but also force; in other words it speaks to both the legitimate and the illegitimate possession and exercise of power. "The meaning of the distinction between legitimate and illegitimate violence is not immediately obvious," he writes.[41] Benjamin offers two kinds of violence, and then provides a third: law-making, law-preserving, and, finally, law-destroying. "Law-making," he says later, "is power making, and, to that extent, an immediate manifestation of violence" (295). Law-preserving is the activity of the state, and the actions of the police constitute both law-making and law-preserving (286–87). The claims to legitimation of these two first forms of violence entail the category of myth. "Mythical violence in its archetypical form is a mere manifestation of the gods," he writes (294). Myth has no need to justify itself; unconcerned with justification, it is unconcerned with justice as well. The only presence that genuinely incorporates the end within the means, and therefore can justify itself with reference only to itself—the illusion of myth but not the truth—is the divine. "Justice is the principle of all divine end-making, power the principle of all mythical lawmaking" (295). A longer quotation is warranted here:

> Just as in all spheres God opposes myth, mythical violence is confronted by the divine. And the latter constitutes its antithesis in all respects. If mythical violence is law-making, divine violence is law-destroying; if the former sets boundaries, the latter boundlessly destroys them. If mythical violence brings at once guilt and retribution, divine power only expiates; if the former threatens, the latter strikes; if the former is bloody, the latter is lethal without spilling blood. (297)

And in the concluding paragraph:

> Only mythical violence, not divine, will be recognizable as such with certainty, unless it be in incomparable effects, because the expiatory power of violence is not visible to men. Once again all the eternal forms are open to pure divine violence, which myth bastardized with law. (300)

That the divine is a new term for the forbidden Messianic is, I think, clear. The opposition between the ideologically sustained, totalizing, mythicizing power of human political agency and the just violence, at once creative and destructive, of the Messianic is clear as well. Benjamin goes further, however, in attributing a Greek archetype to the mythical and a Judaic one to the divine. This Graeco-Judaic distinction implies a commentary on contemporary German culture and ideology.

At stake is what E. M. Butler called, in 1936, "the tyranny of Greece over Germany," in particular the power of the German reception of Greek myths and cultural models to authenticate the desire for cultural totality—in short, the power of aestheticism.[42] The aesthetic culture heralded in Nietzsche's *Birth of Tragedy* is the model of such a reception of Greece and its attendant program for Germany. The Nietzscheans of the 1890s—including, for example, Stefan George on the Christian side and Martin Buber on the Jewish side—favored this aestheticist Nietzsche and ignored the later, post-Wagnerian, critical Nietzsche. George had gone especially far in aestheticizing the violence of the First World War, which he described in terms of a heroic purge. The tentacles of Stefan Georgean hocus-pocus reached close to Benjamin, and included Alfred and Julia Cohn, who were assuming at this times the roles of the architect and Ottilie in Benjamin's personal *Elective Affinities* saga. (His study of Goethe's novel, dedicated to Julia Cohn, was begun in 1921.)[43]

In returning for a moment to "The Task of the Translator," we can see the concerns of these companion critical essays refracted in its argument. All language and languages operate according to the principle of the hidden, forbidden referent, which is the language of God, of "God's remembrance."[44] A translation enters into a dialectic with the original text in common reference to that hidden absolute. The life of the original text and language attains through translation a higher stage of development (*Entfaltung*, which is "governed by a special, high purposiveness"—Kant's *Zweckmässigkeit*).[45] He continues: "Thus translation is ultimately purposive with regard for the expression of the innermost relationship between languages. Impossible for it to reveal this hidden relationship, impossible to recover it; it can, however, represent it, insofar as it realizes it in embryonic or concentrated form."[46] The translation, and the translation process, is thus synecdochical to the forbidden totality of absolute language, as the worldly shard is synecdochical to the divine vessel.

A translation conscious of this ethic will shun accessibility (which amounts to a dissipation of the forbidden reference) and point inwardly to the original language and to the hidden absolute. This principle generated the opening paragraph of the essay and its assertion that no work of art is intended for the reader, viewer, or listener. (A reminder that the essay accompanied Benjamin's own translations of Baudelaire may be in order here.) The success of a translation must be judged according to the incompleteness, and its expression of "longing for linguistic completeness."[47] The essay thus ends in paradox, as it holds that the successful translation must be fragmented, cracked, and therefore faulty as a carrier of meaning. The examples are Hölderlin's Sophocles translations. They expand the German language, but they do not communicate meaning. They reveal

the monstrous and original danger of all translation: that the gates of a language thus expanded and subverted [*durchwaltet*] slam shut and enclose the translator in silence. The Sophocles translations were Hölderlin's last work. Meaning reels in them from abyss to abyss, until it threat-

ens to lose itself in the bottomless depth of language. But there is a stop.
It is granted however to no text other than the holy one, in which meaning has ceased to be the watershed for the flow of language and the flow
of revelation.[48]

It is impossible to know how literally Benjamin wishes to identify holy
scripture with the word of God. But there is a secondary point. The word of
God represents language absolute and *simpliciter*; it is therefore "übersetz-
bar schlechthin": translatable absolutely. (The emphasis here is on the "absolutely": in this light, it was not contrived at all for Paul de Man to make
his notorious remark that on a certain level it makes no difference whether
this phrase of Benjamin's is itself translated as "absolutely translatable" or
as "absolutely untranslatable"—the latter result appearing, by error, presumably, in the French translation of Maurice de Gandillac.) If perfect translatability occurs *only* in a situation of absoluteness, then the everyday process
of translation remains in the realm of untranslatability.[49]

The constant absent presence of this hidden absolute makes living in
language especially painful. The formula is identical in the case of politics
and personal political action. The only strategy for bridging the personal—in
the form of the linguistic or the political—with the universal involves the
aestheticizing redefinition of the universal as a totality within human reach.
This is the strategy, and, I would dare to say, the attraction, of Heidegger's
restoration of authenticity and the house of Being. The point of mediation
between the aestheticizing universal and the unrewarding particular is precisely the mode of thinking and living which Benjamin's intransigence pre-
vented him from finding. On the one hand, the forms of his intellectual and
political exile precluded the aestheticist militancy (and the political irresponsibility) of a Heidegger; on the other, they could not proffer the vantage
point of the Master of Lamb House, who showed enough ingenuousness to
reflect, in 1909: "What indeed could be more delightful than to enjoy a sense
of the absolute in such easy conditions?"[50]

3

Through his lineage, security, and sensibility, Henry James was able to pursue a career and an art with all the distance from historical contingency
that he needed. Walter Benjamin reeled from one contingency to the next,
professionally, personally, politically. James honed his sensibility in his later
years; Benjamin radicalized and politicized his. Yet they do not wind up as
opposites, as authors of texts that have nothing to say to each other. Al-

though I have argued here that the categories of aesthetic form and human language remain absolute for James in ways they cannot remain so for Benjamin, I have also argued that their moral dialogues with the broken vessel of modernity, with its cultural representations and its demands on critical and creative thought, form a solid point of intersection—perhaps of translation. Politics retains a place in James's moral imagination, as the plays of form do in Benjamin.

The late James was particularly sensitive to the question of the legitimacy of his political voice. The theme of politics and art, their confrontation and their incommensurability had been explored most explicitly in *The Princess Casamassima* (1886).[51] The title character stands for the world of wealth and aesthetic taste, as it is introduced to the novel's up-from-poverty protagonist, Hyacinth Robinson. Hyacinth's dilemma is the choice between aestheticism (in the passive sense) and revolutionary politics. He cannot resolve the two imperatives, and the novel culminates in his suicide. But what does the suicide represent: the dissipation of the aesthetic sensibility once political consciousness has revealed the truth about the world, or the victory of the ultimate aesthetic, theatrical gesture? Does Hyacinth resolve this distinction, and does James?

In the 1909 preface to the New York edition, James discussed, five years after *The Golden Bowl*, the development of his own political imagination. He recalled conceiving the novel while "walking the streets" of London with his "eyes greatly open," all the while experiencing "the assault directly made by the great city upon an imagination quick to react." The story of Hyacinth Robinson "sprang up for me out of the London pavement." For Hyacinth and for James at once, "the reward of a romantic curiosity would be the question of what the total assault, that of the world of his work-a-day life and the world of his divination and his envy together, would have made of him, and what in especial he would have made of them."[52] For both Hyacinth and James, politics remains a world perceived and observed, with the security felt by the urban walker who knows he will soon be home.

Walter Benjamin committed suicide at the Spanish border in September 1940. Undoubtedly, his death has encouraged subsequent readers to define his life and his significance as those of a paradigmatic twentieth-century intellectual and political martyr. Yet he died for no political cause, and his participation in political discourse had been theoretically serious but not directly active. Whereas the pathos of his death is obvious, its significance is less so, short of a means of heroicizing his life and thought. It is clear, however, and important that Benjamin lived and died outside the boundaries of aesthetic discourse. This is true despite the high degree of personal

aestheticism (in the passive sense) and *amour-propre* which his biographers
and critical readers have been loath to admit, for fear of compromising his
political and critical profile.

In his best-known work, the 1936 essay on "The Work of Art in the
Age of its Technical Reproducibility," Benjamin identified the critique of
political ideology with the critique of aestheticism. The ideological power
of the aesthetic, he argued, resided throughout human history in the phenomenon of the aura. In religious culture, the aesthetic icon projected an
aura that originated in its contact with the divine. Such contact might be
material and physical, as in the case of a relic, or associative, as in an image or idol. Romantic aestheticism replaced the divine aura with the aura
of genius. In both cultural manifestations, Benjamin argued, auratic power
accrued through a claim of authenticity. What he did not argue systematically was the connection between the physical authenticity of the work of
art and the *cultural* authenticity which the work of art accorded the receptive community that participated in its auratic field. Benjamin's critical and
political rejection of the aura is identical with his rejection of the principle
of authenticity—aesthetic and cultural. He understood with clarity that the
promise of modern aesthetic ideology was to deliver on the anti-modernist
desire for cultural authenticity.

CHAPTER FOUR

Walter Benjamin and Eduard Fuchs

The Collector as Allegorist

I

Between 1934 and 1937, while living in political exile, in financial panic, and in almost total obscurity, Walter Benjamin wrote the life of Eduard Fuchs (1870–1940), a fellow German in anonymous Parisian exile, a Social Democratic feuilletonist turned historian and collector of caricature and erotica. Benjamin called his essay "Eduard Fuchs, the Collector and the Historian."[1] These categories, like the persons Fuchs and (in his own eyes at least) Benjamin, are kaleidoscopic. For Benjamin, the collector is at once bourgeois, fetishistic, and antiquarian, and also, with a different refraction, the historical materialist in the most literal manner. The figure of the collector, distinct, perhaps, from most actual collectors, becomes for him as well an allegory of the allegorist, of the historian as allegorist. The historian is both the nineteenth-century German, totalizing *Kulturhistoriker* and the Baudelairean modernist who lives and chronicles the transient, the fleeting, the contingent. In an intricate play of shadows, Benjamin strives in this essay to produce a shift in the light, so that the bourgeois and the *Kulturhisto-riker*—in himself, in Fuchs, in the vestiges of nineteenth-century European cultural discourses—might, in effect, change sides, and help to reempower the critical and historical consciousness of a desperate European modernity and roll back the expanding cover of fascism. This task needs to be undertaken through a confrontation with material reality.

The goal is a new kind of historical materialism composed of both the collecting of material history and the Marxian analysis of historical process. It is therefore not a question of historical theory but of historical practice. The Fuchs essay thus encapsulates not so much a Benjaminian historical theory, which really does not and could not exist, but rather a Benjaminian historical practice, on which all his writing might be said to depend. In this way, the writing of the Fuchs essay shadows the large project on which Benjamin had been at work since 1927: the history of modernity, the *Passagenarbeit*. To go even further, it contains the promise of a flashback to the logic of his earlier critical-historical writings on the cultural practices of the German baroque and of romanticism. As a component of that flashback, it represents some of the connections between the baroque and the modern which formed Benjamin's historical and critical motivations and work. I want, therefore, to argue that the Fuchs essay can be seen as a prism through which the connecting patterns of Benjamin's historical practice are revealed. Even more strongly: it seems to me that Benjamin himself took stock of this connecting logic through the writing of the essay.

Because the Fuchs essay was written on commission for Theodor Adorno, Max Horkheimer, and their *Zeitschrift für Sozialforschung*, it is likely that Benjamin saw the piece as a chance to take stock of, and even advertise, the principles of his elusive project of the history of modernity. The essay clearly advocates the practice of historical materialism, but if the advocacy is straightforward, the character of the attending practice is intricate. It is the advocacy and not the intricacy in the argument that made the road to publication under the systematic eyes of Adorno, Horkheimer, and Leo Löwenthal a smooth one. A year later, as is well known, Adorno rejected for publication Benjamin's essay "The Paris of the Second Empire in Baudelaire," another, and a more historical, encapsulation of Benjamin's project, on the grounds that it slipped into antiquarianism and failed to exhibit the application of a systematic historical materialism. If Adorno, in reading the Baudelaire essay, was still looking for a statement of theory rather than an instance of practice, then it can be assumed that he had not read the Fuchs essay carefully enough.

Horkheimer's relationship with Benjamin is no less problematic than Adorno's. Horkheimer had completed his own *Habilitation* under Hans Cornelius, the senior aesthetician at the University of Frankfurt, in April 1925 with a thesis on Kant. Weeks later, Benjamin submitted to Cornelius his habilitation thesis *(Habilitationsschrift)*, the study of the origin of the German baroque lamentation play (*Ursprung des deutschen Trauerspiels*, published in 1928). In the aggressive posture of a newly minted *Privatdozent*, Horkheimer read the work first and encouraged its rejection.[2] A decade later, it was he who recommended that Benjamin write on Fuchs for the *Zeitschrift*. His motives were thus clearly complex and possibly combined a genuine

intellectual anticipation with a certain implied distance and even mock-
ery of both Benjamin and Fuchs. In 1930, Horkheimer had defended Fuchs
against charges of obscenity surrounding the publication of "Die grossen
Meister der Erotik."[3] As Rolf Tiedemann suggests, the length of time Benjamin took on the essay shows his "great reservations, or rather, [his] explicit
opposition" (GS 2:13–16). On September 18, 1935, Horkheimer wrote an
encouraging letter to Benjamin from New York (where he had relocated the
Institute for Social Research in May 1934) and, with reference to the Fuchs
essay, offered the following dubious compliment: "The method of grasping
the epoch from small, superficial symptoms seems this time to show its full
strength. You have taken a significant step beyond the preceding material-
istic explanations of aesthetic phenomena."[4] In March 1937, Horkheimer
wrote to Benjamin that the essay furthered the basic theoretical intentions
of the Zeitschrift.[5]

On March 1, 1937, Benjamin wrote to Adorno that his sympathy for
Fuchs and his writings had grown as he worked on them. Benjamin's am-
bivalence about Fuchs parallels Hermann Broch's in regard to Hugo von Hofmannsthal, on whom he was pressed to write in 1947. Whereas Broch had
approached the life of Hofmannsthal as a symptom of an aestheticized age,
he found his object to be a surprisingly compelling analyst of the modernity
that finally defeated him. As his essay progressed, Broch wrote: "Just as a
homosexual relationship develops slowly between the chambermaid and
the lady, so I feel toward H.; with a slight sense of perversity I overcome my
revulsion."[6]

2

The first section of the Fuchs essay opposes historicism to historical materialism. The character of the historicism that is, according to Benjamin, to be
rejected is very clear, even if Benjamin does not rehearse its genealogy. It is
the accumulating conception of history, in nineteenth-century Germany, as
a coherent, linear process, which is stated philosophically by Hegel and then
developed into the academic historigraphic industries of Ranke, Droysen,
Mommsen, and Treitschke, among others. Benjamin calls the narrative principle of this kind of history an epic one. It is a history of "once upon a time,"
he says—of an aestheticized, totalized past. The historian who contemplates
this past (and contemplation is the relevant mode of thought) is thus able
at once to reify a perfect picture of an autonomous past era and at the same
time to infuse that past era into a linear totality that ultimately produces,
and justifies, the present. The antidote to this historicism is historical ma-

terialism, but defined by Benjamin in a highly idiosyncratic manner, to which the attending persona of Eduard Fuchs is appropriated.

Benjamin defines the goal of historical materialism as "a consciousness of the present which explodes the continuum of history."[7] This sounds like, but is not, Marx, and one might go so far as to say that the difference in focus—not necessarily in political agenda—between this statement and the thought of Marx which it seems to echo produces Benjamin's mature sense of history. For Marx, the coming revolution will indeed break the continuum of the past, and that past is a linear and essentially a monolithic process of successive modes of production and their attending modes of social relations and domination. The linearity of the past is the dimension of Hegelianism which Marx never abjures. The linearity of the past is also an instrumentalism in a double sense: the past produces the (liberated) future—in the world as in Marx's writing. Benjamin, however, does not think about the past in instrumental terms. This is not at all to say that he has no interest in revolution. It is to say that the past exists for him—and must exist for the historian he wants to be—with the same dimensionality as the present or the future. Thus, when Benjamin talks about exploding the continuum of the past, he is talking not about breaking the momentum of historical linearity as such but rather about seeing the past not as a continuum. He is advocating a nonlinear historical temporality. For Benjamin, the view of history as a continuum is fundamentally dangerous because it reinforces the ideology of mechanistic progress, which is dangerous no matter into whose hands it falls.[8] With this distinction, Benjamin's concept of historical materialism—politically compatible as it is with that of Marx—moves away from Marxian paradigms as it moves closer to a concept of material history.

Historical materialism is, first, born out of the experience of the present; it thus stands epistemologically on entirely different ground from that of historicism. Rather than claiming to remove the present of the historicizing subject in favor of an autonomous past, which nevertheless functions to generate and justify the present, historical materialism is generated by the desire of the present subject for self-understanding as well as for an understanding of the historical object-world. The method becomes a dialectical (dialogic) relationship with that world, which, in turn, is represented not as an all-encompassing totality but rather in terms of specific material and experiential constructions. History is not the history of thought but the history of experience (a material entity), and the experience of the present is directly implicated in the reconstruction of past experience (not the experience of the past, because there can never be the past). To cite Benjamin's summary paragraph:

Historicism presents the eternal image of the past; historical materialism presents an individual experience [eine jeweilige Erfahrung] with
the past, which stands alone. The replacement of the epic element by
the constructive element proves to be the condition for this experience.
In this experience, the powerful forces that lay bound up in historicism's
"once-upon-a-time" are freed. To place into the work the experience with
history, which is original to every present—this is the task of historical
materialism. It inclines toward a consciousness of the present which explodes the continuum of history. (GS 2:468)

Where does Eduard Fuchs fit in here? As a collector of images—of cari-
catures as well as erotica—Fuchs is appropriated by Benjamin as a kind of
preconscious historical materialist. Fuch's dialogues with the past are on the
way to a full, conscious materialist practice: "an old dogmatic and naïve idea
of reception stands together for him with the new and critical one" (468–69).
With this phrase, Benjamin introduces the principle of a *critical* historical
practice alongside the materialist. He ends the first section of the essay with
an assertion that reveals the extent to which a symbolic autobiography is
underway here: "All courting of a work of art must remain futile, where its
sober, historical content is not met with dialectical understanding [*Erken-
nen*]. This is only the first of the truths to which the work of the collector
Eduard Fuchs is oriented. His collections are the answer of the practician to
the aporias [*Aporien*] of theory" (469).

Fuchs was born in 1870, Benjamin writes, and "formed himself" [*hat
sich gebildet*] in a period in which the competing epistemological paradigms
were those of cultural history and positivism. The "history of culture" [*Kulturgeschichte*] is the twin of historicism. Historical materialism must come
into its own in terms of cultural history. Fuchs's work, as a product of this
period, is implicated by the ideologies of *Kulturgeschichte*, but it points in
the direction of a materialist cultural history. Cultural history thus rejects
the linearity and the aestheticism professed, consciously or not, by *Kulturgeschichte* (the history of culture).[9] Cultural history places the history of
aesthetic objects in a context that includes the corresponding or contributing
"unnamed drudgery of contemporaries": "There is at no time a document
of culture that is not at the same time a document of barbarity. No history
of culture has yet done justice to this fundamental state of affairs, and it can
hardly hope yet to do so" (GS 2:477).

The history of culture is barbaric precisely because it lacks "the destructive impulse that authenticates dialectical thought as well as the experience

of the dialectician" (478). In valorizing certain objects of culture (aesthetic
or other) or bodies of thought, the history of culture casts a shadow over
the lived reality of their production. With an expression of fear explicitly
connected to the year 1937, Benjamin quotes an address given twenty-five
years earlier by Alfred Weber to the convention of German sociologists in
1912 (476). Weber had asserted that "culture exists only . . . when life has
attained the status of a formation [*Gebilde*] liberated from its needs and
usefulnesses."[10] Benjamin answers: "In this concept of culture slumbered
the seeds of barbarity, which in the meantime have germinated. . . . Culture
exists as a kind of artwork. . . . Twenty-five years after these words were
spoken, culture-states [*Kulturstaaten*] have taken it upon themselves as an
honor to resemble such artworks, to be such artworks" (476).

The antidote to this aesthetic discourse of culture and its dangers is thus
a dialectical mode of cultural history, which destroys not the objects of art
or thought but rather their auras. The aura of a historical object or discourse
casts all contextual reality into a shadow realm of marginalization. The destruction of the aura amounts to the reillumination of the margins.

3

My use of the term *aura*, which does not appear in the Fuchs essay, suggests
the presence in the essay's argument of the case Benjamin had made a year
before in "The Work of Art in the Age of Its Technical Reproducibility."[11]
The concept of the aura refers to the power and authority that a unique or
"original" work of art possessed by virtue of its authenticity, and which
disappears, for Benjamin, as the actual object of the work of art becomes a
reproducible entity, as in a photograph or a film, for example.[12] Historically,
the aura and its power had been a function of two basic phenomena. First
the production of art in a religious context endowed the aesthetic object
with a metaphorical association with the divine. "Eternal value and mystery" (*Ewigkeitswert und Geheimnis*), in Benjamin's words, are the auratic
qualities of sacred art. The vacuum created by (in Weberian terms) the disenchantment of the world was filled by the cult of romanticism and its
attending ideology of, again in Benjamin's phrase, "creativity and genius"
(*Schöpfertum und Genialität*) (*GS* 1:473). The point Benjamin makes in his
introduction to the essay is that the stakes are high for the defeat of these
concepts, as their survival into his own period will spell their appropriation
by fascism.

Because the existence of the aura as a quality present in a work of

art is a function of the work's authenticity, one can say that the concept
of authenticity is the one that bridges the work of art and (the work of)
culture. The danger of a fascist appropriation of auratic art lies in the fascist idea—specifically the National Socialist idea—of culture, which is
grounded in an ideology of *völkisch* authenticity. The Fuchs essay, with its
understanding of a cultural history as a materialist history of experience,
argues for a historical conception of culture that offsets a more traditional,
nationalist *Kulturgeschichte* in the same way that postauratic art offsets
auratic art. The Fuchs essay's historical materialism amounts, therefore,
to a postauratic cultural practice. At the same time, it shares and advances
the task of the "Work of Art" essay—that of the critique of cultural and
political aestheticism.

Benjamin's critique of authenticity, in art and in culture (and the importance of art lies in its implications for culture), emerges in clear contradis-
tinction to the contemporary aesthetic and cultural writings of Heidegger,
specifically to "The Origin of the Work of Art."[13] Among the many moves
Heidegger makes in this piece, three are clear: the removal of the work of art
from the quotidian and from the social in general (the separation of "earth"
and essence from "world" and "thing"); the restoration of the aura as an
aesthetic, spiritual, and cultural principle; the carryover of the aura (as the
valorization of the aesthetic) into the reauthenticated, metasocial, meta-
political, cultural world. Heidegger thus intensifies and transforms a traditional formalist discussion of art into an essentialist one that reifies cultural
identity in an unholy alliance with the significant artwork (*Kunstwerk*: the
single, composite noun of the title).

This aesthetic and cultural sanctification is accomplished through the
well-known discussion of Vincent Van Gogh's painting of a pair of peasant
shoes (fig. 4.1). The painting becomes a leitmotiv in Heidegger's argument
because its portrayed object—the shoes—mediates, representationally and,
therefore, potentially philosophically, between earth and world, between a
transcendent essence and a mundane materiality. Heidegger introduces the
discussion of the painting in an intensely tautological paragraph that claims
to introduce the work of art as a thing (its incidental character) but then
gives as examples of "things" objects that are deeply encoded, ideologically,
as cultural-aesthetic essences:

> Works of art are familiar to everyone. . . . The picture hangs on the wall
> like a rifle or a hat. A painting, e.g., the one by Van Gogh that represents a
> pair of peasant shoes, travels from one exhibition to another. Works of art
> are shipped like coal from the Ruhr and logs from the Black Forest. Dur-

FIG. 4.1. Vincent Van Gogh, *A Pair of Shoes*

ing the First World War Hölderlin's hymns were packed in the soldier's knapsack together with cleaning gear. Beethoven's quartets lie in the storerooms of the publishing house like potatoes in a cellar. (19)

The analogies themselves assert the a priori accomplishment of the argument Heidegger is about to undertake. We have in the names Hölderlin and Beethoven powerful metonyms of a nationalistic pantheon. Hölderlin and Beethoven are themselves of prenationalistic generations, but in the 1930s they were received and prized as national and nationalist icons; their works are invoked here, precisely, as resources, and indeed as resources for the nation. And beyond these names, we have a repertory of things that are at the same time blatant and poetic symbols of national essence and identiy, nurturing, and strength: coal from the Ruhr, logs from the Black Forest, the soldier's knapsack, the potatoes in the cellar. The soldier's cleaning gear is hardly limited to the prosaic; it invokes, rather, the militaristic purification of the German soul exalted by Stefan George—and attacked specifically by Benjamin in the closing passages of "The Work of Art." Invoked in general is an economy of hidden resources—strength stored in knapsacks, cellars, and in the poetic recesses of the national mind and body.

Heidegger now takes off by setting the thingly nature of art into an allegorical relationship with its artistic nature. Getting back to the shoes, he introduces a lyric paragraph with the words "And yet—," which at first seems to explode the essentialist character of his argument:

A pair of peasant shoes and nothing more. And yet—

From the dark opening of the worn insides of the shoes the toil-some tread of the worker stares forth. In the stiffly rugged heaviness of the shoes there is the accumulated tenacity of her slow trudge through the far-spreading and ever-uniform furrows of the field swept by a raw wind. On the leather lie the dampness and richness of the soil. Under the soles slides the loneliness of the field-path as evening falls. In the shoes vibrates the silent call of the earth. . . . This equipment belongs to the *earth*, and it is protected in the *world* of the peasant woman. (33–34)

Yet the relationship of the represented object—both the image of the shoes and the image (i.e., the physical painting) itself—to the lived experience of its context serves not to de-essentialize the image but rather to essentialize the context: "Van Gogh's painting is the disclosure of what the equipment, the pair of peasant shoes, *is* in truth. . . . The work, therefore, is not the re-production of some particular entity that happens to be present at any given time; it is on the contrary, the reproduction of the thing's general essence" (36, 37).

For an example of the essentialization of the cultural context into the formal discourse of the attending artwork, Heidegger offers the example of a Greek temple as "a work that cannot be ranked as representational art." But his unconcealed motive is to provide an icon of national culture (like the coal from the Ruhr and the logs from the Black Forest), as soon becomes clear:

A building, a Greek temple, portrays nothing. It simply stands there in the middle of the rock-cleft valley. The building encloses the figure of the god, and in this concealment lets it stand out into the holy precinct through the open portico. By means of the temple, the god is present in the temple. This presence of the god is in itself the extension and de-limitation of the precinct as a holy precinct. The temple and its precinct, however, do not fade away into the indefinite. It is the temple-work that first fits together and at the same time gathers around itself the unity of those paths and relations in which birth and death, disaster and bless-ing, victory and disgrace, endurance and decline acquire the shape of destiny for human being. The all-governing expanse of this open rela-tional context is the world of this historical people. Only from and in this expanse does the nation first return to itself for the fulfillment of its vocation. . . .

The temple-work, standing there, opens up a world and at the same time sets this world back again on earth, which itself only thus emerges as native ground. (41–42)

The rock-cleft valley aside, the structure imagined here is more likely a neoclassical temple in Berlin than a classical one in Athens. (The "tyranny of Greece over Germany" indeed!) The allegorical intent of the invocation of the nation—of the nation as a historical people—is clear. The work of art as "the happening of truth," already tied to the nation as work of art, takes a further step into the explicitly political: "Another way in which truth occurs is the act that founds a political state" (62).[14]

Finally, the "Gestell" of the nation-state as created work of art is succeeded by that of the nation as *preserved* work of art:[15] "The preservers of a work belong to its createdness with an essentiality equal to that of its creators" (71). Preservation is the opposite of commerce, and this opposition maps itself onto the opposition of *Kultur* and *Zivilisation* which controls Heidegger's thinking. He thus dismisses the social dimension of the art work and its afterlife: "As soon as the thrust into the extraordinary is parried and captured by the sphere of familiarity and connoisseurship, the art business has begun. Even a painstaking handing on of works to posterity, all scientific efforts to regain them, no longer reach the work's own being, but only a recollection of it" (68).[16]

If, for just a minute, we absorb Heidegger's essentialist logic and imagine the *Gestell*, or represented figure, that would be the encapsulation of all that is anathema to his aesthetic and cultural ideology, we can without difficulty come up with the figure of Eduard Fuchs. Fuchs the man and Fuchs the allegorical subject of Benjamin's essay provide the archetype of the figure with no place in Heidegger's cosmology. In this respect, "The Origin of the Work of Art" (read: ". . . of Culture") is an unparalleled representation of the work of culture as the work of barbarism.

The intensity of the opposition of Benjamin's cultural practice to Heidegger's cannot be overestimated. The figure of Eduard Fuchs—the displaced (or nonplaced) urban intellectual, materialist, and flâneur—emerges as the modernist antagonist to Heidegger's projection of the regrounded man or woman of the earth. The debate as to who shall inherit modern culture has thus seized on the problem of the reading of Van Gogh's shoes, because of the obvious suggestion of the metaphor of standing in a person's shoes. The question Whose shoes are these? thus becomes the question Who controls (walks the path of) modernity? For this reason, I pursue this discussion a bit further, despite the digressive character of the topic of Heidegger and Van Gogh within the basic outline of my essay. Two more thinkers need to enter the discussion: Meyer Shapiro and Jacques Derrida.

In a short essay of 1968 called "The Still Life as Personal Object: A Note on Heidegger and Van Gogh," Meyer Schapiro joined the most traditional kind of art history (identifying the subject of a painting) to the most subtle and powerful cultural analysis (the meaning of a represented object).[17] With a dazzling piece of evidence, Schapiro argues that the "peasant shoes" of Van Gogh's paintings (there are in fact eight such pictures) are in fact representations of the artist's own shoes. "The philosopher," he says, "has indeed deceived himself" and in fact derived his *völkisch* projection from the idea of peasant shoes: "I find nothing in Heidegger's fanciful description of the shoes represented by Van Gogh that could not have been imagined in looking at a real pair of peasant's shoes" (138). Here Schapiro is pulling out his art-historical credentials, but he does not go on to a formalist argument. Rather, he argues for a historically responsible contextual seeing of the image. The specific painting on which Heidegger said (in response to Schapiro's query) that he had based his discussion does in fact represent, visually and literally, what Schapiro identifies as "the artist's presence in the work":

> When Van Gogh depicted the peasant's wooden sabots, he gave them a clear, unworn shape and surface like the smooth still life objects he had set beside them on the same table: the bowl, the bottles, etc. In the later picture of a peasant's leather slippers he has turned them with their backs to the viewer. His own shoes he has isolated on the floor and he has rendered them as if facing us, and so individual and wrinkled in appearance that we can speak of them as veridical portraits of aging shoes. . . .
>
>   In isolating his own worn shoes on a canvas, he turns them to the spectator; he makes of them a piece from a self-portrait, the part of the costume with which we tread the earth and in which we locate the strains of movement, fatigue, pressure, heaviness—the burden of the erect body in its contact with the ground. They mark our inescapable position on the earth. To "be in someone's shoes" is to be in his predicament or his station in life. For a painter to represent his worn shoes as the main subject of a picture is for him to express a concern with the fatalities of *his social being* [my italics]. (139, 140)

Schapiro concludes with a theatrical unveiling of evidence:

Gauguin, who shared Van Gogh's quarters in Arles in 1888, sensed a personal history behind his friend's painting of a pair of shoes. He has told in his reminiscences of Van Gogh a deeply affecting story linked with Van Gogh's shoes.

"In the studio was a pair of big hob-nailed shoes, all worn and spotted with mud; he made of it a remarkable still life painting. I do not know why I suspected that there was a story behind this old relic, and I ventured one day to ask him if he had some reason for preserving with respect what one ordinarily throws out for the ragpicker's basket.

"'My father,' he said, 'was a pastor, and at his urging I pursued theological studies in order to prepare for my future vocation. As a young pastor I left for Belgium one fine morning, without telling my family, to preach the gospel in the factories, not as I had been taught but as I understood it myself. These shoes, as you see, have bravely endured the fatigue of that trip.'" (140–41)

Gauguin's testimony gives Schapiro the right to assert that the shoes "are the shoes of the artist, by that time a man of the town and city." At stake, as Derrida will say, is the reappropriation of art and modern experience from Heidegger and his essentialist ideology. The shoes are thus "the shoes" of the ungrounded artist in the city—the shoes, also, of Walter Benjamin and Eduard Fuchs. (Our appropriation cannot be complete: in all likelihood, Van Gogh's own evangelical mentality would have made him more comfortable in the company of Heidegger's phantom peasant woman than in that of Eduard Fuchs! His shoes thus walk deeper than his person into the web of urban modernity and its metaphors.)[18]

The fourth and final section of Derrida's book *The Truth in Painting* addresses the so-called "duel between Heidegger and Schapiro" on the question of the appropriation of Van Gogh's shoes.[19] This fourth section carries the virtuoso title "Restitutions of the Truth in Pointing." The French pun is more complicated than its translation, as "pointure" and "peinture" are related by more than sound: "pointure" is a painterly technique, as in Seurat's "pointillage." It is also, as Derrida points out in the chapter's first epigraph, a term in shoemaking having to do with the punching of holes for laces. In other words, one needs only to figure out the title of the chapter to realize that Derrida begins with a breathtaking command of the issues involved in the Heidegger-Schapiro dispute and, furthermore, that his equation—in the very title—of pointing (cobbling) and painting reveals his own association of the shoes with the artist, which amounts to a broad hint that Derrida is on

Schapiro's side. (Derrida's many other treatments of Heidegger, particularly *De l'esprit*, would second such a judgment.) But—"and yet" (the words, a quote from "The Origin," which begin the chapter)—Derrida *does not point*. He does not take sides in his presentation, and in fact he chooses not (or fails) even to mention Schapiro's main evidence—the reminiscence of Gauguin. In the cases of Schapiro and Heidegger, Derrida's rhetoric of egalitarian juxtaposition is disturbing. He presents the case as follows:

> Let us posit as an axiom that the desire for attribution is a desire for ap-
> propriation. In matters of art as it is everywhere else. To say: this (this
> painting or these shoes) is due to [*revient à*] X, comes down to [*revient à*]
> saying: it is due to me, via the detour of the "it is due to (a) me."[20] Not
> only: it is properly due to such-and-such, man or woman, to the male
> or female wearer ("Die Bäuerin auf dem Acker *trägt* die Schuhe. . . . Die
> Bäuerin dagegen *trägt* einfach die Schuhe," says the one in 1935, "They
> are clearly pictures of the artist's *own* shoes, not the shoes of the peas-
> ant," replies the other in 1968, my [Derrida's] emphasis), but it is prop-
> erly due to *me*, via a short detour: the identification, among many other
> identifications, of Heidegger with the peasant and Schapiro with the city
> dweller, of the former with the rooted and the sedentary, the latter with
> the uprooted emigrant. A demonstration to be followed up, for let us
> have no doubt about this, in this restitution trial, it's also a question of
> the shoes, or even the clogs, and going only a little further back for the
> moment, of the feet of two illustrious Western professors, neither more
> nor less. (260)

The rhetoric of Derrida's scrupulously egalitarian juxtaposition of Heidegger and Schapiro is out of control and self-defeating. The mirroring of
the "two illustrious Western professors" is made worse by the deliberately
dismissive locution of "the one in 1935" and "the other in 1968." The enforced symmetry of Derrida's references suppresses the obvious differences
between Schapiro and Heidegger, between the political shadows of the time
markers 1935 and 1968, and—to be completely explicit—between a sup-
porter of National Socialism (in the interest of the same metaphysics of
authenticity elegized in "The Origin of the Work of Art") and his Jewish,
leftist critic. One might argue that Derrida's tone is, ultimately, ironic and
that the ideological schism between his two professors is in fact allegorized
by the years 1935 (a year of the right and its victory) and 1968 (a year of the
left and its defeat, especially in France). But the clumsiness and disdain in

the phrase "two illustrious professors" kills any such play. One cannot avoid the fear that Derrida's intricate and aesthticized discourse absorbs and reflects in its style the same Heideggerian aesthetic ideology that it tends also to unhinge.

What rules of readership should we use in reading such a juxtaposition? It can certainly be argued (and I expect it to be argued against me here) that a debate between Heidegger and Schapiro is a debate between thinkers and interpretive positions, not between ciphers carrying ideological and identitarian burdens. In this way, Derrida's parallel can be said to do honor to both men's thinking, precisely by leaving contextual baggage out. My position on this issue is that there are times when ideological context is inherent in positions that may operate by ignoring or by denying them. For this reason, I argue that Heidegger's imagery of Hölderlin, knapsacks, and cellars is nationalistically determined. Such is the materiality of language, a lesson Derrida himself has taught well.

What are the stakes for Schapiro? His 1968 "Note on Heidegger and Van Gogh" has been reprinted in his collected papers, followed by a piece called "Further Notes on Heidegger and Van Gogh," which carries the date of 1994. Schapiro revisits the controversy and insists on two criteria for interpreting the painting: style and (the artist's) experience. In other words, Schapiro insists on a contextual reading.

That the shoes are Van Gogh's own is not in question. What is in question is the logic of their display:

> Comparing Van Gogh with other artists, one can say that few could have chosen to devote an entire canvas to their own shoes in isolation, yet addressed to a cultivated viewer. Hardly Manet, or Cézanne, or Renoir, hardly even his often cited model, Millet. And of these few—we can judge from the examples—none would have represented the shoes as Van Gogh did—set on the ground facing the viewer, the loosened and folded parts of the shoes, the laces, the unsightly differences between parts of the left and the right, their depressed and broken aspect.[21]

The result of this presentation, Schapiro suggests, is that "one can describe Van Gogh's painting of his shoes as a picture of objects seen and felt by the artist as a significant part of himself—he faces himself like a mirrored image—chosen, isolated, carefully arranged, and addressed to himself" (146).

This self-mirroring aspect of the picture leads Schapiro to see it in conjunction with Van Gogh's previous painting, the 1885 depiction of his fa-

FIG. 4.2. Vincent Van Gogh, *Still Life with Open Bible*

ther's Bible: *Still Life with Open Bible, Candlestick, and Novel* (fig. 4.2). Again, one has to know, and one has to consider it important, that the Bible is Van Gogh's father's. And one has to *see* that the novel in question carries a visible title: it is Emile Zola's *La joie de vivre*. With this contrast of the sacred and profane, the evangelical and the modernist, Schapiro writes, Van Gogh "acknowledges his respect for his decreased minister father and alludes to his own Christian past, but also affirms his devotion to the secular lessons of his admired living author" (149). Might one in this spirit imagine yet another painting—one that does not exist: a phantom ninth image of shoes: a large pair of peasant shoes in the center, offset on the bottom right by a small pair of profane city shoes—those of Emile Zola, Eduard Fuchs, or the still-unknown Captain Dreyfus?

4

Back then to Fuchs. Schapiro leads us back to him nicely. Schapiro, Fuchs, and Benjamin alike demand a materiality and contextualism in the reading of aesthetic objects. Their position returns to a debate in fin-de-siècle art historiography about form versus reference in visual art. As Benjamin turns to this debate and scholarly context at this juncture in the Fuchs essay, we can understand that his move is hardly a nonsequitur. Benjamin's unwitting deconstruction of Heidegger in the name of the figure and practice personified by Fuchs (or Benjamin's image of Fuchs) reaches a moment both of clear symbolic autobiography and of self-distancing in the discussion of Fuchs's opinion of Heinrich Wölfflin. It is here as well that a significant instance of flashback occurs. "Fuchs," Benjamin says, "had to deal with formalism." Wölfflin's Die klassische Kunst appeared in 1899, and his "teaching was on the rise at the same time that Fuchs established the foundation of his work" (GS 2:480). To Wölfflin's position that Quattrocento and Cinquecento styles must be considered autonomously and therefore independently of material conditions or a particular frame of mind, Fuchs responded, in the second volume of Erotische Kunst, with the argument that formal impulses must be explained according to the "mood of the time." Fuchs thus responds according to the precepts of the history of culture and its attendant category of the Zeitgeist, rather than by constructing a critical (in this case destructive) argument against Wölfflin's formalism.[22]

Of course for Benjamin the correct critical approach is that of historical materialism. But here, despite his disapproval of both Wölfflin and—in this instance—Fuchs, Benjamin offers an example of a historical-materialist view of the Renaissance so delicate that it stands in explicit sympathy to Wölfflin's formalism. Wölfflin's formulation, mentioned above, can, he says, "cause offense" to historical materialism but "it also contains something useful." Historical materialism, he says, is interested in the economic and technical motivations of changing attitudes toward beauty. He continues: "As far as the above case is concerned, it would hardly be a vain pursuit to want to know what kind of economically conditioned changes in architecture are coincidental to the Renaissance and what kind of role Renaissance painting actually played as harbinger of the new architecture and as illustration of its emergence—which it itself made possible" (481). Again, we are reminded of "The Work of Art in the Age of Its Technical Reproducibility," in this case the opening paragraph, which set the tone for the argument in general by echoing Marx's insistence on the treatment of the superstructure in a position of dialectical engagement, and not mere reflexivity, with the base.

Implicit in this discussion is a flashback to Benjamin's own hostility to Wölfflin and his early formation of an idea of critique in general and a critique of art in particular in the context of competing models in the history of painting. Very early in his career, Benjamin had taken sides in a crucial "insider's" dispute in the world of art-historical scholarship: that between the formalism of Heinrich Wölfflin and the formal-contextual (I'll explain) approach of Alois Riegl. Thus it was his methodological sophistication in the field of art history which provided the lens for Benjamin's developing critical practice in general and his historical critique of culture in particular. His 1920 Bern dissertation, "Der Begriff der Kunstkritik in der deutschen Romantik" (The Concept of Art Criticism in German Romanticism), addresses Romantic writers, but the model of Benjamin's concept of critique as applied to these writers comes from the methods of art history.

Thomas Levin has commented on the place of art history in Benjamin's work in general by taking precisely the same tack I am with regard to history: "The practice of a certain kind of art history—understood in a broad sense as the critical, symptomatological deciphering of cultural production—was one of Benjamin's primary theoretical concerns."[23] Benjamin probably first read Riegl in 1916, soon after his negative reaction fo Wölf-flin, whose lectures he attended at the University of Munich in 1916. In a ferocious letter to Fritz Radt, Benjamin complained that Wölfflin "does not see the artwork, he feels obliged to see it, demands that one see it, considers his theory a moral act."[24] In his 1929 article "Books That Have Remained Alive," Benjamin cited Riegl's *Late Roman Art Industry* in the company of Alfred Meyer's *Iron Structures*, Franz Rosenzweig's *Star of Redemption*, and Lukács's *History and Class Consciousness*. Levin comments on "Benjamin's rather striking methodological affinity to Riegl—for example, in his shift away from the individual artist toward collective, anonymous works, in the significance accorded to the detail, the marginal phenomenon, the work as a cultural cipher, and so on" (80). Benjamin's rejection of Wölfflin in favor of Riegl operates not on the question of formalism versus nonformalism but on the question of the right kind of formalism. Riegl's attention to form, unlike Wölfflin's, does not, for Benjamin, "close" the visual object, in other words, frame it, in its stillness and self-containedness. The issue of the right kind of formalism is thus the same issue that appears in the discussion of Fuchs, and of Fuchs on Wölfflin.

The principle of Riegl's that became crucial for Benjamin is that of externality as the antidote to self-containedness. Riegl developed this principle in a discussion of Rembrandt's *Anatomy Lesson of Dr. Tulp* (1632) in *Das holländische Gruppenporträt* (1902). Of the six medical students portrayed (along with Dr. Tulp and the cadaver), only one seems to be looking in the general direction of Dr. Tulp's pedagogical scissors. Assuming that Rembrandt was not commenting here on the trials of medical school—an assumption Riegl made without difficulty—we can see how the varied gazes of the painting's subjects, including several cast toward the spectator of the painting, comprise for Riegl the quality of externality. Michael Podro has summarized Riegl's reading of the painting according to the absorption of "internal coherence" (the portrait group, the portrayed event, and the formal structure of the painting) into "external coherence."[25] This external coherence speaks, presumably, the lived cultural contexts of the painting, including the experience of the spectator/viewer. Thus Benjamin writes in his 1933 review article "Strenge Kunstwissenschaft" (Rigorous Study of Art) that "the Dutch Group Portrait" exhibits with particular emphasis "Riegl's masterly command of the transition from the individual object to its cultural and intellectual [*geistig*] function."[26]

It is not difficult to see the importance that Riegl's principle of externality will have for Benjamin's discussions of modernism in nineteenth-century Paris. One of Manet's most explicit borrowings from baroque painting, for example, is the inclusion of the spectator in the gaze and thus in the implied visual context of the painting—a gesture raised to the level of intimidation and insult in the *Olympia* of 1865.

In "Strenge Kunstwissenschaft," Benjamin cites Wölfflin's 1898 *Klassische Kunst*, a citation that may be responsible for the freshness of his discussion of Wölfflin in the subsequent Fuchs essay. Following the citation, Benjamin comments on Wölfflin as follows:

> Wölfflin did not succeed in his attempt to use formal analysis (which he had placed at the center of his method) to remedy the bleak condition in which his discipline found itself at the end of the nineteenth century. He identified the dualism of a flat, universalizing history of the art of 'all cultures and times,' on the one hand, and an academic aesthetic on the other, without, however, being able to overcome it entirely. (84–85)[27]

Benjamin continues his argument interspersed with quotations from Hans Sedlmayer's article "Toward a Rigorous Study of Art" (which had clearly inspired Benjamin's own title). On this new, "rigorous study," Benjamin argues:

> Such a study is not concerned with objects of pleasure, with formal problems, with giving form to experience, or any other clichés inherited from a belletristic consideration of art. Rather, this sort of studious work considers the formal incorporation of the given world by the artist "not a selection but rather always an advance into a field of knowledge which did not yet 'exist' prior to the moment of this formal conquest. . . . We should never be interested in 'problems of form' as such, as if a form ever arose out of formal problems alone or, to put it in other words, as

if a form ever came into existence for the sake of the stimulus it would
produce." (86)

5

The symbolic autobiographical dimension of the section of the Fuchs essay
on formalism, Wölfflin, and the failure of both Wölfflin and Fuchs to form
a critical dialectic evokes much of Benjamin's own intellectual autobiography, from the early interest in the history of art to the conjunction of the
visual and the linguistic in the formation of the early concept of critique as
explored in the dissertation of 1920. The sequential logic at work in the next
section of the Fuchs essay may have something to do with the sequence of
the implied flashback. Fuchs's next "failure," in Benjamin's judgment, is his
inability to grasp the importance of the baroque. In a paragraph on Fuchs's
valuation of the cultural places of caricature and erotic art in periods both
of cultural ascendancy and of descent (in the one they represent "overflow-
ing pleasure" and strength; in the other, "piquanterie" or filth), Benjamin
suggests that Fuchs has nothing to say about those "marginal periods [Gren-
zfälle] where the problematics of these images might prove themselves." For
Fuchs, the historical age of reference remains the Renaissance, and here "his
cult of creativity"[28] gains the upper hand over his antipathy toward classicism (GS 2:484). Benjamin attributes Fuchs's concept of creativity to two intellectual trends: the Renaissance-oriented Kulturgeschichte of Jakob Burckhardt and the [social] Darwinism that was crucial to the self-conception of
the social democrats during their period of persecution under Bismarck. The
most significant result of this composite attitude for Fuchs is his failure to
appreciate "broken artistic epochs [gebrochene Kunstepochen], such as the
baroque" (484).

With this observation, Benjamin's implicit autobiographical flashback
moves forward from his early concern with art and critique (1916–20) to
the large and intricate problematic of his Ursprung des deutschen Trauerspiels (1924–28). By this point, the emerging programmaticity of the Fuchs
flashback may be becoming almost embarrassing. By the sixth section of
his essay, Benjamin announces the Parisian connection that had, in fact,
been one of the original motivations of his confrontation with Fuchs: "The
pathos that traverses Fuchs's conception of history is the democratic pathos
of 1830. Its echo was the speaker Victor Hugo. The echo of the echo are [sic]
those books in which Hugo speaks as the speaker to the afterworld. Fuchs's
conception of history is the one Hugo celebrated in 'William Shakespeare':
'Progress is the stride of God himself'" (488–89).

For Hugo, Fuchs, and Benjamin, nineteenth-century Paris constitutes a topography of hope. The possibility of universal suffrage was the incarnation of progress, of the "democratic optimism" of Hugo's motto *"Qui vote règne:* who votes reigns" (489). Of course the Marxian dimension of Benjamin's thinking in the mid-1930s corresponds to the failure of the promise of hope and the victory of capitalism as a weapon of neobaroque culture—to say nothing of the antiliberal politics that had displaced democratic pathos entirely. Yet that hopeful pathos creates the condition whereby "France is a home even for the collector Fuchs" *(Frankreich ist eine Heimat auch für den Sammler Fuchs).* Benjamin's own attitude toward the line "Progress is the stride of God himself" might be glossed from the mock-biblical tone he uses in the quoted sentences.

But now Benjamin shifts his view and sees Fuchs the collector not as a refracted self but as an undiscovered historical type in his own collection of characters from Parisian modernity:

> The figure of the collector, which becomes more and more attractive the longer it is observed, hasn't yet come into its own. One would think that the romantic storytellers would have no more enticing a figure to which to treat themselves. But one searches in vain among the figures [*Figuren*] of Hoffmann, Quincey, or Nerval for this type, a type motivated by dangerous passions, if also by domesticated ones. Romantic are the figures of the traveler, the flâneur, the gambler, the virtuoso. That of the collector is not found here. (489–90)

The flâneur is of course Benjamin's own archetypal figure for the wanderer in space and time through the modern cityscape, through the equally archetypal space (at least for him) of the arcade. Benjamin here implicates his own project and seems to count himself among the romantic storytellers whose panoramas have overlooked the figure of the collector.

Perhaps Benjamin feels here that he would himself have had to be a little more French to appreciate the collector, the nonsystematic materialist: "Fuchs's French pedigree is that of the collector, the German one that of the historian. The ethical rigor [*Sittenstrenge*] characteristic of Fuchs the writer of history marks him as a German" (492). With at least partial seriousness, Benjamin forms the national types of Germanness and Frenchness into the dialectic of collecting and historicism, of which the imaginary resolution will be the historical materialist. There is an additional dimension to this national dichotomy. Profiting from Fuchs's attention to erotic life as a dimension of culture, Benjamin extends his typology into issues of gender and sexuality. The following passage is the immediate continuation of the one just quoted:

> This rigor made the mark on Gervinus, whose "History of Poetic National Literature" might be called one of the first attempts at a German intellectual history [*Geistesgeschichte*]. It is characteristic of Gervinus, as it is later of Fuchs, that the great creators appear, so to speak, in martial guise and that the active, manly, spontaneous elements of their natures assert themselves at the expense of the contemplative, feminine, and receptive ones.

Benjamin thus avails himself of the somewhat cliché-ridden dichotomy of feminine Frenchness versus masculine Germanness, but in his constant sympathy for the French side of his equations, he justifies himself here with categories shifted into areas of gender. In turning against historicism and systematic theory, he has chosen a French cultural style over a German one. "Benjamin verses Adorno" thus becomes "French style versus German style," and there is sufficient incentive for him to want to justify himself in terms of the gender extension of "feminine thinking" versus "masculine thinking." As Françoise Meltzer points out, Benjamin himself, his archetype of the flâneur, and its closely related type, the dandy, are all subject to a sort of hostile "femininization" at the hand of their contemporaries, for whom cultural and social normalcy is defined in terms of masculine types. The sin of Benjamin, the flâneur, and the dandy is the sin of *acedia*—sloth. The prime masculine type is the working man—the opposite of both the flâneur and the dandy. Benjamin's own lack of permanent employment, whether in academic life or as a critic, was often attributed by friends, including Gershom Scholem, Horkheimer, Adorno, and Hannah Arendt, to his passive and "feminine" character rather than to circumstances beyond his control.[29]

Insofar as bourgeois moralism falls on the German side of the dichotomy, Benjamin faults Fuchs for remaining too much of a bourgeois (or, rather, a burgher, as a German type is at stake) and too much of a German. First, this posture prevents his materialism from taking off. Second, it inhibits his discussion of sexuality, all the attention paid to erotica notwithstanding:

> Clearly, this moralism has a bourgeois [*bürgerliche*] signature. The correct mistrust of the bourgeois [*bürgerliche*] ban of purely sexual pleasure and the more or less fantastic means of achieving it remained distant to Fuchs. . . .

For this reason, the clarification of the sexual-psychological problem
is inhibited. This problem has become particularly important in the period of bourgeois domination. (496)

Benjamin suggests, ultimately, that Fuchs erred in failing to take advantage
of the symbolic analysis of Freud in the *Interpretation of Dreams* and of
psychoanalysis in general.

"The deepest insights into the realm of the symbolic," Benjamin coun-
ters, "he gained at the hand of Daumier" (499). And, back in the realm of
the political, he begins the penultimate section of the essay: "No figure was
more alive for Fuchs than Daumier. It accompanied him throughout his
working life. One might almost say: here Fuchs made himself into a dialectical thinker. At the very least, he conceived of this figure in its entirety and
in its living contradiction" (500). In the most literal sense, Daumier became
Fuchs's material, not only as a scholar but also as a collector. Fuchs was
justly proud to have initiated private collections of Daumier in Germany,
and he did so with justified disdain, Benjamin suggests, for the public collection of the museum, which amounted to the state property of Wilhelm II.
The private collection, controlled as it is by the art market—to which Benjamin is no more sympathetic than Heidegger—has the paradoxical potential
to liberate art from the commodifying and fetishizing power of the market.
As the collection takes shape, the work of art can be liberated from the fetish
of the "master's name." Creative anonymity appealed to Fuchs and generated his esteem for the burial art of the Tang period, on which he wrote.

Liberation from the "master's name" and the "fetish of the master's sig-
nature" disperses the aura. Thus the final step in Benjamin's presentation of
Eduard Fuchs leads him to the principal theme of his own, just completed
"Work of Art" essay. Benjamin quotes Fuchs's *Honoré Daumier* (1:13):

To every time there correspond entirely specific techniques of reproduction. These represent the relevant technical potentiality and are . . .
[Benjamin's ellipsis] of the particular need of the time. For this reason it
is hardly a miraculous phenomenon that every large-scale historical up-
heaval, which brings . . . to power . . . classes other than the previously
dominating ones, routinely involves [*bedingt*] a change in the reproduc-
tive technique of images. (503–4)

Thus Fuchs's attention to caricature, including the work of Daumier, falls
into the appreciation of mass art. In the Fuchs essay's concluding sentences

Benjamin suggests that anonymously produced mass art such as the Tang buried sculptures would "contribute more to the humanization of mankind than the cult of the leader, which is once again to be imposed on it" (505).

6

The figure of Eduard Fuchs in particular and of the collector in general has presence in the notebooks of the *Passagenarbeit,* in particular in *Konvolut* H: "Der Sammler."[30]

> The most decisive thing about collecting is that the object is released from all original functions in order to enter into the closest conceivable relation to itself. This is the diametric opposite of use and falls into the curious category of complementarity. . . . Collecting is a form of practical memory. (H 1a.2)

> The Paris arcades are observed here as if they were possessions in the hand of a collector. (H 1a.5)

> The collector as allegorist. (H 2.1)

> The canon of *mémoire involuntaire,* like that of the collector, is a kind of productive disorder. . . . Voluntary memory, on the other hand, is a registry, which classifies the object with a number, behind which the object disappears. "We must have been there." ("That was an experience.") The nature of the relation between the scatteredness of allegorical props (of patchwork) and this creative disorder remains to be investigated. (H 5.1)

The collector is an allegorist, but his resulting patterns of meaning are capricious, scattered. The Benjaminian collector is not a taxonomist. The alternative is a system of classification in which a strategy of knowledge and control loses sight of the object or object-world. On one side, antiquarianism; on the other, ideology (or, at best, social science). The convergence of the collector and the historian involves the convergence of allegorical thinking and a developed understanding of historical meaning. Is such an allegorical historical practice possible? Benjamin seems to show that it is, but at the same time he refuses (or neglects) to classify either his historical objects or his historical method.

The collector becomes the cipher of an economy omitted from Marx's classifications of use and exchange value: the material economy of memory, or of mnemonic value.

7

Sigmund Freud was one of his century's more famous collectors. "Imagine you are lying on Freud's couch," John Forrester has proposed; "What can you see?"[31] The answer: objects from Freud's collection of Egyptian antiquities. But if you are lying on Freud's couch, you are supposed to be looking inside yourself, recovering your own past. So the collections you see in front of you, should your eyes be open, are the phylogenetic correlatives to your ontogenetic recovery of history. The juxtaposition is not accidental. On both planes, historical recovery has a universalist agenda. A certain view of ancient Egypt in particular, as Carl Schorske has argued, instantiated a universalist, liberal, enlightened cultural heritage, of great relevance to the Jewish liberals of post-1859 Austria.[32] On both planes, the recovery of the past is archeological. That Freud amassed his collectibles exclusively in his study and consulting room, spaces always autonomous from his living quarters, testifies to the antiquities' connection to his psychoanalytic practice.[33] The poet and Freudian patient H.D. remembered her first contact with the display:

> Automatically, I walk through the door. It closes. Sigmund Freud does not speak. . . . I look around the room. A lover of Greek art, I am automatically taking stock of the room's contents. Precisely lovely objects and displayed here on the shelves to the right, to left of me . . . no one had told me that this room was lined with treasures. I was to greet the Old Man of the Sea, but no one had told me of the treasures he had salvaged from the sea-depth. . . . Waiting and finding that I would not or could not speak, he uttered. What he said—and I thought little sadly—was, "You are the only person who has ever come into this room and looked at the things in the room before looking at me."[34]

When Freud took up his residence in exile in London in 1938, H.D. sent him gardenias, which she knew reminded him of Rome. On the accompanying card, as Forrester relates, she wrote the message "To greet the return of the Gods." "This means," Forrester writes, "in their private language, the settling in of his collection of antiques." Freud responded, in precise and slightly unidiomatic English: "I got today some flowers. By chance or intention they are my favourite flowers, those I most admire. Some words 'to

greet the return of the Gods' (other people read: Goods). No name. I suspect
you to be responsible for the gift." Forrester comments eloquently on this
exchange. Freud and H.D.

> had already remarked on the closeness in English between the words
> 'Gods' and 'Goods.' Goods meant to them what is exchanged, and also
> what is highest, most ethical, and aesthetically pure. And this anony-
> mous gift then provoked an elegant thank you that pretended to preserve
> her anonymity. In other words, he will never know for sure whether she
> was the giver or not. But in assuming it, and thanking her, he continued
> the exchange that the play on words between Gods and Goods opened
> up. For Freud, if for no one else, the treasures were continuous with the
> everyday life of analysis, were potentially exchangeable as gifts or for
> money; they were something more than goods, but not quite gods. They
> did not strive for a timelessness beyond the world of goods. (247)

The antiquities collection and the psychoanalytic process worked together as modes of recuperation of a material past in the working through
of a functional subjectivity. Both are defined in terms of exchange: dialogic,
emotional, aesthetic, and monetary. Both are thus limited to everyday life.
Both are allegorical. By the same token, both resist the aestheticization and
resacralization of everyday life through the sublation of the allegorical—the
goodly, if you will—into the godly. Here is the ethical inflection of "the collector as allegorist."

Of course this discussion reinscribes the Heideggerian juxtaposition at
the center of the problem.[35] For Heidegger, in "The Origin of the Work of
Art" as elsewhere, goods must become gods. The Greek temple is the most
paradigmatic and most recuperable site of the work of art (in both senses
of the phrase) and the work of culture, because it is the locus of the godly.
The temple is the site of the gods more essentially than it is the site of the
political, of human exchange. The temple is a symbol, not an allegory. It is,
to be crude, not collectible—except perhaps by an organ of such transcendent capital as the Metropolitan Museum of Art.[36] Heidegger writes: "The
temple, in its standing there, first gives to things their look and to men
their outlook on themselves. This view remains open as long as the work is
a work, as long as the god has not fled from it."[37] In response to which, the
Benjaminian allegorist approaches the temple and plants a sign on which is
written: "gods out."

CHAPTER FIVE

Charlotte Salomon

History, Memory, Modernism

I

In recent years, visitors to the Jewish Museum Amsterdam—scholars and nonscholars alike—have been consistently drawn to the modest, rotating display of the work of Charlotte Salomon. Born in Berlin in 1917, the daughter of a prominent surgeon and from her middle childhood the stepdaughter of a celebrated contralto, Salomon grew up in the privileged, intense, and in multiple ways vexed world of Weimar-Republic Berlin. Salomon's Berlin, her family home in the elegant Grunewald district of Berlin-Charlottenburg, was thus materially similar to Walter Benjamin's. But where Benjamin's family milieu consisted of the more Spartan world of his father's business associates, the Salomon household reproduced the older Berlin atmosphere of the salon: the values and performance of *Bildung* over *Besitz*.

The quarter century that separates these two childhoods enabled vastly different systematic memories. Thus, from his French exile, Benjamin composed his most elegiac work, "A Berlin Childhood Around 1900," a series of vignettes that render significant landmarks of Berlin into tableaux, into paintings, into memory sites, *lieux de mémoire*. Benjamin's project here is manifestly and deliberately one of sentimentalization as a balm against the pain of exile. When Charlotte Salomon made her memories into history and into *tableaux vivants*, she disavowed all sentimentality. Benjamin's scenic memories seem filtered through the palette of Max Liebermann. If Liebermann's palette was invalidated by George Grosz, Salomon seems to know it.

In January 1939, two months after the night of state terrorism known as *Kristallnacht* and its inherent announcement of increased and sanctioned violence against Jews, Charlotte was sent to the care of her maternal grandparents in southern and "unoccupied" France. There, between 1940 and 1942, she produced the single, sustained work for which (and through which) she is known: a body of some 769 notebook-size gouache paintings, with accompanying text and musical references, which the "reader" is supposed to have in his or her head as the "play" unfolds. She called the work a *Singspiel* and entitled it *Leben? Oder Theater?* Salomon consigned the work for safekeeping to a local doctor and member of the Resistance. An apparently apocryphal anecdote claims that she uttered the words "This is my whole life" as she entrusted her work for safekeeping. The question of their factual status notwithstanding, the words carry analytical accuracy as well as poignancy. Shortly thereafter, she was deported via Drancy to Auschwitz, where, five months pregnant, she was murdered at the age of twenty-six, probably upon her arrival on October 10, 1943.

Since the late 1990s, Salomon's work has become increasingly well known. In the fall of 1998 the Royal Academy of Arts in London presented the most comprehensive exhibition to date of *Leben? Oder Theater?* Visitors rapidly increased in number as public appreciation of a life's work of art, history, and memory deepened. Yet the work remained interpretatively as inscrutable as it had proved to be accessible. Over the following three years, the exhibition traveled to three North American museums: the Art Gallery of Ontario in Toronto, the Museum of Fine Arts in Boston, and the Jewish Museum in New York. In 2002 it was shown at the Jewish Historical Museum (Joods Historisch Museum) in Amsterdam, its permanent home. The Jewish Historical Museum Amsterdam is currently expanding and highlighting its rotating display of the work, to meet the increasing interest and recognition.

Leben? Oder Theater? traces its artist's own life, scarred both by domestic tragedy and external political events, in the context of her family and the rich cultural circles within which it moved in 1920s and 1930s Berlin. The images accrue with increasing stylistic as well as narrational intensity, moving from delicacy to deliberate lack of finesse—at times more Giotto than Spiegelman, at times the reverse, with the passion of both and the secular historical commitment of the latter. And they accrue in compositional haste: the work took shape within a space of two years, and probably less, during the artist's exile on the French Riviera in the early years of the Second World War.

In the work's signature image, a young woman kneels at the edge of the ocean, holding brush and paper (fig. 5.1). The paper appears transparent to the ocean, seeming to absorb and duplicate the natural scenery around her. The title of her work in progress is inscribed not on the paper but in sweeping block letters on her back. She appears as both subject and object of the work in question; its creator and its victim. The image now suggests to the spectator a kind of feminine investiture of the position of the prisoner in Kafka's "Penal Colony." Kafka's story focuses on a technology of violence, to the body and to the mind. It describes a machine of execution that kills its victim by inscribing on his back the commandment that his crime disobeyed. (The text's first example is "Honor thy superiors.") And it describes the psychological significance of the moment of death, which occurs when the prisoner "reads" and understands the judicial sentence written on his back. The victim reads not with his eyes but with his wounds; in this manner, "enlightenment comes to the most dull-witted."[1] The prisoner's read-

FIG. 5.1. Charlotte Salomon, *Leben? Oder Theater?*, p. 784. Image captions, translations, and pagination are taken from *Charlotte: Life or Theater? An Autobiographical Play by Charlotte Salomon*, trans. Leila Vennewitz (New York: Viking Press, 1981).

ing of the crime coincides with his understanding of who he is, as defined
by his crime.

Kafka's violence informs Charlotte Salomon's depiction of her work's
title written on the figure's back. This violence mixes with the painterly
and colorful beauty of the image, to the spectator's discomfort. Mediated
through painting and beauty to be sure, self-representation and self-abuse are
fused. For Salomon as for Kafka, self-representation and self-abuse are indeed
fused, as the first depends on the instruments of culture—pens, brushes,
language, images—that act continuously as the instruments of oppression.
Exemplified here is one argument about the nature of modern subjectivity,
in which the subject is folded into a texture of subjection. In one eloquent
reference to this argument and the genealogy that takes it through the work
of Lacan, Foucault, and Althusser, Francis Barker offers the metaphor of the
"tremulous private body": the body as a site of specular invasion, a cultural
predicament in which "the scene of writing and of reading is, like the grave,
a private place."[2]

If this image represents the work as a whole, becomes its signature image at the close of the story, then the work *Leben? Oder Theater?* carries the
same double marking of self-representation and self-abuse: history as narrative and history as trauma. The signature image combines the innocent cliché of the mermaid of Copenhagen with a violent narrative. This signature
image is in fact signature in a more literal sense, as it is the final image of
the 769 that constitute the final work. In the work that has been completed
by the time this final image is drawn and written, Charlotte Salomon has
"covered" herself, written across her body and rewritten her life into a life
that refuses the narrative that others would have written for her. That refusal motivates the work and defines its agenda of recovery. The pun on the
word "recover" is useful here. Charlotte Salomon "recovers" historical narratives: covering them, repeating them, and initiating her own recovery. As
in the plot of Kafka's "Penal Colony," the end-station of the work *Leben?
Oder Theater?*, the moment of this image is thus the moment when its protagonist recognizes the sentence written on her back. But here this is a moment of life and renewal, the moment when the author is able to support
the burden of history on her back.

To speak of the "work" of Charlotte Salomon is to engage an ambiguity
that is at once to be retained and explored: it is to describe at once the project
of survival and the material project of painting, autobiography, and history.
Leben? Oder Theater? is accompanied by descriptive text and references to
musical works, a narrative of her own life in the context of family trauma
and the trauma of Germany and German Jews in the immediate aftermath

of the Nazi accession to power. The work operates through a synaesthesis that resonates with the conjunction as well as competition of seeing and hearing. Charlotte Salomon calls it a *Singspiel.* Griselda Pollock has asserted that *Leben? Oder Theater?* "is one of our century's most challenging art works—but I for one still do not know what I am looking at."[3]

Charlotte had been sent from her home in Berlin to live with her maternal grandparents in January 1939 to escape the deteriorating conditions in Germany. She was twenty-one years old. In early 1940 her grandmother committed suicide, after multiple failed attempts. During the period of these attempts, as Charlotte was trying to persuade her grandmother to remain alive, her grandfather informed her that the family had suffered a large number of suicides, mostly, but not exclusively, of women. Most centrally, he informed Charlotte that her own mother's death in 1926 had been a suicide. At the time, the eight-year-old Charlotte had been told that her mother had died of influenza. Charlotte herself had been named for a maternal aunt who had killed herself in 1919. The force of these revelations was to mark her as the next and possibly final suicide in the family. Explicitly, Charlotte faced the choice between the acceptance of the apparent family curse and its disavowal through some kind of radical self-reinvention. She chose the latter path, and the resulting self-reinvention unfolded through the writing and painting of her life and history in the work that became *Leben? Oder Theater?* The German title carries a sonic remnant of and reference to the question and opposition that its very existence rejects and replaces: *Leben oder Tod*—life or death.

As a work of recovery, *Leben? Oder Theater?* is not in any straightforward way a work of recovered memory, or indeed of memory at all. On the contrary, it is a massive and thorough regrounding of a life and thereby a correction of a pattern of memory that was formed by other people's narratives and quite literally by other people's lies—most portentously the lies of Charlotte's family about the death of her mother. It is a work of history as the production of differentiation, and therefore a correction to that aspect of memory which desires immediacy and identification with its objects and object-worlds.[4] The work seems to know that the conflation of history with memory enables the disavowal of a constructed understanding of the past in a way that is, potentially, both epistemologically possible and materially accurate, in favor of a sentimental narrative that is supplied in other people's terms—other people's memories, other people's histories. *Leben? Oder Theater?* works precisely toward an emancipation from other people's memories and their impositions on the memory of the narrator at the moment she begins the project. The work's "knowledge" of the distinction between recovered history and recovered memory is produced aesthetically, through its elaborate juxtapositions and differentiations of genre (image, music, text), temporalities, and voice (autobiography, history, fantasy).

Leben? Oder Theater? takes responsibility not only for a personal and family history but for the history of German Jewish culture in Weimar Berlin. Indeed, I want to make a case for this work as the most adequate history of modern secular German Jewish culture that I know, and argue that its adequacy is produced through its ongoing recognition and reproduction of German Jewish modernity on the assumption of its multiplicity, its claims, and its contradictions. This is both "a work" in the sense of a work of art, and "work" in the sense of psychological work. It is long and intricate in its engagement of self and history; of the overdetermination of and fissures in collective and personal claims of identity; of trauma and recovery at the level of collective and personal historical experience; of the dialectic of subjectivity and symptomaticity. As such, it performs what I would call the work of subjectivity. It performs this work, moreover, in the sense of a performative speech act. A performative act is by definition a transformative act. As a category, it requires differentiation from a performance in the sense of a theatrical performance, which does not transform reality. At the same time, we know from cultural anthropology and from the newer, related discipline of performance studies that theatrical performances can hold the promise and danger of performative, transformative action. So it seems to me that the performative/performance distinction is analytically crucial, but that the two categories cannot be nearly separated. I bring this up now because this dialectic of performativity and performance is not only the explicit dialectic of the question "Life? Or Theater?" but appears as the most fundamental historical question about the life and claims of German Jewish culture. Indeed, "Life? Or Theater?" was the central question that German Jews asked themselves, if seldom with Charlotte Salomon's rigor.

Leben? Oder Theater?: the two question marks reinforce the opposition of life and theater. Yet the work contradicts the very same opposition. The title asks its reader to engage with the proposition to choose between life and theater. In the context of northern German Jewish cultural norms, this is the opposition of authenticity, reality, and truth on the one hand to theatricality in the sense of artifice, performance, and fakery on the other. The production of authenticity is a claim of German Jewish modernity, the claim of an engagement with the world that strives neither for an essential Germanness nor for an essential Jewishness but to be culturally and existentially authentic in a multiple and flexible manner adequate to the multiplicity and transitoriness of the modern world. This claim, call it modernist authentic-

ity, relies on a disavowal of essentialism, holism, or the search for a defining point of moment of origin. This claim has not been given enough cre-
dence by received traditions of historiography, whether Jewish or German,
whether conceived through an agenda of identity politics or one of identity
dismissal.[5] At the same time, this German Jewish discourse of authenticity should be neither normativized nor sentimentalized, as it produced its
own violence. Specifically, it produced its own form of patriarchal violence
and, subsequently, its own rebellious sons and daughters. These rebels faced
a dual challenge which Jewish historiography has been, in my view, loath
to admit: the dual oppression of internal, Jewish patriarchy and external,
non-Jewish patriarchy, which was in turn often the source and carrier of
anti-Semitism.[6] In Charlotte Salomon's project, the critique of patriarchy
conjoins the private and public story lines.

To write the history of German Jewish modernity involves, I would argue, the recognition of that kind of normative authenticity which hugs the
momentum of a viable historical modernity. I would argue for the theoretical and historical positing of such normative authenticity at the line of distinction between the performative and performance, in other words at that
point where an acknowledgment and indeed an incorporation of the past
allows for at least a degree of emancipation from its intimidating effects, or
aftereffects. Thus the performative is not a simple claim to originality and
the disavowal of repetition, but rather synonymous with the psychoanalytic
principle of repetition with difference. At the same time, such a history of
the modernist culture of authenticity must recognize its ideological and indeed violent components, and thus the high ideological and emotional price
that its adherents paid.

The cultural language of the German Jewish dialectics of authenticity
involved the disavowal of artifice and theater, and this disavowal enabled
easily a culture of almost Puritanical rigidity. Indeed, the legacy of the Mendelssohnian enlightenment might well be called the Protestant culture of
the German Jews. Moreover, and most immediately relevant to the present context, the disavowal of theatricality involved what, in this precise
context, Darcy Buerkle has called the effacement of women. Women were
glibly understandable as the carriers of theatricality, of inauthenticity, and
subsequently also of that more extreme version of theatriality, namely, hysteria. Buerkle thus incisively understands Charlotte Salomon's work as a
drive against the effacement of women.[7] With devastating accuracy, Buerkle
understands Charlotte's basic question—Life? Or Theater?—in terms both
of a reference and of an at least partial adherence to the admonition "mach
doch kein Theater"—don't make a scene; don't make a production out of it.

Buerkle points out that "it is the admonition that women hear in some form or another thoughout the play." Charlotte, or more accurately the Charlotte who narrates *Leben? Oder Theater?*, I think it is fair to say, heeds the anti-theatrical ethic of authenticity, but at the same time undermines its resulting effacement of women. In doing so, she seems, or the work seems, to grasp a crucial distinction between performance and the performative, between "acting" and acting, between representation and presentation.

These analytical agendas and ambiguities determine the work's aesthetic language. It determines the adoption of a Wagnerian self-contradictory aesthetic that is spectacularly theatrical in the very pursuit of anti-theatricality and authenticity: theater that disavows theater, opera that hates opera. Yet to tack onto it the label of *Gesamtkunstwerk* is problematic. It is at once a thoroughly Wagnerian and an anti-Wagnerian work. It makes claims on all the arts, textual, visual, auditory. It carries a leitmotivic underlying structure in all these registers. Yet it is in a stronger way anti-Wagnerian, as it makes no claims to totalization, and indeed uses the interplay of the registers to cancel each one's authority over representation. At every instance, it references the world outside of itself, the opposite of the music-drama ideology which disavows an external world. History is the externality of autobiography—the world as other. The work calls itself a *Singspiel*, paying homage in tone and principle to a Mozartean embarrassment of riches, to a seemingly infinite juxtaposition of forms and genres without the onus of totalization. The prologue reads:

> The creation of the following paintings is to be imagined as follows: A person is sitting by the sea. He [*sic*] is painting. A tune suddenly enters his mind. As he starts to hum it, he notices that the tune exactly matches what he is trying to commit to paper. A text forms in his head, and he starts to sing the tune, with his own words, over and over again in a loud voice until the painting seems complete. Frequently, several texts take shape, and the result is a duet . . .

The *Singspiel* then introduces itself as containing three parts: a prologue, a main section, and an epilogue. The prologue narrates, in paintings supported by tunes and accompanied by texts, original and quoted, the history of Charlotte's family, with all figures carrying mildly parodic pseudonyms, from November 1913, four years prior to Charlotte's birth, until the mid-1930s, several years into the Nazi regime. Besides Charlotte herself, the principal characters are her parents, her maternal grandparents, and her stepmother. The main section is the story of Charlotte's infatuation and possible love affair with her stepmother's singing teacher, Alfred Wolfsohn, who appears in the story under the name Amadeus Daberlohn. The erotic charge between Charlotte and Daberlohn is shadowed by the possible romance between Daberlohn and the stepmother, the well-known contralto Paula Lindberg, who appears as Paulinka Bimbam. Daberlohn claims the amount of space he does partly because of Charlotte's erotic investment in him, but also because he, and the true person of Alfred Wolfsohn who stands behind him, provide the story with its neo-Wagnerian aesthetic, which the author both adopts and scorns: Tristan and Isolde sharing a track with Hansel and Gretel. The third line of this erotic triangle is defined by the erotic aura between Charlotte and Paulinka. And the erotic aura is completely destabilized by the narrator's male self-gendering.

Alfred Wolfsohn was a survivor of the trenches of the Great War, and specifically of a wartime trauma resulting—at least so he said—from being buried alive under the bodies of dead and dying soldiers. He claims to have derived from this experience a theory of the human voice as holding capacities far beyond the human sound range, sounds he remembered from among the dying soldiers. At its extreme registers, according to his theories, which Charlotte represents faithfully and mocks unforgivingly, this extended human voice is tied to the soul. "Voice" becomes the unifier of text and image; specifically the contralto voice of Paula Lindberg a.k.a. Paulinka Bimbam, who is imagined as singing most of the lyrics that are to go through the mind of the reader of the account, as they went through the mind of the painter at work. The three signature tunes, often repeated, are Bach's aria "Bist du bei mir," the Habanera and Toreador Song from Bizet's *Carmen*, the ultimate theatrical, erotic, and—according to Nietzsche—anti-Wagnerian work, and Gluck's aria "J'ai perdu mon Eurydice" from his opera *Orfeo ed Euridice*. Paulinka performs the role of Orfeo in the only operatic role of hers mentioned; Professor Singsong, however, sings it to himself when he is abandoned in favor of Dr. Kann; the Toreador Song is, in turn, Daberlohn's seduction tune.[8]

Throughout, the narrator assumes that the reader/viewer will agree, so to speak, to contribute the musical strand of the story from his or her own internal repertoire. An image will state "to the tune 'x'" and the reader is asked to comply. The text is almost never silent. *Almost* never, because at times the narrator states tersely, "No tune." The music is thus separated from the representational, indeed theatrical, practices of the narrative. Silence is the absence of music.

The final section of *Leben? Oder Theater?* narrates Charlotte's exile to France, and approaches the trauma of the suicide of her grandmother in a mode of aesthetic breakdown, or at least transformation. The *Singspiel* cannot contain the trauma that motivated it. More accurately, it can narrate it, but it cannot contain it aesthetically, as the formal circle that forms the story's formal beginning and end—the passage from the suicides of Charlotte's aunt and mother to the suicide of their mother, has been closed. Since Charlotte chooses to work as a way of choosing life, of choosing not to honor the family curse of the suicide of its women, the act of representation, and its inherent theatricality, becomes the choice of life.

The prologue of *Life? Or Theater?* opens with the suicide of Charlotte's aunt in November 1913 (fig. 5.2). The aunt's name was Charlotte, the name increasing the weight of the burden of repetition. The initial image represents less the suicide of the first Charlotte than the act of taking distance from the act through its very representation. The corpse is represented in a cocoon; a box under that image cites the relevant newspaper entry under the headline "Suicide of an Eighteen-year-old." Beneath the caption are the mourning women of the family: the painter Charlotte's mother and grandmother. On the lower right, the grandfather. But above the grandfather stands a headless male figure, who seems to be a repetition of part of him. Curiously, the grandfather is portrayed as he looked in 1940, rather than as he would have looked as a much younger man in 1913. His bloodshot eyes are the color of the dead Charlotte's dress.

Some seven hundred images later, the same head of the same grandfather appears repeatedly, in the contexts of the final suicide in the family and in the narrative, that of his own wife. In an image whose accompanying text the surviving family members once sought to suppress, the grieving grandfather exclaims to his granddaughter that she might as well complete the cursed circle and commit suicide herself (fig. 5.3). The depictions of the grandfather worsen as his actions seem to worsen in the context of increasing catastrophe. Charlotte and the grandfather have been interned as enemy aliens in the French camp of Gurs, and released after several weeks on the grounds of his frailty and her need to care for him. In the depictions of their difficult route back to Villefranche, Charlotte is depicted as trying to avoid sharing a room or a bed with her grandfather, who in turn is depicted twice as arguing that the two should share a bed because he is in favor of "what is natural" (fig. 5.4).

The depictions of 1940 clearly portray a terror of the grandfather and his apparent sexual overtures to his granddaughter. The more vexed, and ultimately, I think, unresolvable question involves the extent to which the treatment of the grandfather throughout the narrative consists of an expansion of the accusation of incest, and hence the extent to which the legacy

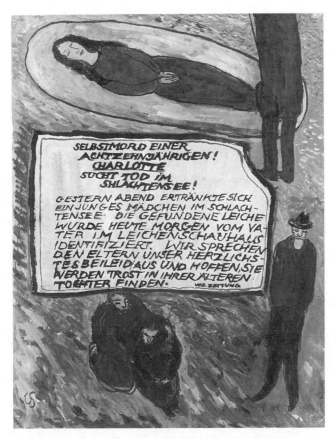

FIG. 5.2. Charlotte Salomon, *Leben? Oder Theatre?*, p. 8. "Suicide of eighteen-year-old! Charlotte seeks death in Lake Schlachten! Last night a young girl drowned herself in Lake Schlachten. The body was recovered and was identified this morning at the morgue by her father. We extend our deepest sympathy to her parents and trust they will find consolation in their oldest daughter. *Vossische Zeitung.*"

of the women's suicide might be connected to this trauma of the patriarch breaking the contract of patriarchy.[9]

Charlotte's own father, the eminent surgeon Albert Salomon—Albert Kann in the story—sustains in the story the other side of patriarchy. He receives for the most part a sympathetic and sometimes adulatory portrayal, and yet he is ultimately accused as well of some responsibility in the breakdown of patriarchal authority, insofar as that authority includes care for children. The accusation is ambivalent, as Charlotte knows that her being sent away to the care of the grandparents in France had been decided in her inter-

FIG. 5.3. Charlotte Salomon, *Leben? Oder Theatre?*, p. 774.
Charlotte: "You know, Grandpa, I have a feeling the whole world
has to be put together again." *Grandfather:* "Oh, go ahead and kill
yourself and put an end to all this babble!"

est. Thus, Albert Salomon's medical eminence is portrayed in the Prologue
in a kind of spoof of Rembrandt's *Cabinet of Dr. Tulp*.[10] But the blood-colored
hospital behind him is the Jewish Hospital (Israelitisches Krankenhaus), the
only institution in which he was permitted to work after 1933. (The red color
of the building might incorporate Charlotte's conscious or unconscious association of the Jewish Hospital with the common anti-Semitic pairing of
Jews and communists, with the charge of *Kulturbolschewismus*.) In a companion image, the despair of Dr. Salomon is represented in the frontal plane
of a triple-planed image; behind him the red hospital has become simply a
swath of red; at the rear of the image a Dr. Tulp scenario has been, literally,
x-ed out (fig. 5.5). (If you remove the people from this image, in other words

FIG. 5.4. Charlotte Salomon, *Leben? Oder Theatre?*, p. 764.
Grandfather: "I don't understand you. What's wrong with sharing
a bed with me—when there's nothing else available? I'm in favor
of what's natural." *Charlotte:* "Don't torment me. You know that I
know exactly what I have to do."

duplicate visually the act of removal of people that is being pictured, you end
up with a desolate visual landscape in the manner of Mark Rothko, about
which more later.)

Albert Salomon's professional, spiritual, political, and erotic *semblable*
and *frère* in this scenario is the conductor Kurt Singer, champion and perhaps sometime lover of Salomon's second wife Paula Lindberg. Singer had
been the deputy director of the Berlin City Opera before 1933. After his dismissal, he conceived and founded the Kulturbund Deutscher Juden in Berlin
as a collective response to Jewish banishment from the musical stages of
aryanized Germany. Through her portrayal of Singer, Paula Lindberg, and

FIG. 5.5. Charlotte Salomon, *Leben? Oder Theatre?*, p. 154. *Tune:*
"Gentlemen, here you see a serious gastric ulcer, but by using the
new method I have invented we can save the patient." "Professor
Kann—out—get out!"

others, Charlotte offers significant insight into the world of the Kulturbund
and its fragile, indeed possibly deluded, place in Germany between 1933 and
1941. One hundred eighty thousand German Jews joined the Kulturbund,
first in Berlin and then in its equivalent chapters in other cities, including
Frankfurt and Cologne, where the repertory was more adventurous than in
Berlin.[11] In Berlin, the seasons were divided into theater, opera, concert music, and cabaret. Operatic repertory included Offenbach's *Tales of Hoffmann*
(a German Jewish work, below the surface), Saint-Saëns's *Samson and Del-
ila,* and Beethoven's *Fidelio.* Beethoven was forbidden to Jewish performers
in 1937. Mozart was forbidden following the *Anschluss* of Austria in March
1938, at which point his Austrian status was reclassified as German. Richard

Wagner and Richard Strauss were forbidden from the outset—one wonders if Strauss ever commented on the fact.[12] Schiller was banned in 1934 and Goethe in 1936. Shakespeare was allowed, but Hamlet's "To be or not to be" soliloquy was not. ("The oppressor's wrong, the proud man's contumely" was deemed potentially subversive, a judgment that led to the censoring of the entire speech.)

Recent historiographical judgment of the Kulturbund and its promoters has been harsh. Thus, Saul Friedländer in his important study *Nazi Germany and the Jews*, understands the project as "fitting Nazi needs": "Apart from the work it provided and the soothing psychological function it filled for part of the Jewish community, the Kulturbund also offered to the surrounding society an easy way to dismiss any potential sense of embarrassment: Aryans who found the regime's anti-Semitic measures distasteful could reassure themselves that Jewish artists were at least permitted to remain active in their chosen professions."[13] As general director, Singer answered to Hans Hinkel, a Nazi appointee as president of the Prussian Theater Commission, who was in charge of the aryanization of cultural life in Prussia. Indeed, the Kulturbund Deutscher Juden, as the association was named in 1933, had to be renamed as the "Jüdischer Kulturbund" in 1934. In April 1935 Hans Hinkel met with delegates of the regional Kulturbünde and informed that their unification into a national association was desirable. Kurt Singer convened the meeting and stated his agreement with Hinkel. In a 1936 speech Hinkel declared that the aim of Nazi cultural policy was that Jewish artists "may work unhindered as long as they restrict themselves to the cultivation of Jewish artistic and cultural life and as long as they do not attempt—openly, secretly, or deceitfully—to influence our culture."[14]

Friedländer's judgment of the Kulturbund's political function may be correct. But it worries me for two reasons as a moral judgment of the entire enterprise. First, it leaves scant room for a dignified portrayal of those participants whose basic decision was to remain in Germany. Second, it stands in the shadow of the general judgment of German Jewish life made, famously, by Gershom Scholem in 1962, namely that the notion of a German-Jewish symbiosis had been delusory from its earliest articulation in the Enlightenment. (Whether we call it the German Enlightenment, the Jewish Enlightenment, or the German Jewish Enlightenment is of course contingent on a position on the very issue being flagged here.) Scholem's claim received an equally famous reply, from another German Jew, the historian George Mosse, who suggested that Scholem was himself the best example of what he claimed never existed. It is ludicrous to speak of a German-Jewish dialogue after 1933, even more so after 1935, and still more so after 1938. But these commonsense judgments belie a historical foundation that commonsense history has been somewhat sloppy about, and that is the fact that the trope "German-Jewish dialogue" assumes the classificatory separation between Germans and Jews that the cultural world of emancipation sought to blur. Charlotte Salomon's depiction of Kurt Singer's emotional and ethical agony thus offers a potential historiographic intervention, even a correction, despite its inarticulate status as art, not historiography.

In a text that remains, to my knowledge, unpublished, Kurt Singer addressed "the work of the Jüdischen Kulturbünde": "Die Arbeit der Jüdischen Kulturbünde: Rückschau und Vorschau."[15] This text requires careful reading for its analytical and symptomatic aspects. The text seems to be an address to the Kulturbund membership, a taking of stock several years into the enterprise. It dates from after 1936. It postdates the forced unification of the various Kulturbünde under the rubric "Reichsverband." The year 1933, he says bluntly, brought to an end a century of emancipation. "The German Jew was isolated" *(Der Jüdische Mensch in Deutschland war isoliert)*—Singer writes, "on the basis of a single law." In the context of the Kulturbund, he probably refers to the Civil Service Law of April 7, 1933, which banned Jews from state-affiliated positions, and which coincided with numerous exclusions and expulsions from more local jurisdictions—such as the April 8 expulsion of Jewish teaching assistants from all universities in Baden, for example.[16] This was for Singer a "violation of the conjunction" *(Raubbau der Konjunktur)* of German Jewish culture. He cites the recent foundings of research centers for the study of Jewish cultures independent of such conjunction—Jewish, Hebrew, and Yiddish poetry, and an archive for Yemenite and Palestinian music. But these efforts stood apart from the self-understanding of German Jews who identified with European culture, and who expressed their sense of conjunction through hybrid formations, one example of which is the music of Mahler. It seems to me that Singer demonstrates conceptual as well as political courage when he addresses the German-Jewish "conjunction" in the post-1933 political and ideological climate. Because of "the unity with Western culture" *(Aus Verbundenheit mit westlicher Kultur)* a Jewish culture for Jews could not be established in Germany from "one day to the next" *(von heute auf morgen)*—a phrase from Schoenberg. He makes oblique reference to the decision of the newly formed Kulturbund to open its 1933 dramatic season with Lessing's *Nathan the Wise*—an obvious choice, Singer remarks, but an atavistic one with no bearing on the present moment. "A goal, a plan, a constructive theater-idea was lacking." Again, the self-criticism strikes me as extraordinary. Singer pledges the new mandate of the Kulturbund in terms of the expression of contemporary Jewish culture, and he states explicitly that this principle of autonomy/separation is the basis of the compromise with the regime. Autonomy is coterminous with exclusion. He announces the new name "Bund für jüdische Kultur" and proclaims "Hic Rhodus, hic salta." Singer seems to know that this compromise is made with the devil.

Kurt Singer died in Theresienstadt in 1944. Obviously one can say that he should have left Germany in 1933, as did Bruno Walter, Erich Kleiber, and the non-Jewish Fritz Busch. But Singer's insistence on maintaining German Jewish aesthetic life in Berlin within monstrous and shrinking parameters cannot be dismissed too lightly.

In the address cited above, Kurt Singer invokes the music of Mahler as a discourse of cultural hybridity. The musical repertory of the Kulturbund included much Mahler. The 1935 issue of the almanac of the Kulturbund—the first of two—included an essay by Dr. Anneliese Landau entitled "Gustav Mahler: Der Unzeitgemässe": Gustav Mahler against his time. Here, the fin-de-siècle outsider becomes an allegory for his own reclassification by the Third Reich as an excluded Jewish composer. Landau cites Mahler's understanding of musical composition as "building a world for oneself": "sich eine Welt aufbauen." In this constructive act, nature becomes the metaphor through which particularity is linked to the universal. Mahler and his music become a kind of suspended language through which the possibility of Jewish universalism, now suspended, might be grasped. Mahler's compositional, or rather his "composed world"—seine komponierte Welt—the piece reads,

> is neither a Jewish world nor a Christian world, it knows no partiality, it is the image of an all-encompassing being. If one wants to find something Jewish in Mahler, it can be encountered in the restlessness of his search for God, in his eternal questioning of the How and Why of things, the quality that sealed his friendship with the Jewish poet Siegfried Lipiner. Shortly before his death, he wrote to Bruno Walter: "What thinks in us? Acts in us? Remarkable! When I hear music, when I conduct, I hear the most precise answers to my questions, and I am clear and sure. Or rather, I feel quite clearly that these are in fact not questions." But one can find just as much in Gustav Mahler that is Catholic and Buddhist, as he was at once musician, poet, and philosopher.[17]

Landau writes with purple prose but proceeds carefully nonetheless. Her Jewish universalism does not disavow Jewish particularity but refuses its

isolation. With the phrase "if one wants to find something Jewish in Mahler
. . ." she engages the painful ambiguity of an act shared by pro-Jewish and
anti-Semitic agendas. The convergence of the particular and the universal
constitutes a principle of the so-called Jewish Enlightenment. This, one can
infer, is the didactic argument for the Kulturbund's Mahlerism, as imparted
to its reading public in its almanac. Moreover, it may also be judged a metonym for the Kulturbund's general agenda.

For logistical reasons, Kulturbund musical programming stressed
Mahler's song literature, with the *Lieder eines fahrenden Gesellen* performed most often by far—I count four performances between January 1935
and September 1940. The First Symphony was performed in late November
1938 and again twice in late April 1939. The Second Symphony, the so-called
Resurrection symphony, was performed on February 27, 1941. A review of
this concert, by one Micha [Israel] Michalowitz, appeared on March 7 in
the *Jüdisches Nachrichtenblatt* (the informational newspaper sanctioned
by Hermann Göring following the Kristallnacht ban on the Jewish press).[18]
Michalowitz's rhetoric doubles the rhetoric of the music itself—exalted universalism and transcendence. Gustav Mahler's universalism was based—as
universalism often is—in majoritarian positioning; this is the musical work
that follows his religious conversion. For German Jews—performers, listeners, reviewers, to enter ecstatically into this rhetoric of universal transen-
dence, in 1941, can clearly be described as delusionary and perhaps even
as psychotic. The idea of a performance by the Kulturbund in 1941 of the
Resurrection symphony, with its exalted passage from abjection to inclusion
to apotheosis, seems to me embarrassing to the point of obscenity. But such
judgments are too glib.

Paula Lindberg and her biography enter the narrative of *Leben? Oder
Theater?* with her marriage to Albert Salomon—Albert Kann, in the story.
The text reads:

> L'amour est enfant de Bohème, il n'a jamais jamais connu de loi.
>
> The wedding was celebrated in Paulinka's home town of Kurzenberg-
> am-Rhein. Her father had been dead for many years. But her mother was
> still alive and was frequently moved to tears at the wedding.
>
> Meanwhile, a very good friend of Paulinka's, an extremely famous
> man, the general manager of an opera house, sat in his box listening with
> a critical ear to a new production of Orpheus and Eurydice. Orpheus's
> aria "Oh, I have lost her" seemed to be rendered with particular expres-
> siveness and feeling.

The repetition of "jamais jamais" suggests that Charlotte wants her reader to sing along with the music. Less consciously, the reference to the death of Paula's father rehearses Charlotte's possible feeling of the death of her father on the occasion of his remarriage.

We now have several pages of Paula's biography. She meets and sings for "the famous Professor Klingklang," the conductor Siegfried Ochs (1858–1929) (fig. 5.6). Short strokes in red, orange, and white begin at the top of the image as the orchestra players and resonate at the bottom as pure sound. When Paulinka Bimbam is recognized, interpellated, by this demigod of music, she becomes the source of this sublime sound (fig 5.7). Another image portrays Paula's contract with Professor Klingklang and her abandonment of her real name. Klingklang crosses out the name Levy and replaces it with Bimbam. Paula Levy had indeed become Paula Lindberg as her career took off; now Paula Lindberg becomes Paulinka Bimbam. We have here a thick concatentation of Jewishness, music, and motherhood, and an opaque disquisition on origins and authenticity. Paula becomes the source of divine rays of sound as she covers her own origins, this at the moment when she usurps the place of Charlotte's dead mother. Paula's voice, and the brushstrokes that depict it, have the modernist quality of the abstract sublime. The abstract sublime merges with the authentic, as authenticity is unbound—not without pain—from origin.

The following image (fig. 5.8) shows Paula's first concert and her musical, musical-erotic bond with Professor Klingklang. As the text makes clear, she sang the Bach aria "Bist du bei mir." Next (fig. 5.9) we see the *Allgemeine Deutsche Musikzeitung* acclaiming Paula as an extraordinary singer of Bach. "Paulinka became a singer," says the text. "She sang sacred songs—almost always in churches." Music without theater. One might call it the German-Jewish aesthetic, the aesthetic of J. S. Bach as transmitted by Felix Mendelssohn. (It was, we need to recall, Mendelssohn who returned Bach to musical currency with his landmark performance of the *St. Matthew Passion* in Berlin in 1829. The restoration of Lutheran music, Mendelssohn said at the time to his co-participant Eduard Devrient, required the services of an actor and a Jew.) Thus Paulinka's identification with Bach performs a cultural identification that is a century old. Just as the form of *Leben? Oder Theater?* suggests that Charlotte "heard" the music that supplied her references, thereby incorporating a musical dimension at the very least as a correlative into her visual composition and style, we can understand that aesthetic incorporation to be a dimension as well of the historical record that she portrays. If the Protestant culture of the Berlin Jews remains a narrative

FIG. 5.6. Charlotte Salomon, *Leben? Oder Theatre?*, p. 63. "Just a moment, young lady!" the professor called out, as she was about to leave the hall after the lecture. "Here's a ticket for my concert tonight!" And she goes to the concert and listens reverently and afterward takes him a bunch of violets. "Oh, professor, that was wonderful!" And he invites her to come and see him some time.

"We are the family of the famous Professor Klingklang. Who is this?"—"We are the daughters of . . ."—"I am th . . ." "I am the son of that famous . . ."—"And this is my wife." And he wanted to try out her voice and discovered that in her throat lay a glorious gift for singing. *Tune: "Come all ye seraphim . . ."*

FIG. 5.7. Charlotte Salomon, *Leben? Oder Theater?*, p. 67. As for her
old name, however, she had to abandon it, and her gave her the name
Paulinka Bimbam.

of "assimilation," then the resulting cultural experience or indeed cultural
hybridity is understood here to have been deeply and sincerely experienced.
In Mendelssohn's shadow, Siegfried Ochs was known for his championship
of sacred choral music and most specifically for his restoration to the performance repertory of J. S. Bach's B Minor Mass, in the 1880s. Charlotte
celebrates Paulinka as Ochs's last discovery, and includes a deathbed scene
(corresponding to the date 1929) in which Professor Klingklang bids farewell
to the devastated Paulinka.

Klingklang/Ochs's death moves Singsong/Singer into the story's leading
musical position, and makes him the wooer of Paulinka. Singsong/Singer
plays Beckmesser, one might suggest, to Daberlohn's Walther von Stolzing.
According to Charlotte's narrative, Paula refused to marry Kurt Singer to

FIG. 5.8. Charlotte Salomon, *Leben? Oder Theater?*, p. 68. And then came her first concert. "At my dying and at my rest, be Thou with me, With joy I go to my dying and to my rest." And she sang only for him. *Professor:* "I did it only for her." *Paulinka:* "I sang only for him." It was really wonderful.

preclude her career becoming absorbed into his. Paula marries Albert Salomon, and Charlotte immediately records her own combination of jealousy and "ardent love" for her prospective stepmother.

The narrative returns briefly to Paula Lindberg and Kurt Singer after fifty pages, in the context of the Nazi accession (figs. 5.10 and 5.11). Paula sings, and Nazis in the audience yell "Get out"—"Aus/Raus"—to Kurt Singer, who is then portrayed in lonely suffering. An image (fig. 5.12) portrays the agreement between Kurt Singer and the *Reichskulturkammer* for the founding of the Kulturbund Deutscher Juden. Singsong states "The honor is mine," and under his breath, "You filthy swine."

FIG. 5.9. Charlotte Salomon, *Leben! Oder Theater?*, p. 69. And
Paulinka became a singer. She mostly sang sacred songs—almost
always in churches. *Paulinka Bimbam sang Bach with extraordinary
success. We are greatly indebted to Professor Klingklang for this
new discovery. —Allgemeine Deutsche Musikzeitung.* But she sang
only for him. *To the same tune: "Be Thou with me . . ."*

What is the source of the fictional name Paulinka Bimbam, which in
Charlotte's story replaces the adopted name Lindberg, itself a substitute for
Levy? The childlike syllables of the name "Paulinka Bimbam" resonate multiply. The name Paulinke appears in the popular children's anthology *Struw-
welpeter*; final *e*'s tend to transmute into *a*'s when an Eastern European aura
is desired (a move that would be biographically inaccurate in this instance
but not irrelevant to the structure of the work's humor overall). "Bim bam"
appears as a diminutive of the name "Benjamin," and as nonsense syllables
in varied musical settings.[19]

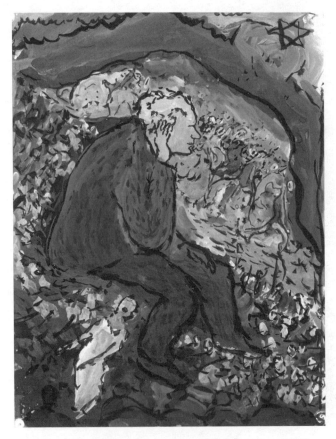

FIG. 5.10. Charlotte Salomon, *Leben? Oder Theater?*, p. 158. *Dr. Singsong:* "One might establish a Jewish theater—that would be a big help to all the artists." *Tune: First movement of Mozart's "Eine kleine Nachtmusik."*

To my ear and sense of context, the most resonant source for the name Bimbam in *Life? Or Theater?* is Gustav Mahler's Symphony No. 3. It is not only that it appears there, but its stylistic and emotional character and use relate directly to Charlotte Salomon's own invocation. The symphony's fifth movement, by far the shortest of the six, carries the title "What the angels tell me." It succeeds the movement that might be called the symphony's navel: the austere setting of Nietzsche's "O Mensch, gib Acht; was spricht die tiefe Mitternacht!" (O Man! Take heed! Deep midnight speaks!)]. Within the symphony's massive structure, this little movement seems charming and inconsequential, a memory of childhood. The syllables "bim-bam" are sung by a boys' and women's chorus, joined later by a solo alto voice. All

FIG. 5.11. Charlotte Salomon, *Leben? Oder Theater?*, p. 159. "I'll write out the bylaws and take them to the Ministry." *Same tune.*

share the narrative of a poem from *Des Knaben Wunderhorn*. "Es sungen drei Engel einen süßen Gesang," sing the children, identifying with angels and receiving the reward of a motherly voice. The imagery and rhetoric of the childlike and the fantasy of angels delivering the presence of the mother to the grieving daughter are consistent with those of *Leben? Oder Theater?* For Mahler as for Charlotte Salomon, the childlike carries weight as a dimension of adult experience. The memory of childhood is recaptured as a dimension of the historical constitution of the self.

Paula Lindberg sang a good deal of Mahler with the Kulturbund between 1933 and her departure from Berlin in 1939, but she never sang the Third Symphony, which was never performed under Kulturbund auspices. I find no direct evidence whatsoever for the tracing of the name Paulinka Bimbam to

FIG. 5.12. Charlotte Salomon, *Leben? Oder Theater?*, p. 164.
Minister: "It's been a pleasure, you would've been just the man. A
pity I can't use you here. But if you should need me, don't hesitate to
call on me." *Dr. Singsong:* "The honor would be mine." (Under his
breath—"You filthy swine.")

this music. But it makes sense to me, not only for the circumstantial presence of Mahler in Charlotte's musical world, and indeed not only for the
cultural and ideological resonances of that music, but most directly for the
combination of the naïve and the sentimental, to use romantic terms, or of
the philosophizing and the childlike, to use more accurate ones. Nanette
Salomon has suggested that Charlotte's images resemble those of Ludwig
Bemelmans, specifically those of his *Madeline* series, inaugurated in 1939.
These are, of course, children's books. Nanette Salomon argues that such
images carry art historical but also cultural-historical resonance.[20] A similar
case is to be made for Mahler's musical rhetoric, where childlike voices are

incorporated into intricate symphonic structures. Sometimes these incorpo-
rations descend into kitsch, but the fifth movement of the Third Symphony
does not do so. There is, I would argue, no kitsch here as the childlike voices
of this movement do not—as Charlotte's images do not—recapture a lost
innocence of childhood. The children's voices are preceded and subsequently
overtaken by the gravity and enormity of the surrounding movements. The
alto solo herself participates in this movement, but her voice is defined by
the leitmotivic tones and Nietzschean text in the previous movement: *O
Mensch, gib Acht, was spricht die tiefe Mitternacht.* In this way Charlotte
Salomon's *Leben? Oder Theater?* might be described as Mahlerian in rhetoric: vast and dark in its narrative while at the same time hailing the outlook
of the child and consoling itself with reminders of innocence. Innocence is a
desire of the child, as it is for the historicizing adult, and not its property.

Among the prominent performers of the Kulturbund Deutscher Juden
was Magnus Davidsohn, who was born in Silesia and had served as chief
cantor in the Fasanenstraße synagogue in Berlin. In 1899, as a young man, he
had sung the bass solo in Beethoven's Ninth Symphony under the baton of
Gustav Mahler, who returned to Prague from Vienna to conduct this Prague
Festival performance. Davidsohn's account of his meeting with Mahler is
related as follows by Peter Gradenwitz:

> Mahler . . . was apparently so much impressed by the young man's per-
> formance that he invited him to join him for a cup of coffee at a coffee
> house he knew from his youth. He was very moved when he heard that
> the singer came from a traditional Jewish family and had studied the
> art of a synagogue cantor. Mahler requested him to come with him to a
> music room and asked the singer to sing Hebrew tunes for him and to
> explain their modal foundations. Mahler argued that the tunes had little
> interesting musical content, but when he heard the singer improvise on
> some prayer texts he whispered with a dry voice: "Yes, this is religious.
> That's how I heard them as a child. From the old precentor in the small
> village temple." There were no more words, remembered the singer—
> "And suddenly Mahler sits down at the piano. He plays. He improvises.
> Phrase after phrase as I improvised them, and he added to the melodies
> wonderfully blossoming harmonies. It was as if he had to overcome vio-
> lent inner emotions. Nothing was spoken anymore. Mahler left and said
> cordially, 'I shall remember you.'"[21]

What is "religious" for Mahler includes the desire for return but not the
claim of return; it includes improvisation, reading, and commentary but not

repetition and only the most private and individualized of rituals. We have a unique insight into Mahler's inner life, into an intimacy of high emotionality and low sentimentality. The image offered here remains, to my ear, entirely compatible with Adorno's summary comment:

> What is Jewish in Mahler does not participate directly in the folk element, but speaks through all its mediations as an intellectual voice, something non-sensuous yet perceptible in the totality. This, admittedly, abolishes the distinction between the recognition of this aspect of Mahler and the philosophical interpretation of music in general.[22]

In Mahler as in Salomon, the childlike is a trope, the flagging of a mode of desire, reproduced cannily and without kitsch, and with the moral and political responsibility inherent in the recognition that the exit from history is impossible. One might call this modernist historiography, modernist epistemology.

We can recall that the sixth and final movement of Mahler's Third Symphony returns the rhetorical aesthetic of absolute music and repeats, in scope and rhetoric, the gravity and musical narrativity of the massive opening movement. As such, it offers a Mahlerian moment as diametrically opposed and as musically distant from the rhetoric of the Second Symphony as one might imagine: the abstract sublime, one might suggest, as opposed to representational kitsch.

The Epilogue of *Leben? Oder Theater?* carries scenes from Charlotte's flight from Berlin: an image of herself seated in front of an empty suitcase (fig. 5.13) and an image of the train moving out of the station (fig. 5.14). The empty suitcase carries an interesting historical untruth, as Charlotte was in fact allowed to leave with only an overnight bag and a tennis racket, to represent her departure to the border authorities as a weekend trip.

The Epilogue is interrupted at one point by a kind of comic interlude, captioned "The German Jews." This is late in the game, about the time of Kristallnacht. It offers a lighthearted but devastating send-up of a performance of authenticity where performance eclipses the performative. The result is violence and the victim is Charlotte. In the section's principal image, the extended Salomon family is seated around the dining table (fig. 5.15). The conversation begins with Albert Salomon's remark "First I am sending away my daughter." The narrator's caption describes the scene as one where

FIG. 5.13. Charlotte Salomon, *Leben? Oder Theater?*,
p. 670, epilogue.

each participant "is so preoccupied with himself that at a dinner party a silent observer feels as if he were in a goose pen."

At different but not opposite ends of a spectrum, the maternal grandfather and Albert Salomon are depicted in terms of their responsibility for the
transmission of paternal law, in which both adherence to the law in terms
of the protection of women and the breaking of the law, in the possible suggestion of sexual violence, bring about the despair of women. It is this cycle
of transmitted violence which *Leben? Oder Theater?* strives to break. It
succeeds in doing so, both as a personal therapeutic odyssey for its author
and as a work of art.

In this context I would like finally to engage some of the aesthetic terms
with which the work *Leben? Oder Theater?* refers to historical violence and

FIG. 5.14. Charlotte Salomon, *Leben? Oder Theater?*, p. 678, epilogue.

works through it. I believe that it does so by matching an aesthetic language of formal reference to the painterly past with a therapeutic language of historicization and recovery. The issue that unites the aesthetic and therapeutic programs of the work is that of the suicide of women. The narrative begins, as we have seen, with the suicide of the first Charlotte, Charlotte Salomon's aunt. After an account of her parents' marriage, the story moves to the death of Charlotte's mother. The method of this suicide has to be constructed materially in order to be established historically. The mother killed herself by jumping from a window, and with this historical correction—recall that Charlotte had grown up in the belief that her mother had died of influenza— the window becomes the leitmotiv for the death of women (fig. 5.16).

Charlotte recalls her mother telling her of the pleasures of heaven, of imagining "Wouldn't it be nice if I were an angel and brought you a letter?" She remembers asking her mother not to forget to leave the letter on the windowsill (fig. 5.17). The image depicting the death of Charlotte's mother is a double frame: a large window which "frames" the life of Fransziska Salomon and a small, floating window which functions as a metonym for the falling body. The mourning grandmother is depicted repeatedly in front of

FIG. 5.15. Charlotte Salomon, *Leben? Oder Theater?*, p. 650, chapter four, *The German Jews*, of whom each one is so preoccupied with himself that at a dinner party a silent observer feels as if her were in a goose pen. *Albert:* "First of all, I'm sending away my daughter." *Woman to his right:* "And we're going to Australia!" *Man to her right:* "And what will you do?" *Sculptor:* "And I'll go to the United States and become the greatest sculptor in the world." *Paulinka:* "We'll be staying here for the time being." *Mr. Blahn:* "And I'll go to the United States and there I'll become the greatest singer in the world." *Daberlohn's fiancée:* "And we're going to America, aren't we, Mucki—" *Maid:* "Take this piece, Professor, it's the best one."

FIG. 5.16. Charlotte Salomon, *Leben? Oder Theater?*, p. 140.
"Now she no longer stands there. Ah me, in a different place
she now abides."

the window (fig. 5.18). And when Daberlohn is depicted, later on in the work, in a pensive reverie, he is also depicted in front of the window, "standing," as the caption says, "like many a woman, at the window." The window is a woman's space, and the transgendering of Daberlohn mirrors the transgendering of the artist Charlotte under his influence. At its most abstract, the window is pictured alone, with the signature divisions of the image into horizontal rectangles of single colors, the color red signifying blood and death.

This image has a genealogy, tying Charlotte's story with invocation—by her and by her readers—with art historical practices, claims, and tropes. I would suggest that the parent of this image is the romantic depiction of the window as the site of both transcendence and death and in particular the

FIG. 5.17. Charlotte Salomon, *Leben? Oder Theater?*, p. 26.
Franziska: "In Heaven everything is much more beautiful than
here on earth—and when your Mummy has turned into a little
angel she'll come down and bring her little lambkin, she'll bring a
letter, telling her what it's like in Heaven, what it's like up there
in Heaven." Franziska was of a somewhat sentimental disposition.
She would often take the child to bed with her and tell her about a
life after death in celestial spheres, a life that was said to be simply
glorious and for which she seemed to have a terrible yearning, and
she often asked Charlotte whether it wouldn't be wonderful if her
mother were to turn into an angel with wings. Charlotte agreed that
it would, only she asked her mother not to forget to tell her in a
letter—which she was to deliver personally as an angel and deposit
on Charlotte's windowsill—what it was like up there in Heaven. *To
the same tune.* (The tune captioned for the previous picture is *"The
Christmas tree is bright with candles."*)

FIG. 5.18. Charlotte Salomon, *Leben? Oder Theatre?*, p. 147.
"... this is the thanks I got for it!"

site of women. In 1805 Caspar David Friedrich painted the window of his studio; in 1822 he famously placed his wife in the same space, gazing outward (fig. 5.19).

In 1951, Mark Rothko found his mature style in the modernist play of transcendence and death and the limits of representation, with a canvas that hovers between life and death and at the same time offers an unintended homage, I think, to the geometry and colors of Charlotte Salomon's work.[23]

The historical work performed by Salomon's images leads me to place them into dialogue with Friedrich and Rothko.[24] I see a bond of kinship in the images of Friedrich, Salomon, and Rothko that involves the language of modernism, specifically the tension provided by the simultaneity of the

FIG. 5.19. Caspar David Friedrich, *Woman at the Window.* (artres)

engagement with transcendence—of life and its representations—and at the same time the refusal to fall under its spell, in other words the refusal to agree to the representation of the transcendent. This is the position Freud cites in the opening pages of *Civilization and Its Discontents* with the help of a citation from Grabbe: *Wir können aus dieser Welt nicht fallen*—we cannot fall out of this world.

Charlotte does not shy from the representation of death in the form of its violent residues: corpses and blood. What she does not portray is any kind of transcendence from life, death, world, or history.

Griselda Pollock suggests that Charlotte Salomon's images might be understood according to Benjamin's notion of the theater of memory. I would second that suggestion, but with a qualification. The qualification rests in what I see to be Salomon's framing of the theatrical gestures she uses, which coincide with the critical framings of her own memories. Thus the phrase "bim-bam" puts the quotation marks of historical distance around the memory of childhood it invokes.

Although Charlotte Salomon's work seems never to make the choice between life and theater that its title proposes, it does, outside the structure of that choice, embody a fundamental choice of life. Surely this is one way to read the signature image of the girl on the rock: the burden of history is born on the back, while the figure herself faces into the open. This reading is consistent with Charlotte Salomon's life after completion of the work. She married a fellow refugee, Alexander Nagler, and became pregnant. In September 1943 both were arrested and deported to Auschwitz, where Charlotte was murdered on arrival. When she suspected that her arrest was imminent, she consigned the body of *Leben? Oder Theater?* to a doctor friend. Albert Salomon and Paul Lindberg survived the war, and reclaimed the work, which is now owned by the Jewish Museum of Amsterdam.

The Nazi persecution of European Jews is inseparable from Charlotte Salomon's life and work for the obvious reason of its emergence in exile. Salomon's death in Auschwitz is an equally essential fact, perhaps the historically paradigmatic fact of her biography. At the same time, however, Auschwitz is not the telos of her life, as it cannot be understood to be the telos of modern Jewish or modern German Jewish life. Micro- and macrocosms speak identically to this assertion. In relation to Salomon's life and to Jewish life, Auschwitz must be understood to be at once alien and inalienable: both absolutely relevant and absolutely irrelevant. I hope that the force of this ironic, necessary contradiction is apparent. It is, I would argue, the contradiction that needs to inform the placement of the Holocaust within a trajectory of Jewish history. It would seem to me both vulgar and ludicrous to suggest that Salomon or her work transcend Auschwitz. But their deliberate, painstaking, self-aware, and I would hazard to say Mahlerian choice of life stands uncompromised.

CHAPTER SIX

Arnaldo Momigliano and the Facts

I

In the fourteen-line preface to the collection *On Pagans, Jews, and Christians*, published in 1987, the year of his death, Arnaldo Momigliano offered the following summation:

> The treble tradition—Jewish, Classical, and Christian—that I have inherited as a Jew and as an Italian invited exploration and clarification, but did not carry inside it the seeds of any dramatic conflict. The spirit of the Risorgimento is still active in Italy. The conflicts in which I have been involved during my life—and the resulting cruelties—have other origins.[1]

At once incisive, lucid, and cryptic, these words represent a style of thinking that Momigliano's readers and students know well. This chapter will engage the character and ramifications of what I take to be the passage's three assertions. First is the assertion that the triad of classical culture, Judaism, and Christianity did not evolve and need not—indeed must not—be understood as immanently incompatible or conflicted. The "treble tradition" that they made contained no "seeds" of its own dissolution. It is not really clear whether Momigliano means that this specific Jewish-Italian composite contained no such seed or whether he means that cultural encounters and history itself have none, in other words that history does not operate and must not be understood via metaphors of determinism, whether drawn from biology or elsewhere.

Second is the assertion that the treble tradition survives in modern times as a political possibility created by liberalism and as an intellectual possibility enabled by historical memory and knowledge. In the Italian context, liberalism is understood as the emancipatory energy and promise of the Risorgimento. The Risorgimento stands for the nineteenth-century nationalism of liberation, a nationalism similar to pre-1848 liberal nationalism in Germany but one to which history and posterity have been kinder. The Risorgimento thus abides as a carrier of liberalism, whose antagonists and undoings came from the outside: from the Holy See between 1860 and 1929; from fascism after 1922. This summary and Momigliano's evocation of it follow Benedetto Croce's grounding post-1945 assertion that the two decades of fascism constitute an exception in the liberal trajectory of modern Italian history. Italian liberalism pursues an idea of multicultural compatibility, one that was perhaps evident also in the German Enlightenment of the previous century. Thus, *Judentum* and *Italianità* recuperate the lost ideal of *Judentum* and *Deutschtum*. Momigliano in his life and work found liberalism in many contexts; to their trajectories in modern Italian, British, and secular Jewish history he paid particular attention.

Third, and least transparent, is the assertion that the twentieth-century collapse of this co-habitation of cultural traditions, of this multicultural promise—a collapse in which anti-Semitism forms a basic element—has "other," i.e. external origins. Other and external to what?—the reader will ask. To the Risorgimento? To liberalism? To Italy itself?

Arnaldo Dante Momigliano (1908–87) devoted a career of six decades to the study of the classical world (or the pagan world—a term he shared with Aby Warburg and others) of Greece and Rome, the Jewish world, and the Christian world. Through the history of classical scholarship, the history of historiography, and the history of scholarship in general, he pulled the ancient world into the modern one. His model was not one of *Nachträglichkeit* or unconscious legacy, like those of Freud and Warburg, although he was surprisingly and deeply sympathetic to such dimensions of culture and analysis, his positivist style and empirical emphases notwithstanding. His paradigm of the intellectual historical record as well as its recuperation was one of conscious knowledge, of the cumulative scholarly knowledge of the past and its varieties. But as the history of knowledge is also the history of the limits of knowledge, Momigliano always had an eye on these limitations and their motivations. Scholars were for him not dry-mouthed Casaubons, spending too much time with the dead, but rather full-headed and full-blooded Jacobs, struggling with the angels of history toward the inevitable display of their own limitations—empirical, archaeological, political, personal.

The cultures and institutions in which Momigliano lived and worked form a second tripartite picture. Trained at the University of Turin, he taught

there and in Rome between 1929 and 1938, when the anti-Semitic legislation
of Mussolini's regime forced his dismissal. Although he declined to return to
Italy after the war, turning down an invitation to join Croce's new institute
in Naples, he never relinquished his Italian citizenship and traveled only
with an Italian passport. In 1964 he joined the faculty of the Scuola Normale
Superiore in Pisa. His exile in England had taken him first to Oxford; after
the war he taught at the University of Bristol and in 1952 he was appointed
professor of ancient history at University College London. His inaugural address on that occasion, "George Grote and the Study of Greek History," paid
homage, in Karl Christ's words, "to the great liberal tradition of University
College," as well as to British liberalism itself.[2]

In the United States, Momigliano's principal university affiliation was
with the University of Chicago, where he first visited in 1959. On his retire-
ment from University College in 1975, he accepted a position as the Alexander White Visiting Professor in Chicago, which he held until his death. He
arrived in the fall for an annual seminar for faculty and graduate students,
and again in the spring for another seminar and a series of public lectures.
In the fall quarter of 1979 he co-taught a seminar on Max Weber's *Ancient
Judaism* with Edward Shils. I was a student in this seminar during my first
quarter in graduate school. Among its many extraordinary aspects was the
demeanor of Edward Shils, whose default comportment would prove to be
overbearing on most topics and especially on Max Weber. In Momigliano's
presence, however, he guilelessly took the position of a student, a subject
position he echoed in the booklet he published privately to record the memorial service held for Momigliano at the University of Chicago in October
1987. "He was one of the greatest scholars of his age," Shils wrote then,
"perhaps of any age."[3]

Throughout my years as a graduate student at the University of Chicago
in the early 1980s, the fall quarter began, ritually, with the arrival of Momigliano. I mean this in a literal sense, as the task consistently fell to one
or more of us of meeting him at O'Hare Airport—always on a Sunday afternoon, always on TWA Flight 771 from London. The trip and flight seemed
hardly to disrupt his personal aura and routine, defined by a three-piece dark
grey winter suit and a barrage of books, loose papers, and small note pads
equipped with carbon paper. Although he preferred being met at the airport
by his students, he also relished telling the story of his one-time Chicago
adventure with an Italian-American taxi driver who persuaded him to make
detour on the way from O'Hare Airport to Hyde Park in order to adjudicate
a neighborhood dispute between two rival pizza parlors, each one of which
carried the name "Leaning Tower of Pisa" and insisted in a grandiose mu-

ral that the tower leaned in a direction different from that portrayed by its rival. On that occasion, Momigliano settled the case and was driven free of charge to Hyde Park.

With us students, his person and his articles safely in the car, he would immediately stake out the first topic of conversation, always with the opening phrase "As you know . . ." He used the same phrase in the classroom, and it is the only stock phrase of his that we assumed to be empirically false. "As you know," he said, on one of these occasions, seated in the front seat of the car and still circling the lower-level arrivals concourse of the airport, "I have never in my life tasted wine or seen a film. Today, however, I had the curious experience of looking up from my reading and realizing that the film they were showing was in fact a biography of an old friend of mine." I was mystified, but the facts followed. The friend was Harold Abrahams, 100-meter gold medalist at the 1924 Olympics and long-time director of athletics at Cambridge thereafter; the film was *Chariots of Fire* (1981). The film tells the stories of several runners, each with his own social and religious contexts and passions. Abrahams's story is that of the trials of the Jews in interwar Britain, especially in the universities, and specifically at Cambridge.

The claim that he had never tasted wine or seen a film was matched, to my memory, by a statement he made in the more formal setting of his biannual seminar in Harper Library Tower: "I have never understood Kant," he said. "One thing that marks me as an historian is never to have understood Kant."

Wine, film, and Kant might therefore be understood to share a status for Momigliano as objects of mystification and thus necessarily of disavowal. More accurately, they share a status in his rhetoric of disavowal, a rhetoric that consistently sought to distance itself from areas of indeterminacy that could too easily evolve into the ground for ideology. He thus disavowed indeterminacy and ideology in favor of the facts of history and a consistent rhetorical and enacted appeal to the dignity of the fact. At the same time, the fact was not the whole story; the fact did not make history. The "true collector of facts"—as Momigliano described Herotodus—paves the way for the witness to truth. Thus the force of his dedication of the 1961–62 Sather Lectures "To the memory of Gaetano Salvemini, Marc Bloch, Johan Huizinga, Simon Dubnow, historians and witnesses of truth."[4]

The fact serves as the gateway to the true and the real, and thus at the same time to the empirical, material, and political responsibility of the historian. It follows that Momigliano should have had a developed relationship to antiquarianism, to the understanding of history as a collection of minutiae. Antiquarianism did not amount to historiography but served it and indeed protected it. Momigliano thus pulled antiquarianism from the jaws of its nineteenth-century dismissers, including Hegel and Nietzsche, as well as from the long tradition of Italian Hegelianism as inherited in Momigliano's lifetime by Benedetto Croce.

Momigliano's relation to antiquarianism might be understood as a strategic identification that would provide a check on the temptation of historical understanding to overreach legitimate epistemological boundaries. Here may lie one of the many differences between Momigliano's antiquarianism and Eduard Fuchs's, as celebrated by Walter Benjamin. Momigliano's check on historiography's epistemological claims countermands Fuchs/ Benjamin's allegorization and consequent expansion of the historical referent.

Its limiting function notwithstanding, however, antiquarianism offered Momigliano its own mysteries. From one the Sather Lectures of 1961–62, published as *The Classical Foundations of Modern Historiography*, called "The Rise of Antiquarian Research":

> Throughout my life I have been fascinated by a type of man so near to my profession, so transparently sincere in his vocation, so understandable in his enthusiasms, and yet so deeply mysterious in his ultimate aims: the type of man who is interested in historical facts without being interested in history.[5]

The carefully calibrated purple touches in the opening phrases—more Hamlet than Herodotus in their tone—seem to me to prepare the sarcastic tone of the phrase following the colon. I remain unconvinced by the sincerity and force of the praise of "the type of man who is interested in historical facts without being interested in history." On the one side, Momigliano's respect for the antiquarian does not make him interchangeable with the connoisseur or the collector. As Kenneth Sacks has observed, connoisseurship departs from antiquarianism, in Momigliano's typology, in its fussiness, narcissism, and remove from historical context.[6] Neither would one argue for any proximity with the collector's practice of Eduard Fuchs. The *theory* of collection as a mode of allegory, however, might well have elicited Momigliano's interest and sympathy, had it been presented to him in such terms. On the other side of the question of antiquarianism, the proposition of facts without history might provide some ground, or at least a metaphor, for a critique of historicism (in the Popperian sense).

The "archetype of all antiquarians" is identified in the essay's second paragraph as Nicolas-Claude de Peiresc:

When confronted by the *Dialogues d'Oratius Tubero*—the Sceptic publication of François de La Mothe Le Vayer—Peiresc disclaimed any understanding of such deep thought: "moi qui ne cognoys rien en toutes ces grandes élévations d'esprit." But three days later he made to his friend Gassendi one of his most forceful statements, against those centuries "de grande simplicité" in which one believed everything "sans autre preuve que de simples conjectures de ce qui pouvoit avoir esté." (56)

Where is the antiquarian, and how is he respected, in Momigliano's homage to the eighteenth century as the age that "performed the greatest rescue operation for forgotten civilizations [including China, India, and the Celts] humanity had ever witnessed," but whose "consequences were felt only by professors, philosophers, poets, and cranks"?[7]

Antiquarianism—especially as treated in the 1950 essay "Ancient History and the Antiquarian"—guided Momigliano, as Carlo Ginzburg has written, in his "detachment from Croceanism."[8] From Ginzburg's use of the term Croceanism we can reasonably infer the whole and varied apparatus of Italian idealism, which outpaced positivism in Italian intellectual fashion by the 1890s and ultimately divided into two camps: on the one hand, that of Croce himself, a philosophical conservative who steered resolutely and consistently clear of fascism, and that of Giovanni Gentile, who served as Mussolini's first minister of education from 1922 to 1924.

Karl Christ cites the same essay with a harsher judgment of antiquarianism, and of Momigliano's view of antiquarianism. "For the antiquarians taught"—and here Christ cites Momigliano—"'how to use non-literary evidence, but they also made people reflect on the difference between collecting facts and interpreting facts.'"[9] Commenting on Momigliano's 1944 study of "Friedrich Creuzer and Greek Historiography," Christ writes: "Already at this point it was clear that Momigliano's understanding of the history of historiography did not imply absorption in the sterile, antiquarian inventory of tradition."[10]

Antiquarianism functions as a foil to the excesses of history, including those of traditions of national historiography in the nineteenth century, and thus as a partner to empiricism, a necessary but not sufficient condition of historiography. Put another way, empiricism and its rhetoric have shadows. Antiquarianism may also serve as a foil to what might be described as bureaucratic knowledge or the bureaucratic organization of knowledge, whereby vast sums of material are organized to the avoidance or repression of epistemological and political responsibility.

We can consider, for example, the essay "The Rhetoric of History and the History of Rhetoric: On Hayden White's Tropes":

> In the other research in which I happen to be involved—the characterization of so-called Jewish Hellenism—the element of novelty is less apparent and, at least to me, less important. I am a Jew myself and I know from my own experience what price Jews had and have to pay to be Jews. I am not collecting facts for academic purposes when I try to understand what moved the Jews to refuse assimilation to surrounding civilizations. But I could choose to give an answer to this question in religious and moral terms. If instead I choose to clarify my ideas on this matter in historical terms and I make the Greco-Roman period the central point of reference for my quest, I subordinate myself *ipso facto* to what the specific evidence (the Books of Maccabees, Philo, the Gospels, Flavius Josephus, the *Mishnah*, etc.) will tell me. Of course I am not bound to confine myself to what the evidence tells me. I may add whatever other considerations I like. But I shall have to be careful to keep my private thoughts separate from the evidence I use. Whatever ideological considerations guide my research, I shall be judged by my use of the evidence.[11]

Or: "We must face the facts": a statement from the preface to *Alien Wisdom: The Limits of Hellenization* (1975)—which counts at the same time as his most poetic book.

In *Alien Wisdom*, the subtlety of the historical facts Momigliano wants to face, along with the subtlety of his mode of engagement, are perhaps most apparent. The short book has a preface of fourteen lines, exactly the length of the preface, cited above, to *On Pagans, Jews, and Christians*. This one is more matter of fact. It acknowledges warmly the hosts of the two institutions, Cambridge and Bryn Mawr, which had hosted, respectively, the Trevelyan and Flexner Lectures in which the argument and sweep of *Alien Wisdom* were first worked out. But the preface faces a dedication page of a poignancy unique in Momigliano's work, a dedication to the memory of his mother, including her place and date of birth—Turin, 1884—and the fact of her death: "campo nazista di sterminio 1943."

Alien Wisdom traces the Hellenistic confrontation of the Greeks with four other civilizations—the Romans, Jews, Celts, and Iranians, of which they had known only the last in a previous period. Momigliano calls this confrontation an *intellectual* event—"an intellectual event of the first order," giving "international circulation to ideas." The Greeks had known the

Persians as a conquering empire; now "Rome replaced Persia as the empire by which the Greeks were directly challenged." "Only the Jews and the Iranians stood up to the Romans, as they had stood up to the Seleucids. The Jews had not a chance, but in the course of their toils one of their minority groups acquired autonomy and challenged the Roman Empire in a more fundamental manner than the old worshippers of the Temple of Jerusalem had ever done."[12]

Momigliano understands the violence of empires as intellectual as well as physical violence. Carthaginian culture, he writes, "was murdered by the Romans." The "murder" of Carthaginian culture (to an extent distinct from Carthage itself) by the Romans exposes a high level of historiographical affect, suggesting that for Momigliano, Carthage carried an overlay of "Semitic" identification just as it did for Freud, who famously made Hannibal a personal hero in his battles against Rome. As a result of their disappearance, Momigliano continues, Carthaginian ideas are opaque to historians. In the second century B.C., the Greeks and Carthaginians shared the fear of Rome. Rome also had a strong impact on the "intellectual relations" of those cultures who felt its power, including the relations between Greeks and Jews, Celts, and Iranians.

Hellenistic Greek became the Mediterranean *lingua franca* because no literate Greek commanded a second language. Other Mediterranean cultures were bilingual. The Jews used Greek to communicate with others but also among themselves. The Jews both "remained convinced of the superiority of their beliefs" and at the same time absorbed "many Greek notions and customs in the process—and ultimately found themselves involved in that general confrontation of Greek and Jewish values which we call Christianity."[13]

"The influence of Rome on the minds of those who came into contact with it was quick and strong."[14] The Romans had little sense of or interest in the international: "They paid the Greeks to teach them their wisdom and often did not even have to pay because they were their slaves."[15] Inscrutably, the Romans learned Greek and about Greek culture while fighting the first two Punic Wars against Carthage; at this time the interest was not mutual. "We shall never be able to decide," Momigliano concludes his first lecture, "how much of the success of Roman imperialism is implicit in this determined effort by the Romans to speak and think in Greek." "The command of a foreign language meant power to the Romans." And in a coda intended, presumably, more for Cambridge than Bryn Mawr: "Compulsory Greek, we all agree, is indispensable for the upkeep of an empire; but is compulsory Latin necessary to save oneself from an empire?"[16] How if at all one saves oneself from an empire—and indeed whether one should—is a question he does not raise.

In a chapter of *Alien Wisdom* on the historians Polybius and his follower Posidonius, Momigliano comments on imperialism as a general phenomenon, despite the fact that the concept belongs to the turn of the twentieth century. Although Polybius accepted Roman hegemony over Greece, he "was obviously worried about the future of a state which had to resort to terror in order to maintain its supremacy."[17] Posidonius offered a "negative analysis of Roman rule," but "it did not escape him that the barbarous West was involved in the crisis."[18] Posidonius's partially justified reputation, Momigliano writes, "of being a religious soul" accounts for his attribution of the sacred aura of Roman power: "He therefore lends some support to that candid scholar of unimpeachable erudition, Aurelio Peretti, who, in the year 1942, tried to persuade himself (and if possible his readers) that no man of Indo-Germanic blood could have protested against Rome: only Jews and other Orientals scribbled Sibylline oracles against the ruling power."[19] Peretti was presumably not interested in the Jews in 1942; Momigliano was and continues to be in 1975. The allegorical reach of the reference to Peretti is explicit but not precise. One wonders to what extent Momigliano favors Peretti's view of ancient Jewish resistance so as to give the same aura to the Jews of fascist Italy.

Momigliano analyzed Hellenism and cosmopolitanism in the early work perhaps most important to his career, his 1934 study *Filippo Il Macedone: Saggio sulla storia greca del IV secolo a.C.*[20] Cosmopolitanism as a category of both history and historiography precedes the study of Philip, however. It forms a principal agenda of Momigliano's first monograph, his study of the Roman Emperor Claudius: *L'opera dell'Imperatore Claudio*, published in Florence in 1932.[21] The preface inserts the book into the preceding decade's revisionary work on Claudius, as enabled by archaeological finds and the pioneering work of Michael Rostovtzeff (*Social and Economic History of the Roman Empire* [Oxford, 1926]). It discloses its own agenda as that of writing the history of the Roman Empire via the history of Claudius's reign, and specifically of tracing the *reality* of the empire's "monarchic and cosmopolitan constitution" out of the survival in *appearance* of the Roman republic.[22] In this context, cosmopolitanism is an attribute of empire and the centralization of power, synonym of a metropolitan ideology that looks outward to the cultures it conquers and controls, and not the attribute of a culture of exchange, multilinguality, and indeed multicultural experience. In this sense, cosmopolitanism assumes and identifies with the position and power of the metropolitan subject position. It differs fundamentally from the decentralizing assumptions and agenda of internationalism. To such cosmopolitans, aliens will have no wisdom to offer.[23]

The Momigliano I knew as my teacher consistently interrogated histori-cal writing, or one dimension of it at least, as an allegory of the historian's contemporary concerns. Indeed, as we shall see below, in his final written sentences he interrogated his early work in precisely such terms. Thus I think it is fair to suggest that if Momigliano were to have been reading this work as written by another historian, he would no doubt have interrogated its status as an allegory—witting or unwitting, intentional or functional, favorable or unfavorable—of the fascist regime in Italy. Momigliano's 1931 Claudius invites such speculation on its own terms. Claudius's will to power has an imperial as well a domestic agenda. In the chapter called "The Poli-tics of Centralization" *(La politica di accentramento)*, Momigliano writes that all of Claudius's efforts were conceived in contempt of the authority of the Senate.[24] This autonomy drove both his foreign endeavors, with a strong focus on the loyalty of the army, and (in particular distinction from the po-litical style of his predecessors), his domestic ones. From the book's opening paradigm of the republic sublated by the cosmopolitan empire, the study introduces Claudius himself as an intellectual—an *erudito*—and proceeds to examine his policy on religion, specifically his reintroduction of the cult of Rome and the celebration of the founding of Rome.[25] For Claudius, the cult of Rome accompanied the cult of the emperor.[26] So far as Claudius's treatment of religions is concerned, the case of the Jews supplies the most evidence.

"The Jews," Momigliano wrote here in 1931, "were a religion and a people; and Claudius, in keeping with his preferential politics toward the provinces, wanted to maintain peace with the latter, while repressing the active proselytism of the former, as recently fueled by the new ferment of the Christian predicament, as yet indistinguishable from the synagogue."[27] Claudius's predecessor Caligula had initiated what Momigliano anachro-nistically calls "a necessarily anti-Semitic politics": "una politica neces-sariamente antisemitica." Caligula's "anti-Semitic" program included what Momigliano names "pogroms." Claudius reversed these tendencies, in acts including the restoration of citizenship to the Jews of Alexandria, as re-counted authoritatively by Flavius Josephus.[28]

Though the study of Philip of Macedonia (finished in 1932 and published in 1934) is often referred to as biography, it is not, as the title makes clear. Rather, the study takes up explicitly and with explicit homage J. G. Droy-sen's 1833 "discovery" ("*scoprire*"—the quotation marks are Momigliano's) that Philip's person and reign stand not at the conclusion of Greek history but at the moment of its transformation from a collection of autonomous cities into a single Hellas united in one bundle: *in un fascio solo*. This is the jargon of the regime. Droysen's motivation, Momigliano argues, was the desire to find the Hellenistic foundations for the mediation between classicism and Christianity.[29] Following Droysen, Momigliano argues that Philip's Macedonian state rose according to a cosmopolitan rather than a national model, which already in Philip's time reveals the basis of Alexander's supernational state.[30] In Momigliano's usage, then, the cosmopolitan equals the supernational. Does the cosmopolitan supernational also equal the imperial?

The penultimate and longest chapter of *Filippo Il Macedone* is called "The Conflict of Ideals": *Il conflitto degli ideali*. Here a clearer potential allegorical argument comes into relief, one which in fact places the young Momigliano on the side of the Italian liberals (Croce as well as Gaetano De Sanctis, Momigliano's *Doktorvater* at the University of Turin). For here the ideals of Philip are juxtaposed against those of his Athenian rival Demosthenes. On the one side, Philip summoned Aristotle to his court as the tutor for his son Alexander. This was undoubtedly, Momigliano asserts, a political act. Aristotle served the father as well as the son, providing grounds for Philip's absorption of the multiplicity of Greek cities into a unified whole, which for him meant under Macedonian control. The point was to control Greece without conquering it, to reconcile with Athens. One means to this end was the assimilation of Greek thought, especially Isocrates, "the father of all fourth-century panhellenism."[31] Thus would intellectual legitimacy contribute to the power that would avenge the defeat in the Persian War and reconquer Egypt as well. On the other side: Demosthenes, the democrat and possible pluralist, who recognized the legitimacy of Persian rule in Egypt.[32]

The book ends with a portentous opposition of liberty and despotism and indeed a warning about the abdication of liberty to despotism. The final paragraph carries an opaque and labored syntax, a rhetoric that seems to turn inward into itself, possibly to protect itself. What it clearly fears is the slippage from liberty to despotism. It is perhaps this rhetoric which Momigliano recalled, in preparing the new edition just before his death in 1987, in his cautious retrospective alliance with the Italian liberals and anti-fascists of the early 1930s:

> But—to repeat—such an abdication before Philip was in its intentions no different from many other projects/longings to introduce a new order in Greece for the use and advantage only of the Greeks, while the superimposition upon the interests of one single people was implicit in Philip and explicit in Alexander. And therefore nothing questions more the ra-

tionality of the passage from a freedom that ignores the freedom of others to despotism than the discovery how the Greeks, in their labored effort to overcome that freedom, achieved nothing else—even without a precise awareness of this—but the invocation and preparation for despotism.

Ma—ripetiamo—questa abdicazione davanti a Filippo non era nelle intensioni diversa dai molti altri vagheggiamenti di introdurre un ordine nuovo in Grecia ad uso e vantaggio dei soli Greci, mentre in Filippo era implicito e in Alessandro esplicito il sovrapporsi agli interessi di un popolo solo. E perciò nulla ci fa più pensosi sulla razionalità del trapasso dalla libertà ignara della libertà altrui al despotismo che lo scorgere come i Greci nel travaglioso sforzo di superare quella libertà non giungessero ad altro, sia pure senza rendersene esatto conto, che ad invocare e preparare il despotismo.[33]

On February 17, 1933 ("Year 11"), Mussolini wrote to Francesco Ercole (his minister of education between 1932 and 1935) about his concern that the history of Rome was being "massacred" by historians hostile to his regime, "no matter whether they are anti-fascists, Catholics, or Jews." Of particular concern to him were the "noted Catholic propagandist" Gaetano De Sanctis and three of his students, all named as Jews: Attilio Levi, Claudio Treves, and Arnaldo Momigliano. Mussolini described Momigliano as the "author of various biographies [*memorie*], completely superficial, without originality of point of view [*pure affrattate, senza originalità di vedute*]."[34]

Momigliano used the occasion of a book review in 1980 to evaluate Mussolini's turn to anti-Semitism in 1938.[35] As per his custom, he understood motivation in terms of both political strategy and personal idiosyncrasy. For Mussolini in 1938, Momigliano wrote, anti-Semitism "was above all used to distract the attention of the majority of the Italians from their own difficulty," including the now obvious fact "that the conquest of Abyssinia had solved none of the economic and social problems of Italy." On the personal side, Mussolini's connections to Jewish figures, including his former mistress Margherita Sarfatti, are well known. Less well known (and unmentioned, Momigliano points out, in the book under review) was Mussolini's resentment of Jewish socialist circles in Milan which had excluded him, and his longstanding contempt for Claudio Treves, his rival for the leadership of the Socialist party and its journal *(Avanti)* between 1912 and 1914, with whom he had fought a bloody duel in 1915.

As we have seen, in his 1991 tribute "Arnaldo Momigliano and the History of Historiography," Karl Christ gives emphasis to the 1952 inaugural lecture at University College London, "George Grote and the Study of Greek History," as an homage "to the great liberal tradition of University College," as well as to British liberalism itself. Christ understands the lecture as the "high point of the first postwar phase in Momigliano's concern with the history of historiography." The exposition provided, in Christ's summary, "a deeply informed survey of the modern historiography on ancient Greece, an analysis of the crisis in this field, and one of the most vigorous arguments for its significance." What crisis? Momigliano began, Christ continues, with the late eighteenth-century work of William Mitford and John Gillies, "works which ushered in a new epoch in the British historiography of Greece." "What was really new"—here Christ quotes Momigliano—"was, however, political discussion embodied in a Greek history." Neither Momigliano nor Christ maps the terms of what both are classifying as historiographical allegory, i.e. the political discussion of the contemporary world, here Georgian England, alongside an empirically valid discussion of ancient Greece. This allegorical investment of eighteenth-century historiography in general, of eighteenth-century ancient historiography in particular, is best known through the example of Edward Gibbon's Roman history, in which Rome's decline under the pressures of Christianity mirrors the perceived threat of Catholicism and "popery" to the well-being of Britain. Christ is entirely right not to be surprised by Momigliano's acceptance of allegorical investment as a legitimate partner to historiographical and empirical responsibility. Momigliano, Christ writes, now connects the work of Mitford and Gillies to the previous continental European and Irish work of C. M. Olivier, the Abbé de Mably, and Thomas Leland, emphasizing particularly (Christ's phrase) Leland's comparison of Philip II of Macedonia with Frederick the Great. Leland, we might observe, compared Philip II with the monarch whom Kant honored as the voice of Enlightenment; now Momigliano brings the same ancient monarch into the historiographic (if not historical) world of British liberalism. "Thus," continues Christ, "under the rubric of the history of historiography, Momigliano reestablished, as it were, his own, personal ties to 'Filippo il Macedone.'"[36]

Momigliano's *Filippo Il Macedone* opens, as Christ recounts, with references to Karl Beloch and George Grote. "Above all," observes Christ, "Momigliano praised Johann Gustav Droysen." Wrote Momigliano: "Droysen in fact recognized for once and for all that the essential characteristic of Hellenism is the constitution of a cosmopolitan civilization." Continues Christ:

But this was a return to the early Droysen—the "primo Droysen"; Momigliano rejected the "secondo Droysen" of the second edition of the *His-*

tory of Hellenism, which appeared in 1871, just after the founding of the German Empire. For Momigliano, this "second Droysen," the historian of Prussian politics, had emphasized the power of politics of national unification through the parallel of the roles of Macedonia and Prussia. The early Droysen, on the other hand, had taken the priority of fundamental religious problems as his starting point.[37]

For Christ, then, the 1934 study of Philip II establishes a constant argument for ancient historiography and political allegory according a cosmopolitan ideal and against the ideologies both of empire and of nationalism.

For a 1987 new edition of the Philip study, Momigliano wrote a new preface. It begins with the categorical contextualization of the edition of 1934 into "the years 1929–1934, the years in which it was conceived and written and which were of particular significance for a Jew such as myself, already deeply concerned about his freedoms—and not only political freedom but religious as well."[38] (The same context would apply to the book on Claudius.) In 1929, Momigliano continues, a book called *La dissoluzione della libertà nella Grecia antica* appeared, which argued its case from a position approximate to but not identical with the fascist position.[39] The book was criticized by the liberal voices of Gaetano De Sanctis and Benedetto Croce. Momigliano recalls his own position at the time as being more equivocal, and indeed based on his reading of Croce on Benjamin Constant. From this work of Croce, Momigliano had developed a sense of the differences between ancient and modern conceptions of liberty, as well as a sense of the varied and evolutionary quality of the conceptions and politics of liberty in the ancient Greek world. Thus, Demosthenes's idea of freedom is not Christ's: *La libertà de Demostene non era la libertà di Cristo.* Could he have added *la libertà di Grote* as well? Momigliano seems to imply here that Croce's own historiography was subtler than his polemics, and that it was the former which he himself had emulated as a young scholar in a difficult political period. In 1987, in what was in fact to become his final published statement, Momigliano recalled his study of Philip as an initial consideration of the evolution and varieties of ancient liberty—political and religious—which would preoccupy him for the next fifty years, for all his life.

These are some of the questions to be addressed to Momigliano's historiography, indeed to the history of his historiography. Did the subtlety of Momigliano's grasp of the ancient world, which he believed to be greater than Croce's, produce a more subtle history of ancient freedom? Or did the allegorical imprint of his work in the early 1930s bear a politically less defined—or indeed less liberal—position with respect to the fascist regime and the function of ancient historiography as contemporary political allegory? Or does a significant distinction need to be made between religious liberty and political liberty? Or are the fissures that open in Momigliano's assertions and recollections of a liberal position not the fissures of political contingency but in fact those of liberalism itself?

There is a significant circumstantial complication to this issue as well, which Karl Christ does not address. This has to do with Momigliano's vexed personal relation to Italian fascism. Here too, or here especially, the facts do not provide answers.

Like one third of the eligible Jewish population of Italy and the vast majority of Italian academics, Momigliano joined the National Fascist Party (P.N.F.). He was encouraged to do so by his mentor Gaetano De Sanctis. De Sanctis also went in, despite his liberal persona. Momigliano contributed four entries to the *Enciclopedia Italiana* under Giovanni Gentile's editorship, which appeared in four volumes between 1929 and 1937. Some collaborators remember that partaking of this project "was equivalent to being in the good graces of the regime. And many coveted that" *(equivaleva ad essere nelle buone grazie del regime. E molti vi appetivano).* However, many Jewish anti-fascists like Nello Rosselli (later killed with his famous brother) and Rodolfo Mondolfo (later exiled in Argentina) wrote for the encyclopedia, and this may have to been seen under Gentile's search for consensus and against fascist extremism. Momigliano, Gentile biographer G. Turi says, resembled many who thought they could take "material bread" from Gentile while receiving "spiritual bread" from Croce. And Momigliano, he adds, was one of many who repented later for going too far in their endorsement of the regime. ("Alcuni si illudono di prendere da Gentile solo il 'pane materiale' ricevendo quello spirituale da Croce, come Arnaldo Momigliano, pentito in seguito per aver avallato un'opera del regime col solo fatto di avervi collaborato.")[40]

These specific biographical facts as well as aggregate, demographic ones of which they are a part have been generally known. They are disturbing and difficult to process, emotionally and analytically. The adherence to fascism follows a wide spectrum from survival under a dictatorship to allegiance to it. Cruelly as well as ironically, allegiance and the need for survival increased between 1922 and 1938 as the regime became increasingly brutal. Leading milestones along this path include the murder of the socialist leader Giacomo Matteotti in 1924, the invasion of Ethiopia in 1935, and the introduction of racist and anti-Semitic legislation in 1938, along with the tightening of the alliance with Nazi Germany that the legislation signified. But that path was itself inconsistent. The Nazis' assassination of Austrian Prime

Minister Engelbert Dollfuss, who as the transformer of the first Austrian Republic into an Austro-Fascist state had been a protégé of Mussolini's, infuriated the latter and produced not only a temporary rapprochement with Italy's Jews but a meeting with Nahum Goldmann, head of the World Jewish Congress, and Mussolini's own declaration: "I am a Zionist."[41]

Beginning in the early 1960s, Renzo De Felice and others have shown that the regime remained popular throughout the population for most of its twenty-two-year life, and that it claimed statistically comparable levels of adherence among the tiny minority of Italian Jews, who numbered under 50,000 in 1938.[42] This fact became retroactively more sensitive with the Mussolini-Hitler alliance, the persecution of Italian Jews and the deportation and murder of many of them. German Jews were never able to become Nazis. There is no statistic to contemplate, and the counterhistorical, moral question as to whether German Jews would have become Nazis if they had been able to is a question that historians have not had to ask, although courageous thinkers have often mulled it over, if usually in private and informally. In Italy, Jews could become fascists and did. After 1938 and in historiography that succeeded Renzo De Felice, the question of anti-Semitism in Italy has continued to vex. Momigliano's 1980 review of Meir Michaelis's book, cited above, shows this. Momigliano remarks, with a critical edge, that the confines of Michaelis's study limit his treatment of anti-Semitism to foreign policy issues and to the terms of Mussolini's alliance with Hitler. Relations between Mussolini and the Italian Jews lasted unproblematically into the Ethiopian invasion and Declaration of Empire in 1935, when many Italian Jews supported Italy's actions with an eye on the liberation of Ethiopia's ancient Jewish community. They failed to realize that Mussolini was playing a racist card that would fan anti-Semitism.

Alexander Stille's 1991 book *Benevolence and Betrayal: Five Italian Jewish Families Under Fascism*, provided the kind of cultural analysis that Momigliano had found missing (though understandably so) in Michaelis's book. Stille's first portrait is of the Ovazza family of Turin. Ernesto Ovazza was a member of the P.N.F. and president of the Jewish Community of Turin in the 1920s. His son Ettore, an ardent fascist in 1922, founded a "militant new Jewish fascist movement" in 1934 (when anti-Semitism was beginning to appear both in the regime and in the population, in correspondence with Hitler's accession in 1933), and remained a fascist in and after 1938, when he helped to burn down the offices of a Zionist newspaper in Florence "in a last, desperate attempt to prove his loyalty to the fascist cause."[43] Ettore Ovazza publicly accepted the July 1938 racial laws as a "necessary sacrifice." The language here supplies an uncanny echo of Momigliano's 1932 characterization of Caligula's politics as "necessarily anti-Semitic." Likewise, the council of the Turin Jewish Community voted "to maintain its position of unqualified support for the government."[44] Between July and November of 1938, certain Jews, party members and military members especially, could be designated as *discriminati* (literally, discriminated), in other words exempt from the racial laws. The second set of racial laws, however, passed on November 17, 1938, expelled all Jews from the P.N.F. as well as from all state-controlled positions, including university professorships.

In 2001, the Italian journal *Quaderni di storia* published a letter that Momigliano wrote on November 3, 1938 to Giuseppe Bottai, Mussolini's minister of education, pleading exemption from the racial laws on the grounds of his own and his family's loyalty to the fascist party and cause. The letter generated sustained response and debate in the popular press, including a pair of prominent articles in the main Roman newspaper *La Repubblica*. In the letter, Momigliano introduced himself as a professor of Roman history at the University of Turin, and requested that his position with respect to "the problem of race" be considered in the context of four criteria, pertaining to supporting documents attached to the letter. First, Momigliano had himself volunteered for service in the militia (M.V.S.N.) during the Ethiopian campaign. Second, his father Riccardo, "a fascist from Year 1," had served the regime as party secretary and treasurer of the party branch (the *fascio*) in his Piedmontese home city of Caraglio and had confirmed his loyalty to the regime during the Matteotti affair of 1924. Third, his father had not presented himself for further military service as a result of an injury sustained while serving during the winter of 1915–16. Fourth, his mother had received a bronze medal from the minister of war and had served as political secretary of the women's branch of the Caraglio *fascio.*

The *Quaderni di storia* as well as a follow-up article in *La Repubblica* juxtaposed the letter against a letter written two years later from Oxford to British authorities, in which Momigliano affirmed his and his family's longtime antifascist credentials, placing himself in the antifascist, liberal company of Gaetano De Sanctis and Benedetto Croce, and citing his father's friendship with the prefascist liberal leader Giovanni Giolitti. The *Quaderni*'s editor, Luca Canfora, was thus moved to ask, "Which one is the authentic Momigliano?" His answer: the first one, the fascist Momigliano of 1938, a subject position succeeded and replaced by a strategic reinvention of the past from the subject position of the exile and potential enemy alien in Britain. Canfora's position, implicitly endorsed by the author of the first piece in *La Repubblica*, offers itself as especially damning insofar as its object is a historian. In a rejoinder, Alexander Stille wrote a long exposé of the ground he had covered in *Benevolence and Betrayal*, urging placement of Momigliano's vexed picture in the context of the political trajectories of the Italian Jews under fascism as portrayed in his book.[45]

Canfora's question strikes me as the wrong one. At the level of political affiliations and activities, the biographical record of Momigliano and those of family members may conceivably be adjudicable with documentary support, although contradictions and category confusions (formal affiliation on the fascist side and personal friendship on the liberal side, for example) may remain. The more important question is whether an "authentic" persona can be found behind these documents and texts, especially when the persona at stake is a scholar and historian whose public presence and legacy are themselves largely functions of texts. What this story corroborates and indeed insists on in the history of scholarship in general as well as for the history of Momigliano's scholarship in particular is the extraordinary complexity and volatility of categories which readers might want to understand as clear differences and choices, and which we in fact may have the intellectual as well as political responsibility to distinguish as clear choices in many contexts: liberal versus fascist.

Momigliano's writing in the 1930s shows a clear sense of the historical and political dichotomy of liberalism and fascism, of the Risorgimento and the dictatorship. Then and always, he placed the Italian Jews, including members of his own family, on the side and in the service of the Risorgimento and its legacy in Italian parliamentary democracy. These convictions stand in clear contradiction to his personal actions, specifically and especially to the letter of November 1938, which was written in despair and which may or may not be interpretable in that context alone. What is fascinating and possibly more disturbing is the ambiguity on these issues evident in his scholarship of this period. In Momigliano's early scholarship, the liberal and the fascist do blur at the level of the cosmopolitan.

⚬

In his 1952 inaugural lecture at University College London, "George Grote and the Study of Greek History," Momigliano honored and claimed the legacy of Grote not as much for history as for political philosophy and practice—notably the arguments of British liberalism in general and of philosophical radicalism, John Stuart Mill, and Sir George Lewis in particular. Grote was, as Momigliano certainly knew, a close friend and frequent visitor of both John Stuart and James Mill. The elder Mill had named a son (born in 1825, nineteen years after John Stuart) George Grote Mill. Completing his enclosure by the philosophical radicals, Grote lived in Jeremy Bentham's former country house, Barrow Green, where John Stuart Mill had spent part of his childhood.[46] Momigliano's own refashioning as a British liberal seems to have been part of his agenda. Empiricism and liberalism combine in their shared understanding of the dignity of the individual as subjective agent or as object of analysis:

> When all is said, it remains true that Grote possessed the all-redeeming virtue of the liberal mind. He was determined to understand and respect evidence from whatever part it came; he recognized freedom of speech, tolerance, and compromise as the conditions of civilization; he respected sentiment, but admired reason.[47]

In a review essay from 1999, "Arnaldo Momigliano: Pace e Libertà nel Mondo Antico," a review of a lecture series of the same title given in Cambridge in the winter of 1940 and published in 1996 under the editorship of Riccardo Di Donato, Emilio Gabba argued that these lectures confirm a consistency evident throughout the 1930s, including the review of Croce in 1931, the monograph on Philip II of Macedonia of 1934, and the entry on imperial Rome in the *Enciclopedia Italiana* of 1936.[48] Specifically it concerns an account of the Roman Empire that was increasingly at odds with the instrumental and ideological use of the Empire on the part of the Italian fascist regime. The peace of empire did not produce liberty; the weakness of empire came however to sanction functionally the valorization of inner, spiritual peace, a value championed by emergent Christianity. Thus, political liberty was internalized as moral liberty.[49]

Gabba's account of Momigliano's analysis of late Roman political and inner freedom offers a striking parallel to Carl Schorske's argument of liberal crisis in the late Habsburg Empire and the postliberal turn to interiority, as exemplified in Freud and psychoanalysis. In the introduction to his study *Fin-de-siècle Vienna: Politics and Culture,* Schorske recalled that his own sense of American liberal crisis in the 1950s had informed his understanding of late imperial Austria.[50] Schorske's work, like Momigliano's, continued to operate with liberal politics and liberal epistemology as its main frame of reference, but with perhaps a greater sense of melancholy. As I have suggested, however, it is not clear that the distinct liberal historiography and epistemology of Momigliano's British period were already in place in the Italian writings of the 1930s.

By "liberal epistemology" as an anchor of cultural history I have in mind values of transparency, rationality, and the occasional rhetoric of anti-theoreticism. In the American context, and especially in the context of my generation's reading of the generation of Momigliano and Schorske, the distinction between anti-theoreticism as a rhetoric—sincere but strategic—and anti-theoreticism as an ideology would seem crucial.

At the same time—and here I return to the shadows of empiricism— liberal epistemology deploys categories and metaphors of nontransparency. In Momigliano's language, we might trace the usage of such categories as "the person," "mentality," "intuition," and "mystery," the last of which I will return to in a moment. G. W. Bowersock investigated the first category in his 1991 essay "Momigliano's Quest for the Person," losing control, in my view, in his final sentences: "Momigliano's quest for the person, in the sense that Marcel Mauss had tried to define it, was in part, as Momigliano's writings had shown it had to be, a quest for one particular person. That was himself."[51]

Melancholy or not, liberal epistemology has lost ground in recent cultural history. Cultural history has paid increasing attention to what might be called the other side of Herodotus: the exotic rather than the antiquarian. Looking to psychoanalysis as well as to anthropology for interpretive paradigms, it has found the exotic in the familiar as much as in the distant, making the uncanny—the *unheimlich*, which is also the *heimlich*—into its most deployable trope. The power of the uncanny, especially the uncanny object, has generated various initiatives in microhistory, which comes quite close to antiquarianism in its choices of objects of analysis but then zooms out into macrohistory via the symbolic functions of its objects.[52]

"The most difficult thing" (I am quoting the 1972 essay "A Piedmontese View of the History of Ideas") "is to know what one still means by an idea; attitudes, propaganda, dreams, subconscious needs, symbolic figures are included."[53] There is less hostility to this inventory than there might initially seem. In any case, the 1974 essay "Historicism Revisited" states that "the right of psychoanalysis . . . to be treated as a tool for historical research has been asserted."[54] Propaganda, however, is not admissible. In this vein, the essay that is perhaps the most moving and the most revealing, "Reconsidering Croce" (1966) states: "He hated the idealization of war and imperialism. He knew the difference between the search for truth and propaganda and despised those who mistook the latter for the former. He never changed his attitude on this point—which explains his later hostility towards the Fascist regime."[55]

Two successive paragraphs in the Croce essay contain the following two assertions: "Beyond individual situations, Croce saw nothing but mystery," and "Grace, Providence, humility, are not words Croce uses rhetorically or analogically. They exactly define his attitude to life—which is one of acceptance of mystery and weakness."[56] I doubt that the contradiction between these two propositions cannot be reconciled. This is the duality of mystery as obfuscation and ideology, on the one hand, as the epistemologically and ethically necessary marker of the boundaries of knowledge, on the other.

2

Late in his career, Momigliano's interest in Jewish multiplicity and cosmopolitanism found expression in a series of essays on German Jewish thinkers. Figures to whom he had paid continual attention in the context of the history of classical scholarship (Jacob Bernays in an essay from 1969 and Eduard Fraenkel in another from 1971, for example) and, in the same context of classical scholarship, figures like Droysen (1970) who had sustained connections to German Jews, were now joined by Gershom Scholem (1980), Walter Benjamin (also 1980), and Leo Strauss as subjects of analysis.[57]

Momigliano had reviewed Scholem's magnum opus *Sabbatai Sevi: The Mystical Messiah* in 1975. Scholem's study of seventeenth-century pan-European false messianism, first published in Hebrew in 1957, amounts to a baroque, alchemical mixture of positivistic, document-driven circumstantial reconstruction and unwieldy historical allegory, the latter in the image of the allegorical theorizations of his friend Walter Benjamin. In his 1980 essay "Gershom Scholem's Autobiography," Momigliano attempted to separate Scholem's positivistic achievement, the work of a "great historian," from the Romantic and indeed nationalistic nineteenth-century historiographic and ideological models which also inspired him. To deploy another one of Momigliano's contexts and metaphors, the idea was to rescue the "primo Droysen" in Scholem's scholarship from the "secondo Droysen" that permeated the same body of work. Momigliano opposed nationalism to liberalism, and writes as a liberal in support of liberalism. At the same time, however, he draws a distinction between Jewish nationalism, and its preeminent articulation, Zionism, and European, especially German, nationalism. There is clear identification with Scholem in the lines "Scholem remains Scholem, not a nationalist, not even a religious Jew, but a man who is certain that the beginning of truth for a Jew is to admit his Jewishness, to learn Hebrew, and to draw the consequences—whatever they may be (which is the problem)."[58] As usual, Momigliano introduces sharp humor and becomes cryptic at the extremes of his articulated personal and political emotions.

For Momigliano to turn to Benjamin directly is more of a surprise. He alludes to Benjamin in the essay on Scholem. Whereas Scholem "fully en-

dorsed esotericism" as an object of Jewish historical record and therefore of
contemporary scholarship and analysis, Benjamin found his subject position there: "Reticence, allusiveness, and ambiguity were characteristic of
Walter Benjamin."[59] The essay on Benjamin is a review of two biographies
by Werner Fuld and Giulio Schiavoni, and it cites both scholars' view (now
commonly accepted, for reasons Momigliano points to) that Scholem not
be considered wholly reliable as a source of information about Benjamin.
Benjamin's problem, Momigliano glosses, was his lack of exposure to the
sources, from Hebrew to Catholic theology to Soviet Marxist theory:

> Benjamin himself described Kafka (and thus himself) to Scholem as the
> commentator of a truth lost and no longer recoverable (letter from Paris
> dated June 12, 1938): "he has renounced truth in order to stick to what
> is transmissible, the *haggadic* element." Benjamin embodies the sadness
> of the critic who no longer has faith in the intellectual tradition upon
> which he is commenting. A comparison comes quickly to mind between
> Benjamin and Attilio Momigliano, a much less original critic, but equal
> to Benjamin in his honesty and subtlety as one who experienced a simi-
> lar situation. Attilito lived and survived in the name of poetry, because
> he had not lost his faith in the Italian literary tradition to which he had
> devoted his life.[60]

The (Benjaminian) work of allegory hardly needs to be pushed another small
step for Attilio to become Arnaldo, for poetry to become history, for the Italian literary tradition to become the Italian liberal one.

"In his humorous but at the same time quite serious after-dinner speech
at Brandeis University," Karl Christ wrote in 1991, "Arnaldo Momigliano
looked back on his own intellectual development":

> In a sense, in my scholarly life I have done nothing else but to try to un-
> derstand what I owe both to the Jewish house in which I was brought up
> and to the Christian-Roman-Celtic village in which I was born.

"In a certain sense," Christ continues, "this sentence contains the key not
only to Momigliano's intellectual impetus, but also to the core of his scholarly work."[61] Only the "nothing else but" may strike a false note. The task
Momigliano identified for himself, the task of tracing the historical lines and
potentials for cosmopolitanism in a world that both politics and scholarship
have organized into artificial and often violent patterns of separation, is an
enormous one. The facts. The facts add up, bringing no clarity, and no con-

solation. Biographical facts remain troubling. Historical fact includes the existence of the treble tradition in its ancient and modern form, the existence of a multicultural world in which individuals belong to multiple cultures. On this count, historical fact expands into historical truth.

◦◦◦

In her essay "Truth and Politics," first published in the *New Yorker* in the aftermath of the controversy around her *Eichmann in Jerusalem* (1961), Hannah Arendt asserted that factual truth, unlike philosophical truth, "is always related to other people." The assertion sounds counterintuitive, as we might presume that the easiest kind of fact to adjudicate would most likely concern the natural, physical world. The passage reads:

> Factual truth, on the contrary, is always related to other people: it concerns events and circumstances in which many are involved; it is established by witnesses and depends upon testimony; it exists only to the extent that it is spoken about, even if it occurs in the domain of privacy. It is political by nature. Facts and opinions, though they must be kept apart, are not antagonistic to each other; they belong in the same realm. Facts inform opinions, and opinions, inspired by different interests and passions, can differ widely and still be legitimate as long as they respect factual truth. Freedom of opinion is a farce unless factual information is guaranteed and the facts themselves are not in dispute. In other words, factual truth informs political thought just as rational truth informs philosophical speculation.[62]

Momigliano often deployed the rhetoric of the historian as storyteller. But he did so at a distance, citing stories rather than telling them directly. I will conclude with three of them.

"The story is by now famous," Arnaldo Momigliano wrote as the opening words of a 1966 essay on Giambattista Vico.[63] "When at Harvard Gaetano Salvemini was told that a complete English translation of Vico's *Scienza Nuova* was about to appear, his enthusiasm was unbounded: 'L'Inglese è una lingua onesta. Di Vico non rimarrà nulla'" (English is an honest language. Of Vico, nothing will remain). Such was the protest by an Italian positivist against the use and abuse of Vico in the Italian idealistic tradition.

The essay leaves Salvemini behind and proceeds to analyze Vico as a Roman historian, plotting a complicated interpretive practice that advocates the reading of this hermetic and idiosyncratic thinker not only in the light of his posthumous readers but in the light of "those later philosophers and historians who never read him." As an Italian liberal and positivist at Harvard, Gaetano Salvemini served at once as *semblable* and foil to Momigliano. Positivism was for Momigliano a necessary but not a sufficient condition for historical scholarship. The rules and ethics of facts and evidence were never negotiable. But scholarship's human interest and interpretive animus aimed regularly, in Momigliano's work, beyond the questions that the facts could answer. For this reason he respected Vico more deeply than his compatriot Salvemini did—as the cited essay shows. But he was equally suspicious of him. The paradigm Vico enabled is that apparent resolution of the two faces of the present's regard for the past: myth and history. Vico enabled what several contemporary scholars have called "mythistory."[64]

The story exemplifies Momigliano's refined, never explicitly theorized hermeneutic. The person, the individual, to use the jargon of classical liberalism, contains its mysteries and often, perhaps always, leaves the positivistic historian in the dark. So with culture in general. Momigliano recognized, indeed cherished, that leap into speculation, insisting only and always that the historian "face the facts" and thus the boundary between what is knowable and what is "difficult to know."

Second, from an essay of 1986:

Gertrud Bing, the Director of the Warburg Institute, used to tell with great gusto a story that apparently has not found its way into the biography of Aby Warburg by Ernst Gombrich. Bing happened to be in Rome with Warburg, the founder and patron saint of the Warburg Institute, on that day, February 11, 1929, on which Mussolini and the Pope proclaimed the reconciliation between Italy and the Catholic Church and signed a concordat, the first bilateral agreement to be reached between post-Risorgimento Italy and the Church of Rome. There were in Rome tremendous popular demonstrations, whether orchestrated from above or from below. Mussolini became overnight the "man of providence," and in such an inconvenient position he remained for many years. Circulation in the streets of Rome was not very easy on that day, and it so happened that Warburg disappeared from the sight of his companions. They anxiously waited for him back in the Hotel Eden, but there was no sign of him for dinner. Bing and the others even telephoned the police. But Warburg reappeared in the hotel before midnight, and when he was reproached he soberly replied something like this in his picturesque German: "You know that throughout my life I have been interested in the revival of paganism and pagan festivals. Today I had the chance of my

life to be present at the repaganization of Rome, and you complain that
I remained to watch it."[65]

Through the anecdote itself and the tone in which he tells it, Momigliano
suggests how Aby Warburg, in many ways a tragic figure himself, chose to
represent the rise of fascism as a comedy.

On one occasion in Chicago, he entertained his students with a story
carrying the same function. Apparently Mussolini had a favorite archaeologist, a dubious scholar and a party hack, who once claimed to find stone
fragments carrying inscriptions that revealed previously unknown burial
sites of the Kings of Savoy on the Piedmontese mountain of Superga. The
inscription fragments as presented by this scholar had read:

NICOLA FU RE DI SUPERGA.

When rearranged by a non-fascist archaeologist, however, the fragments
read:

FUNICOLARE DI SUPERGA.

CHAPTER SEVEN

Leonard Bernstein in Vienna

Wien Stark Bewölkt: heavy clouds over Vienna. The title of Peter Weiser's memoir of musical life in postwar Vienna carries a rich symbolic resonance.[1] Obliquely but clearly enough, and in a fine deployment of a local, melancholy wit, its author, the sometime director [*Generalsekretär*] of the Wiener Konzerthaus, refers at once to the fog and the greyness, the burden and the ambiguity, through which postwar Austrian culture attempted to find its way back to legitimacy and decency. Austria after 1945 had a *Vergangenheit* but no clear way to *Vergangenheitsbewältigung.* As is well known, the Moscow Protocols of 1943 named Austria the first victim of Nazi aggression, thereby bracketing indigenous complicity in the *Anschluss* of 1938 and impeding the formation of a collective discourse through which the years 1938–45 could be adequately and responsibly understood. Anti-Semitism, the key element in local complicity with the National Socialist regime, had of course an Austrian history much older than the Third Reich. Karl Lueger, Vienna's fabled fin-de-siècle mayor and Christian Social leader, was the impresario of anti-Semitism as a political tool. After 1945, many Austrians tried to downplay Lueger's anti-Semitism. As a cultural prejudice and a political tool, Lueger's anti-Semitism wa constituted differently from the racist version of the Nazis. But it was neither benign nor irrelevant to the latter version. The fact that Lueger stands in effigy on the Ringstraße still today reminds us all that anti-Semitism remains unfinished business in postwar, post-Waldheim, post-Haider Austria. Perhaps uniquely, Austria's historical consciousness remains more postwar than post-Cold War.

For the city of Vienna, the violence of the years 1938–45 spelled the collapse of cosmopolitan culture. Vienna had never worn its cosmopolitanism lightly, but had certainly taken it seriously. The cosmopolitan and the international were categories of opprobrium in the Nazi ideological lexicon, associated with Jewishness *(Judentum)*, with the inauthentic, the external, indeed with the poisonous. Vienna the city of music *(Die Musikstadt Wien)* was now the city without Jews: *"die Stadt ohne Juden."*[2] After 1945, the rehabilitation of Viennese culture faced a complicated irony. On the one hand, the return to economic, political, and cultural health meant the recapturing of international prominence. But on what foundation: the global, the German, the Austrian? And where, in this program, to understand the position and reintegrative potential of the surviving and often prominent Jews who had formed a part of cultural life until 1938?

The high profile of musical life in Vienna highlighted the question of Jewish return. Predictably, the focus was on major personalities. The last pre-*Anschluss* artistic director of the Wiener Operntheater (named Staatsoper by the Nazi Regime) had been Bruno Walter, né Schlesinger, a Jewish convert to Catholicism and a close associate of Gustav Mahler. The two candidates for the directorship of the postwar Wiener Staatsoper were Karl Böhm and Clemens Krauss, both of whom had served the Nazi regime loyally. Bruno Walter, Marcel Prawy has observed, was noticeably absent from the discussion ("stand bezeichnenderweise nicht zur Diskussion, und wurde auch nicht gefragt"). Though Prawy cannot say whether Walter would have accepted such an offer, he asserts nevertheless that "Austria should have asked": "Österreich hätte es jedenfalls stellen müssen."[3]

Bruno Walter did not return to Vienna; neither did Josef Krips.[4] Outside the conducting field, the picture is more mixed. Arnold Schoenberg was invited to return to Vienna; his health failed before he could entertain the possibility. The musicologist and critic Max Graf returned in 1947 to help found the postwar Wiener Festwochen, the annual springtime Vienna cultural festival. Most visible and most popular of the returning emigres was probably Marcel Prawy himself (1911–2003), who returned to Vienna as an American soldier to embark, before long, on a long career as a dramaturg and central administrator at both the Staatsoper and the Volksoper.

With the key patronage and support of Ernst Marboe, the director of the federal theater administration *(Bundestheaterverwaltung)*, Prawy strove to localize for the Viennese audiences the kind of musical theater that had first come to Austria as an organ of occupation culture and American propaganda. This is American musical theater, on whose coattails Leonard Bernstein arrived in Vienna. In September 1952 the Volksoper had hosted the traveling production of Gershwin's *Porgy and Bess.* Prawy recalls, with crystalline

Schadenfreude, that Clemens Krauss stormed ostentatiously out of the theater in protest soon after the first performance began. For Krauss, apparently,
cultural guardianship meant the exorcism of the foreign, and *Porgy and Bess*
counted as multiply "foreign." As recent scholarship has made clear, the
ideological lexicon of anti-Semitism targeted the Jewish, the black, and the
American as interchangeable categories of otherness and danger. *Porgy and
Bess,* of course, fit all of these categories.

In 1956 Marboe encouraged Prawy, according to the latter's account, to
bring Bernstein's *Wonderful Town* to the Volksoper. This was Bernstein's
European debut as a composer. The predictable anecdotes accumulated. As
Prawy recalls, the announcement of Bernstein's engagement provoked on
administrator of the Volksoper to remark: "It must be some friend of Prawy's
from his emigration period, as the name itself suggests." An unmistakable
Viennese intonation drives the German utterance: "Wie der Name schon
sagt, anscheinend irgendein Freund von Prawy aus der Emigration."[5]

Bernstein thus came first to Vienna as a composer, and as an American
composer. Prawy cites Bernstein's evaluation of the American musical as
follows: "Das Musical ist keine moderne Form der Operette, sondern der
embryonische Vorläufer einer zukünftigen amerikanischen Oper, die noch
auf ihren Mozart wartet" (The musical is not a modern version of operetta,
but rather the embryonic predecessor of a future American opera, which still
awaits its Mozart).[6] As is well known, Bernstein's musical diversity shadowed his career both as a blessing and as a curse. It brought both popularity
and suspicion. Always aware of this predicament, Bernstein seemed particularly aware of its complicated relation to his reception in Vienna. "Ich mache
Musik—I make music," he told an interviewer of ORF Austrian television in
1966, seated in the studio outfitted in a new, made-to-order Loden/Trachten
jacket, chainsmoking through the interview: "Symphonien und Broadway."
Leonard Bernstein personified hybridity and indeed exulted in it: Clemens
Krauss's greatest phobia.

Leonard Bernstein's conducting debut in Vienna is the story that people
remember. Humphrey Burton, his most conscientious biographer, devotes
a chapter to the episode, which he aptly calls "The Conquest of Vienna."[7]
Bernstein arrived at the end of February 1966 to conduct Luchino Visconti's
production of Verdi's *Falstaff* at the Staatsoper, opening on March 14. He
had triumphed with the same work at the Metropolitan Opera in 1963, in a
production by Franco Zeffirelli, Visconti's protégé. In its Austrian context,
however, the work resonated, symbolically and politically, in new and contingent ways. Its most celebrated performances there had been conducted

by Arturo Toscanini in 1929, with the forces of Milan's La Scala on tour.
Toscanini conducted the work in Salzburg in the summers of 1935, 1936,
and 1937, in the celebrated affiliation with the Salzburg Festival made possible by his refusal to conduct in Nazi Bayreuth. *Falstaff* appeared on the
Salzburg schedule again in 1938, but was offered without Toscanini, who
had withdrawn from Salzburg in the aftermath of the *Anschluss*, as he had
done from Bayreuth five years before.

This was Bernstein's second visit to Vienna. A first one in 1948, to conduct the Vienna Symphony Orchestra, had left him with a disagreeable
memory of the city.[8] Humphrey Burton describes Bernstein's first encounter with the members of the Vienna Philharmonic in 1966:

> He tended to talk too long to orchestras when he was nervous. After ten
> minutes or more of instructions in his still rather halting German, the
> players became impatient. The *Vorstand*, the orchestra's elected chair-
> man, pointed discreetly to his watch. Bernstein took the hint and began
> the music for the first scene. It was a love affair from the first downbeat,
> he remembered later. "We were off and flying. By the third bar there was
> no catching us and we knew this was a lifetime relationship."[9]

On March 8, halfway into the rehearsal period, he wrote from the Hotel
Bristol to Helen Coates, his one-time piano teacher and longtime personal
secretary and confidant:

> Dear Helen,
> Here I am in the middle of my second week in Vienna, with highly mixed
> feelings. The work goes marvelously, in general, with ups and downs
> (mostly ups)—and the opera and orchestra people are paying court to an
> embarrassing degree. They want me to take over everything—operas,
> tours, concerts, Lord knows what. Ovations from the orchestra, etc. The
> cast is generally fine, Fischer-Dieskau extraordinary.
>   But so far it's been nothing but work, day and night. I've seen the Bris-
> tol and the Opera House—nothing of Vienna or the countryside. Which I
> hope to remedy as soon as this schedule lets up, if it ever does. . . . Much
> time goes to the press—interviews, TV, etc. I'm a very reluctant hero.
> And the elections here depressed me somewhat: Nazi-looking demon-
> strations in the square outside my window. There's still something about
> a shouting German crowd that makes my blood run cold. I don't know if
> I shall ever really *love* Vienna.[10]

Following the premiere on March 14, Bernstein sent a telegram to Coates containing the words "GLORIOUS SUCCESS PUBLIC PRESS EVERYTHING." Humphrey Burton reports an audience ovation of half an hour and forty-eight curtain calls. Music critic Karl Löbl, a Karajan devotee and as such not immediately sympathetic to Bernstein, proclaimed Bernstein "world class on the podium. A genius in the service of Verdi." Rudolf Klein's report from Vienna appeared in the *New York Times:*

> Since the departure of Herbert von Karajan from the Vienna State Opera, no conductor has been so extolled in this house as was Leonard Bernstein for the premiere of his production of the opera *Falstaff.* He certainly deserved the ovations: his work achieved the maximum both on stage and in the orchestra. Moreover, one never had the impression that here was a dictator issuing commands with an iron will. Quite the contrary, each musical phrase came forth as improvised, as if of itself, without any compulsion. . . . A union of praise followed—and in the very papers that have found nothing right with the State Opera since Mr. Karajan left. A comparable production of *Falstaff* has not been seen since the already legendary performances under Toscanini.[11]

Humphrey Burton again:

> Legends grew up around Bernstein immediately. One concerned the single rose mysteriously left on the conductor's desk each night before he entered for the performance. The donor, it was rumored, was Karajan's divorced second wife. Certainly Bernstein thought so.[12]

On March 19, Bernstein wrote to his parents, Sam and Jennie Bernstein:

> Dear Folks:
> At last I have a minute to write you. I am enjoying Vienna enormously— as much as a Jew can. There are so many sad memories here; one deals with so many ex-Nazis (maybe still Nazis); and you never know if the public that is screaming *Bravo* for you might be someone who 25 years ago might have shot me dead. But it's better to forgive, and if possible for- get. The city is so beautiful, and so full of tradition. Everyone here lives for music, especially opera, and I seem to be the new hero. What they call "the Bernstein wave" that has swept Vienna has produced some strange results, all of a sudden it's fashionable to be Jewish.

For his ORF television interview, mentioned above, Bernstein dressed in his "traditional Austrian loden coat [Burton's description], made to measure":

> "I wear it as a therapy against German Nationalism," he told an English journalist, "which I still remember and still dislike." But he had no compunction about making music in Vienna, whatever his doubts about his musical partners. Although [Staatsoperndirektor] Egon Hilbert could point to his resistance to the Nazis, the business manager of the Vienna Philharmonic—the trumpeter Helmut Wobisch—had been active in the Nazi party from 1933 onward. Bernstein brushed aside his past: he would refer to him openly as his "SS Man."[13]

The ORF interview (and the Loden coat) come up in another memoir of musical life in Vienna, that of the Vienna Philharmonic's longtime concertmaster Otto Strasser. Strasser had first met Bernstein in Salzburg in 1959, at a reception for the New York Philharmonic. Strasser writes that the reception took place "auf der Judenbergalm bei Salzburg—on the Jews' Mountain Meadow," not far from where he had himself grown up "in einer Straße namens Judenbergweg—on a street named Jews' Mountain Way"! Forty years later, one shudders at the remark's deployment (however unconscious) of anti-Semitic cliché, its implication that the very soil and streets of Salzburg combine in anthropomorphic suspicion to mark the Jew as a Jew. How unaware Strasser seems of his own entrapment in anti-Semitic ideology and cliché! But he is not without insight, nevertheless. Strasser quotes from a statement of Bernstein's about the character Falstaff:

> What really struck me was the sentence he wrote with regard to Falstaff: "He was basically motivated to win sympathy for himself, and understood superbly how to make the circumstances of a foreign country suitable to him." This is clear from his first television interview, for which he, the American, appeared in Austrian folkloric dress.

> Was mich wirklich dann fesselte war der Satz, den er anlässlich des Falstaff schrieb: "Er war jedenfalls bemüht, Sympathien für sich zu gewinnen, und verstand es ausgezeichnet, sich den Gegebenheiten eines ihm fremden Landes anzupassen." Das stelle ich schon be seinem ersten Fernsehinterview fest, zu dem er, der Amerikaner, in einem österreichischen Trachtenanzug erschien.[14]

Does Strasser really mean "the American"? Or does he mean "the Jew"? Or are these ever interchangeable, the first more respectable, more *salonfähig* than the second?

Bernstein's personal encounter with Austrian politics—in words and gesture, in what he said and what he chose to wear—reflects a personal style that consistently conflated the emotional, the sensual, and the sentimental. And this conflation sealed the so-called love affair with Vienna. It is a Viennese conflation as well. What can be called Viennese takes refuge in sentimentality, disavowing its own cosmopolitan and critical alter-ego. Here we can recall Hannah Arendt's allergy to this style of being, as expressed in her hostility to Stefan Zweig. The two parties understood each other. Moreover, in courting each other, Bernstein and Vienna were performing roles in an uncontrollable, overwhelming, and intricate historical drama.

Surpassing even Bruno Walter, Bernstein was identified internationally with the music of Gustav Mahler. He instilled the taste, indeed the love, for Mahler with his New York Philharmonic audiences, especially through the Mahler centennial season of 1960–61. In Vienna, he intervened decisively in the predicament that Gerhard Scheit and Wilhelm Svoboda have recently identified in the title of their book, *Das Feindbild Gustav Mahler: Zur antisemitischen Abwehr der Moderne in Österreich.* (The Hostile Portrayal of Gustav Mahler: The Anti-Semitic Rejection of the Modern in Austria).[15] Between 1945 and 1966, they report, the Vienna Philharmonic played Mahler 29 times; between 1967 and 1991, 126 times. Bernstein leads in this period with the number of performances at 51, followed by Bruno Walter with 34 and Claudio Abbado with 31. Bernstein is the only conductor to have led the orchestra through Mahler's entire orchestral oeuvre.[16] Vienna's "Mahler Renaissance"—a term used often in the local press—was thus due largely to Bernstein.

When the performances of *Falstaff* were done (and recorded), Bernstein and the Vienna Philharmonic performed a program of the Mozart B-flat Piano Concerto (with Bernstein conducting from the piano) and Mahler's *Das Lied von der Erde.* The latter was recorded, along with the *Falstaff.* "I've been up to my ears in *Das Lied von der Erde,*" Bernstein wrote to Helen Coates on April 1; "too little time to study and rehearse it. But how I love it: I think it will be beautiful. Dieskau sings it like a god." According to one biographer, Bernstein's work on Mahler in Vienna made him "more committed to Mahler and his music than even he had ever been before. More than that, [Bernstein] said, 'it made me feel more Viennese.'"[17]

In 1966 Peter Weiser was planning a Mahler Festival for the following year. He visited Bernstein at the Bristol Hotel and invited him to return to

Vienna to conduct the Second Symphony. Bernstein asked whether it was true that Weiser had first offered the full cycle to Karajan. Weiser admitted this to be the case, upon which Bernstein asked why Weiser had answered truthfully, not a Viennese habit. Weiser explained: "I'm not from Vienna. I'm from Mödling" (a close suburb).[18]

The "conquest of Vienna" in 1966 produced not only subsequent invitations but invitations celebrated as homecomings. This status found expression in the two works that Bernstein conducted at the Staatsoper: *Der Rosenkavalier* in 1968 and *Fidelio* in 1970. "Insider" works for an "insider" conductor. The concertizing relationship with the Vienna Philharmonic flourished as well, producing a legacy of recorded repertory well into the 1980s. At the Volksoper, meanwhile, *West Side Story* arrived in 1968. Marcel Prawy proposed that Bernstein conduct *West Side Story* himself in Vienna, an offer Bernstein reacted to with enthusiasm but also declined, in light of his obligations to the Staatsoper.[19]

The measure of Bernstein's Viennese embrace was stretched furthest, however, in 1981, when his *Mass* was staged at the Staatsoper. The event unfolds as a catalogue of unlikelihoods. Bernstein's *Mass* strives to overcome cultural and aesthetic boundaries and reconcile all their relevant differences. It is a mass written by a Jew, an homage to pop music and 1960s pop culture set in the idioms of symphonic and choral writing. The work pushes hybridity to new limits, possibly beyond its limits. Its contradictions resonate differently in Vienna than in the United States.

At home, *Mass* was written for the 1971 opening of the Kennedy Center for the Performing Arts in Washington, D.C., a center named for John F. Kennedy, the United States's only Catholic president. Bernstein's first memorial to Kennedy had carried a Jewish aura; the Kaddish Symphony (No. 3) of 1963 was dedicated to the just assassinated president. The Kennedy Center evolved under the eye and patronage of Jacqueline Kennedy Onassis, a personal friend of Bernstein's. In a different key, however, for Bernstein the foray into American Catholicism meant a flirtation with the radical social protest associated with the Berrigan brothers. His contact with them—including a brief consultation with Philip Berrigan at the Danbury Federal Correction Institute, where Berrigan was serving a sentence for allegedly plotting to kidnap Henry Kissinger—brought Bernstein under the ever zealous surveillance of the Federal Bureau of Investigation and its notorious director, J. Edgar Hoover. Hoover wrote: "Important government officials, perhaps even the President, are expected to attend [the Kennedy Center opening] and it is anticipated that they will applaud the composition without recognizing the true meaning of the words." "But," Humphrey Burton astutely adds to his account of the episode, "the prayer *Dona nobis pacem* was hardly open to misinterpretation at the height of the Vietnam War."[20]

Mass carries the subtitle *A Theatre Piece for Singers, Players, and Dancers*. It demands two hundred performers, including several choral ensembles, a children's chorus, a dance ensemble, two organs, and a rock band costumed onstage as street musicians. Its hybrid musical idiom notwithstanding, its principal controversy lodges at the intersections of religion, politics, and theatricality. *New York Times* music critic Harold Schonberg, never friendly to Bernstein, dismissed the work as "pretentious and thin . . . a pseudo-serious effort at re-thinking the Mass that basically is, I think, cheap and vulgar. . . . a show-biz Mass, the work of a composer who desperately wants to be with it."[21] So did Harold Schonberg play Nietzsche to Bernstein's Wagner, excoriating *Mass* as Nietzsche had excoriated Wagner's in many ways similar effort, his *Bühnenweihfestpiel* (play for the consecration of the stage), *Parsifal*. Nietzsche decried *Parsifal* as "Rome's faith without the text"; Bernstein's critics dubbed *Mass* Rome's text without the faith.[22]

So, in fact, did many of his friends. In June 1972 the impresario Sol Hurok produced *Mass* at the Metropolitan Opera House in New York. Hurok attended the daily rehearsals, and received from his co-producer Martin Feinstein the daily reports of weak ticket sales. He received one such update in the company of Marcel Prawy, to whom he reportedly turned and whispered: "Prawy, ich glaube, das Schreiben von Messen soll man den Goyim überlassen" (Prawy, I think we'd better leave the writing of Masses to the Goys).[23]

The Viennese life of Bernstein's *Mass* is largely ignored by his biographers.[24] Rudolf Gamsjäger, general manager of the Staatsoper, worked to arrange a Viennese production of *Mass* immediately on its 1971 Washington premiere; the initiative floundered, due in part to Gamsjäger's troubled relationship with Bernstein's most determined Viennese champion, Marcel Prawy. In 1973, Peter Weiser imported a student production from Yale University. Catholic authorities in Vienna did indeed object to the work, specifically to its depiction of a crisis of faith brought on by God's failure to provide peace. Peter Weiser in fact secured the personal support and intervention of Vienna's Franz Cardinal König, who went so far as to allow posters advertising the work to be displayed in the Stephanskirche. Never to be upstaged, Prawy observes, Bernstein arrived in Vienna for this initial foray there of *Mass* directly from Rome, armed with photographs of his audience with Pope Paul VI. *Tannhäuser* redux! In 1981, *Mass* did reach the Staatsoper, in Prawy's German translation. Prawy recalls the Viennese reception as mixed: "Es gab Jubel und Buhrufe; der Maestro quittierte den gewohnten Jubel und die ungewohnten Buhs mit dem gleichen Lächeln" (There were cheers and boos; the Maestro greeted the habitual cheers and the unusual boos with the same smile).[25]

A more thorough analysis than possible here would examine Prawy's text to determine how, if at all, the decidedly 1960s idiom of the American original was reproduced for the Viennese ear. The American text (the text that supplements that of the Latin Mass), by Bernstein and Stephen Schwartz, indulges in heavy idiomatic clichés that have not aged well. Within and around the work, Bernstein never hesitated to promote his sentimental ecumenicism. In a 1972 interview for *High Fidelity*, he spoke of the work as both Catholic and Jewish. It is Catholic in form, text, and theatricality; the traditional Mass, he suggests, "is also an extremely dramatic event in itself—it even suggests a theatre work." His own *Mass* may be construed as Jewish, he suggested, "based upon the intimacy with God which Jews have always felt, especially in the diaspora, in exile, in ghetto living." "Several people have told me that they thought *Mass* was a 'Jewish' work, and I know what they mean."[26]

Bernstein's sentimental ecumenicism dismantled different kinds of boundaries: on the one hand, those of cultural and aesthetic rigidity; one the other, those of historical as well as aesthetic integrity. His "conquest" of Vienna was grounded in an extraordinary quality of music and musicianship, as any random moment from the recording of *Falstaff* will prove. But the sentimentality, the *Schwärmerei*, is also an important element in the story, a story that is both Bernstein's and Vienna's. Bernstein's style played to a structure of desire on the part of Viennese musical culture, and of Viennese culture in general. Bernstein restored Mahler, but his Mahler was itself not immune to the sentimentalization through which, and for which, he spoke for a mythical Vienna whose patrons were the Strauss family more than Mahler himself or, indeed, than Arnold Schoenberg. In Vienna, in other words, Bernstein was a sentimentalist, not a modernist. When, in 1982, a second prominent American Jewish conductor and champion of Gustav Mahler arrived in Vienna—Lorin Maazel—the difference of personal style and symbolic resonance proved overwhelming. Maazel's rapport with the Viennese public proved troubled and short-lived.

Leonard Bernstein brought to Vienna—brought back to Vienna—both cultural riches and cultural fantasy. For his Viennese fans, Bernstein conjured the aura of a vanished past that had been marked by the delicate coexistence of cosmopolitanism and sensuality, passion and humor, synthesis and contradiction, Jewishness and *das echte Wien*. He restored not Jewish life but a certain aura of Jewishness that seemed to revive a less problematic era and a less problematic structure of collective memory. He did this with uncanny instincts for local style—musical style and cultural style. It is hard to say whether Bernstein's intervention and its local reception constituted serious engagements with Austrian history and reality or whether they constituted rather the mutually shared desire to escape from history and reality; whether, finally, Bernstein and Vienna together flattered their own shared cultural fantasies, their own melancholy narcissism.

CHAPTER EIGHT

Grounds Zero

History, Memory, and the New Sacredness
in Berlin and Beyond

I

In September 2001 the new Jewish Museum Berlin unveiled a permanent exhibit of "two thousand years of German Jewish history." The installation was pitched largely—and successfully—to laypersons and to the young, most of whom continue to arrive in large organized school groups. The historical exhibit's narrative of cultural difference, emancipation, and destruction filled and transformed the empty interiors of Daniel Libeskind's museum building, which for a period of almost three years had been visited as a shrine to human and cultural disappearance by close to 350,000 people. Many of these visitors expressed the hope that the structure would be kept empty, as the de facto Holocaust Memorial it was not intended to be.

Libeskind's museum building is deliberately inhospitable. It is a multiply jagged, metallic structure, whose shape and angles are often described as a Star of David that has been pried open. It does not compromise the moral and historical difficulty of the issues to which it speaks: namely, historical rupture, violence, trauma, and loss generated by the persecution and murder of German and other Jews between 1933 and 1945. The building's demands and inhospitality recall Walter Benjamin's understanding of the dynamics of translation, whereby a text in a new language is never intended for its reader but rather as an engagement with the unavailable ideal of "language itself."[1]

The filled museum quickly became, along with the Pergamon Museum of antiquities, one of Berlin's two most visited museums. The school groups arriving from all regions of the recently enlarged Federal Republic deliver legions of young people who statistically "have never met a Jew" and who know nothing about German Jewish history. The majestic historical narrative they consume is tailored to their ignorance and to their needs, as the observing historian—and this chapter—must keep in mind.

The Jewish Museum Berlin was not built for the historians but for the sake of historical knowledge as a dimension of public, civic responsibility. Though the latter is a value few professional historians would disavow, we serve it nonetheless through multiple filters, professional, linguistic, etc. On the popular level, the relation of historical knowledge to public responsibility differs markedly across cultural and national boundaries. Such responsibility lodges at the center of a postwar German public sphere that has taken up forcefully the enforced engagement with the Nazi past. In this concluding chapter I want to recognize the Jewish Museum Berlin's place at the center of practices of history and memory that are professional and public, nationally diverse but also internationally linked. I cannot make these categories discrete and for this reality principle I apologize to the reader. Moreover, for reasons that I hope will become clear as my analysis develops, I will not introduce or refer to the JMB according to the jargon of the *lieu de mémoire* or the "site of memory." Rather I will argue that the rhetorical and emotional desire to merge history and memory has repressed the substantial tensions that persist between these two tropes, often with highly problematic results. This problem informs the Jewish Museum Berlin as it does recent historical work, both written and built, both professional and public. Refusing the choices called for by much debate within the historical profession since 1990 or so, I do not think that historical thinking, professional or not, should or indeed can merge history and memory; nor can it "choose" a model of "history" as a fully rationalized, scientific discourse or a model of "memory" as an authentication of the past which in turn makes moral demands on the present. Rather, I will argue that historical understanding in its resistance to ideological appropriations requires an active dialectic between the distance and presence of the past to the historian, a dialectic that thus invalidates the opposition of history and memory.

The realized architecture of the Jewish Museum Berlin catapulted Libeskind into the position of perhaps the world's leading practitioner of a discourse whose theoretical ground he had occupied for some time: the architecture of memory. Specifically, the memory of violence, disappearance, and death. Before Berlin, his single built structure had been the Felix Nussbaum Museum in Osnabrück, dedicated to the work of this single artist, who was murdered in Auschwitz. In the spring of 2003, Libeskind was named "master architect" of the new World Trade Center site in New York. The architecture of memory is still young.

In Libeskind's discursive and constructed contexts, memory involves post-traumatic recovery, the sustained reference to historical trauma, the presence of absence. The last of these, the presence of absence, is to my mind the most problematic, both as an abstract principle and as a model for an actual, built material structure. Structure turns absence into presence, thus transforming the remembered, absent other into a representation by— and potentially a projection of—the remembering self. In an essay called "Trauma"—the title itself performing his aesthetic of minimalist theatrical-ity—Libeskind suggests that trauma is the cultural inheritance of "every-one" born after the Holocaust, generations who must perforce understand history in terms of a void and a gap: "a gap which in time becomes obliter-ated and which generates in itself an even greater emptiness in the posthis-torical world."[2] In architecture, Libeskind writes, "the void is a space." In other words, a reference to absence, loss, and the irrecuperability of the past becomes, perhaps in a necessary contradiction, an act of representation. In this context, during a debate in New York about the proposed designs for the World Trade Center, Leon Wieseltier questioned the very possibility of a monument to memory, suggesting that all monuments are ultimately about themselves. Attentive to this problem, recent interventions by Rosalind Krauss, Andreas Huyssen, James Young, and several conceptual artists have tried to advance the idea of the counter-monument, where the absent past would not be immediately contradicted by an act of representation. Young, for example, highlights the work of Horst Hoheisel, whose 1995 submission for the design of the "Memorial for the murdered Jews of Europe" (eventually designed by Peter Eisenman) was called "Blow Up the Brandenburg Gate," arguing for the creation of an empty space by doing just that.[3]

Libeskind's architecture of memory marks out hallowed interior as well as exterior spaces on formerly secular, civic ground. The Jewish Museum Berlin juxtaposes a jagged, scarred, and multidirectional structure (fig. 8.1) against the preexisting City Court House, a building in which E. T. A. Hoff-mann had once worked, whose form resonates with historical continuity but whose Berlin location, close to the site of the Berlin Wall, does not. In the Cold War period this structure housed the Berlin City Museum. The city's original post-1989 plan for its new Jewish Museum was to house it in the building combined with its other foci. The project's revisions both redefined the Jewish Museum as a separate institution and then moved the museum space into a new structure beyond the confines of the baroque courthouse. The earlier alternative would have involved the representation of Jewish history as a "wing" of the history of Berlin—possibly juxtaposed against the history of the military and the display of armor, and this had begun to appear absurd to the museum planners. The history of German Jewry as represented

FIG. 8.1. Jewish Museum, Berlin, exterior. All photographs in chapter 8 are by the author.

in the new German capital and in the city where their murder was organized required its own story and its own institution. Yet, museologically and historically, the decision has its complications, placing as it does the history of the Jews on a field separate from the history of other Germans. Here the museological quandary duplicates the historiographical one: giving the Jews "their" history adopts a functionally nationalist paradigm for the organization of historical patterns and groups which may do violence to the subject positions of precisely those whom the gesture seeks to redress.

Libeskind's winning design created a structure of literal as well as symbolic impenetrability. The old building, sadly, now serves mainly as an entrance, security, and service point (restaurant and gift/book shop). Exhibition spaces are largely confined to the new structure, which is accessed through its basement via a stark, black descending staircase. The message of descent into a heart of darkness can be lost on virtually no one. Moreover, the inaccessibility of the new structure's interior suggests the unavailability of a destroyed past. Access to that history requires first the negotiation of spaces commemorating genocide; access to a secular narrative of cultural life (which includes, to be sure, religious life) follows the negotiation of a sacred commemoration of an absolute fact of our time and consciousness:

namely, the Holocaust. Thus the visitor who has descended the staircase is faced with three "axes" that open from the new structure's lowest level: the axes of exile, Holocaust, and continuity. The axis of exile leads into a garden, consisting of a raked and hence vertiginous space punctuated by forty-nine imposing, angled columns (fig. 8.2). Forty-eight of the columns are filled with soil from Berlin; the forty-ninth is filled with soil from Israel. Yet it is the number 48, as Libeskind repeats in numerous contexts, which refers to the year of the foundation of the state of Israel. The axis of death leads to a cavernous darkened void ("void" being a trope of preference in Libeskind's work), into which small groups of people are ushered, to the other side of a large door which is shut behind them. The referent is the gas chamber. All this flirts, it seems to me, with kitsch: numerological kitsch, theatrical kitsch, historical kitsch.[4]

Least vulnerable to the experience and indeed accusation of kitsch is the so-called axis of continuity, an intimidating staircase that climbs two stories to the top of the building and to the beginning of the narrative of 2000 years of German Jewish history. The visitor climbs, literally, out of darkness, commemoration, and rupture into the lightened world of historical narrative. The climb might be understood as that out of darkness and into light, reason,

FIG. 8.2. Jewish Museum Berlin, Garden of Exile

and historical science. The German Jewish past is now rehistoricized, having been removed from history by the facts and representation of genocide. More problematically, the museum's stepwise presentation might be understood as the progress from (sacred) memory into (secular) history. Here, this move combines with the transfer of museological authority from Libeskind himself to the museum's curators. The curators must now take care (as I believe in fact that they do) not to imply the simultaneous shift from a Jewish epistemology of memory to a German epistemology of history.[5]

The exhibition spaces continue to refer to the building's general architecture of memory, but now a shrine about the Holocaust is asked to produce a historical narrative that knows nothing of the Holocaust, with the exception of the short and supremely inadequate coverage of the years after 1933. Having climbed three stories of stairs, the visitor is greeted on the top floor, at the entrance to the permanent exhibition, by a tree of life, to which guests (mainly children, one would presume) are invited to attach paper fruits holding their names or greetings. The historical narrative begins here, gaining quickly in density and in supporting visual as well as narrative materials as time passes and evidence thickens. Its two thousand years begin with the Roman colonization of the Rhine and a displayed copy of Emperor Constantine's decree from the year 321, allowing the appointment of Jews to the papal court. Medieval life is summarized via a holographic account of life in Mainz, Speyer, and Worms. The "thicker" representation of early modern life gains focus via three figures, as I will discuss in more detail below: Glikl bas Judah Leib (Glückel of Hameln), "Jud Süß," and Sabbatai Sevi. The road into the modern opens with the Enlightenment and its hero, the philosopher Moses Mendelssohn.[6]

That the museum visitors are asked to negotiate an elaborate labyrinth of death ultimately to earn, as it were, an entrance into a panorama of life strikes me as a sensitively conceived antidote to the claims of kitsch, some of the kitschy aspects of the enterprise notwithstanding. Even more objectionable, for example, than the so-called Holocaust Void, is Menashe Kadishman's installation in one of the other voids, "a mass of loose round metal slabs," in Amos Elon's summary, "with holes for eyes, mouths, and noses. We are supposed to step on these faces and, presumably, in the metallic clatter on the stone floor hear the victims' voices and remember them."[7] Thus, a built metaphor of historical closure, rupture, and impenetrability gives way, allows access, indeed, contradicts itself in the invitation to enter a historical world after all. In this way Libeskind's structure proves more successful, in my view, than Rachel Whiteread's more modest but similarly conceived Jewish Memorial in Vienna, which fills a portion of the city's medieval Judenplatz with a completely closed, impenetrable monolith of outturned bookshelves. These outturned books redouble the message of the past as unopenable, irretrievably lost. But the monument's rhetoric collapses in the unintended message that the books are themselves denying access; the "people of the book" appear themselves responsible for their loss to the world, in space and in time. More successful on this issue of the agency of violence is Micha Ullman's memorial to the Berlin bookburning of May 1933 on its site, the Bebelplatz in front of the law faculty of the Humboldt University. Ullman asks spectators to look down through a glass plate and gaze on a small cube of whitewashed, emptied bookshelves. The books have clearly not evacuated themselves. (See fig. 8.3.)

The filling of Libeskind's structure transformed sacred into secular space, absence into presence, the cult of memory into the work of history. The historical narrative that filled these spaces came together (or not) in complicated and vexed ways. The Berlin exhibition was assembled by a group of curators, informed by an academic advisory board, and supervised finally by a chief curator, Ken Gorbey, whose major achievement had been the redesign of the National Museum of New Zealand (Te Papa Tongarewa). There were debates and personnel changes, a process which in its personal and ideological vexations recalled the making of the Musée d'Orsay in Paris in the mid-1980s. In Paris, a team of historiographically oriented curators had been summarily replaced by art historians as a result of the "mid-term" elections of March 1986. The display of great art in its historical contexts (including politics, economy, and industry) seemed to the political right to conjure the same dreaded Marxism which indeed informed the historiographic formation of the many of the original curators. Berlin also spent the 1990s purging its historical museums of Marxism but not to the extent of purging history itself, for which Germany had other paradigms. Berlin's museums never attempted anything so radical as the convergence of art and history. The Jewish Museum Berlin never doubted its role as a disseminator of historical knowledge. In a museum a visual narrative must dominate, often reducing its displayed art to the status of a document or an example, and sometimes compromising its own explanatory task by fetishizing its objects of display: Moses Mendelssohn's spectacles, for example.

Berlin's initial result—and the word initial is important here as the curators have signaled, generously, that they intend to revise and refine—suffers from two predictable anxieties, about coherence and about audience. Correctly, the curators targeted an audience of open-minded and generally ignorant secondary schoolchildren. The narrative suffers from excessive coherence, providing a panorama of Jewish "identity" and success that turns into tragedy in 1933. Thus, in the anxious service of coherence and communicability, a history that might produce infinite variety is pulled together as a monument. Two fallacious totalities, "Jews" and "Germans," are posited and then displayed together and apart.

Here the plot thickens. The Berlin curators cannot be faulted for not consulting available, international scholarship. The problem lies here. The curators consulted perhaps too well. The general historiographic moment supports the curators' decisions. The curators and scholars who assembled this grand narrative of two millennia of Jewish history found themselves also in a historiographic context that is itself in sore need of reworking, at a moment of a certain scholarly plenitude and, unfortunately, plateau. Milestone works are still fresh. On one side, for example, *The Yale Companion to Jewish Writing and Thought in German Culture, 1096–1996* defines, expands, and refines the repertoire of German Jewish writing across time, space, and genre.[8] It provides no general interpretation and does not seek to do so. No totalization, linear or other, can be reasonably inferred from this collection; at the same time it makes no general claim to withstand or critique existing totalizations of the ground it covers. On the other and more crowded side, the four-volume synthetic history sponsored by the Leo Baeck Institute, *German Jewish History in Modern Times*, does offer a holistic narrative (close to that of the Jewish Museum Berlin), as implied by the volume titles: "Tradition and Enlightenment 1600–1780"; "Emancipation and Acculturation 1780–1871"; "Integration in Dispute 1871–1918"; "Renewal and Destruction 1918–1945."[9] German Jewish internal coherence, structural separation from non-Jewish society, and indeed an apocalyptic teleology are implied. The same arguments inform Paul Mendes-Flohr's very erudite and elegant book *German Jews: A Dual Identity*, in which the category of "bifurcation" (*Zweistromland*, in Franz Rosenzweig's metaphor), dominates, as well as older paradigms such as assimilation, acculturation, and subculture.[10]

On a more popular level, the Viennese-born Israeli writer Amos Elon has recently published an honorable and readable book called *The Pity of It All: A History of Jews in Germany 1743–1933*.[11] Elon's title implies a "lachrymose" teleology in the mode of Heinrich Graetz, the late-nineteenth-century historian of German Jewry. Any such linear narrative, encompassing the period of emancipation and ending in 1933, would imply such a trajectory. The year 1743 makes that result more certain, as does the opening gambit of Elon's introduction:

> In the fall of 1743, a fourteen-year-old boy entered Berlin at the Rosenthaler Tor, the only gate in the city wall through which Jews (and cattle)

were allowed to pass. The boy had arrived from his home town of Des-
sau, some one hundred miles away. . . . For five or six days he had walked
through the hilly countryside to reach the Prussian capital. We do not
know whether he was wearing shoes; it is more likely that he was bare-
foot. The boy, later famous throughout Europe as the philosopher Moses
Mendelssohn, was frail and sickly, small for his age.

The metaphors pile up. They are reinvoked in the book's last lines, which
flags Hannah Arendt's train speeding out of Berlin "in the opposite direction taken two centuries earlier by the boy Moses Mendelssohn, on foot,
on his way to fame and fortune in Enlightenment Berlin."[12] Interestingly
enough, the Jewish Museum Berlin finds in Arendt a similar antipode to
Mendelssohn's articulation of the Enlightenment. In one of the most successful and arresting details, a jagged corner in a passageway is filled by a
television monitor showing a four-minute interview clip in which Arendt,
in the well-known German television interview with Günter Gaus in 1964
(cited in chapter 1), reflects on the moment of finding out about Auschwitz.
In my observations, most viewers find themselves taking in her account
two or three times.

Elon's own lacrymose synthesis was in evidence as well in his generally
perspicacious review of the Jewish Museum Berlin's newly unveiled permanent exhibition for the *New York Review of Books*. "The continuing tragedy
and not infrequent despair of socially integrated, assimilated, and enlightened German Jews is overlooked" in the permanent exhibition, he wrote.
This judgment is consistent with his larger point, which I would strongly
endorse: "a curious scarcity of historical tension is characteristic throughout—tensions between German Jews and Gentiles and tensions within German Jewish communities." And, most forcefully: "During the Weimar years,
there was no such thing as 'Jewish life.' There were, as Gordon Craig once
put it, 'half a million individual Jews who were busily building their own
lives' and like most other Germans pursuing points of view along many different and independent lines." In this vein, Elon correctly asserts, internal
Jewish arguments go unaddressed, "including bitter debates over Zionism
and the tensions between native German Jews and *Ostjuden*." Here Elon
takes issue, tacitly, with Michael Brenner's book *The Renaissance of Jewish
Culture in Weimar Germany*, which masterfully demonstrates the rebirth
of German Jewish interest in the cultures of East European Jewry but also
makes good on its own Buberian title by suggesting at once a historical and
normative move from the panoply of variety and difference toward a general
rediscovery of cultural authenticity.[13] According to this paradigm, secular-

ity cannot be adequately distinguished from assimilation, i.e. from cultural loss, and the desire for originality combines too readily with the desire for origins.

Amos Elon, in the introduction to his book, aptly invokes the 1933 publication of the Centralverein deutscher Staatsbürger jüdischen Glaubens (the Union of German Citizens of the Jewish Faith): a 1,600 page compendium called *Jews in the Realm of German Culture*.[14] The founding goal of the Centralverein, as its name makes clear, was to define German Jewry as nationally fully German. The contemporary question is to what extent the JMB repeats this agenda. The problem here would be the convergence of identity and nationality rather than the convergence of *Deutschtum* and *Judentum*. Predictably and understandably, the museum gives most space and attention to the years of Jewish integration, from the Enlightenment through Weimar. As mentioned above, the quick survey of earlier periods is punctuated by the presence of a fourth-century decree of the emperor Constantine and the holographic reconstruction of medieval Jewish communities. Medieval pogroms and expulsions are given short shrift, as is the Reformation period and Luther's treatment of the Jews. The ambiguities of the early modern period are summed up by three paradigmatic profiles—of Glückel of Hameln, of the Jud Süß in his various literary and cinematic incarnations, and, most bizarrely, of Sabbatai Sevi, the false Messiah of the mid-seventeenth century. The Enlightenment is personified, predictably, by Moses Mendelssohn, who receives not only a shrine but a relic, as already noted, in the form of his spectacles.

The historical case of Jud Süß involves Joseph Süss Oppenheimer, a court Jew *(Hofjude)* to the early eighteenth-century Duke Charles Alexander of Württemberg. As Mordechai Breuer recounts, Süss Oppenheimer bolstered the duke's private financial interests and monopolies, alienating both fellow Jews and the local Protestant majority, the latter particularly so in the aftermath of Charles Alexander's conversion to Catholicism. When Charles Alexander died suddenly in 1737, Süss Oppenheimer was arrested and executed.[15] The story remained obscure until the publication of Lion Feuchtwanger's novel in 1925, whose allegorical reference to the murder of Foreign Minister Walter Rathenau in 1922 was clear to most of its readers. As Michael Brenner recounts, Feuchtwanger "initially intended to write a novel about Rathenau . . . but he ultimately pondered 'the same problematics, only two centuries earlier.'"[16] Now, if Breuer's account of Süss Oppenheimer's participation in ducal corruption and controversy does not impugn the anti-Jewish dimension of his demise, it does complicate the story considerably. It thus compromises the allegorical control of Feuchtwanger and his reader, as Rathenau's case—his own controversial personality notwithstanding—cannot be closely compared to Süss Oppenheimer's. The JMB, in choosing to highlight the case of "Jud Süß" does take on the curatorial responsibility of maneuvering through the perils of the case's reception, by Jews, such as Feuchtwanger, as well as by anti-Semites, such as the makers of the celebrated Nazi period film. What should "Jud Süß" in fact be called upon to represent?[17]

The representational problem is more severe still with the case of Sabbatai Sevi, the false Messiah of the 1660s. Gershom Scholem's magisterial account of 1957 placed Sabbatai and Sabbateanism at the center of a Jewish history whose contours Scholem had already redrawn: namely a history of mystical passion that competed with the earlier historical paradigms based on law, text, and tradition. For Scholem, Sabbateanism formed the popular result of Kabbalism, the textual tradition suppressed by rationalist historiography. Yet to target Sabbatai Sevi as representative of the new Jewish historiography is quite different from placing him at the center of Jewish history. Here again, the curatorial logic is opaque, and not readily clarified by an allusion to the demands of popular museology.

Amos Elon's book has a companion in W. Michael Blumenthal's *The Invisible Wall: Germans and Jews, A Personal Exploration*.[18] This book accrued a functionally official status on its publication one year after its author had been named director of the Jewish Museum Berlin in 1997. Born in Berlin (in Oranienburg, to be precise) in 1926, Blumenthal and his family emigrated eastward to Shanghai and finally to San Francisco, where he began a meteoric career in international economics that included service as Jimmy Carter's secretary of the treasury. *The Invisible Wall* connects a general history to portraits of Blumenthal's ancestors, from his immediate family to key figures such as Heinrich Heine and Giacomo Meyerbeer, who appear on branches of the Blumenthal family tree. The book sold well in the United States but even better in the German translation that appeared in 1999. Its general argument resembles Elon's as it does the general presentation of the museum that Blumenthal did much to enable between 1997 and 2001.

Elon, Blumenthal, and the JMB offer parallel summational, synthetic narratives that one might describe (perhaps a bit tendentiously) as consistent with the cosmology of the Leo Baeck Institute. This venerable institution was founded in 1955 with branches in Jerusalem, London, and New York (and since 1989 has a "working committee" in Berlin) with the purpose of preserving and transmitting modern German Jewish culture. This narrative of modernity tends toward totalization, offering a linear story of a Jewish community through triumph and tragedy. Triumph involves the uses of a hard-earned emancipation, the creation of a culture of overrepresented achievement whose favored trope involves comparison with the Italian Renaissance. Tragedy involves the persistence of anti-Jewish prejudice and politics, its evolution into an allegedly scientific discourse of anti-Semitism in the 1870s and its successful instrumentalization into an extreme nationalist and exclusionist politics, culminating in the Nazi-led crimes of 1933–45. The historical and factual structure of this argument is not in question. The problem lies in the tendency of the general picture to remain loyal to a Wilhelmine-period assumption of the essential integrity of the German nation and hence of the "problem" of Jewish participation in it. The problem is nationalism: German nationalism, significantly more so than Jewish.

In this context, the distinction too regularly elided is that between German culture and German national culture. That elision constitutes precisely the ideological work of 1870–71, in other words the absorption of Germany into the unified state and then, swiftly, into empire. For German Jews, the elision is a double one. First, it collapses the distinction between Jewish subject positions and Jewish object positions. Thus the assertion that the Jews were, subjectively, Germans just like other Germans merits full agreement, in my view, as a gloss on modern subject positions from the Enlightenment onward, surviving the Nazi takeover and inspiring a rich and well-known émigré culture throughout the world. A German Jewish subject position (or subjectivity) that cannot choose or give priority to one of these positions is an experience to be respected by historians and quite independent from the parallel reality of anti-Semitism, which by definition involves the objectification, classification, and exclusion of Jewish from German subjectivity and status. The obvious historical reality that must be mentioned here is that of the 200,000 German Jews murdered by the Nazis. The second dimension involves Jewish participation in the ideological moment of 1871, an ideological investment that continues to inform what I am calling here, somewhat provocatively I realize, the "Leo Baeck cosmology." Thus, the Germanness of the Jews is rendered indistinguishable from the German nationalism of the Jews, and hence an investment which was always problematic from an ideological point of view. The historiography that does not differentiate historically or critically between Germanness and German nationalism takes on a normative investment that finds both Jewish legitimacy and Jewish pleasure in the importance, self-importance, and legitimacy of the German national project.

To be sure, the politics of Zionism have made it difficult for Jewish thinkers to take critical distance from nationalist projects in general; German Jewish historiography after 1945 may fall, paradoxically, within this general parameter as it continues to take pleasure in the memory of German national inclusion. Between 1890 and 1930, the Centralverein and the Zionists preferred opposing national arguments but remained twins in their mutual embrace of nationalist models of culture.

In an important review article, David Sorkin has described the governing paradigm of the Leo Baeck Institute's four-volume *German Jewish History in Modern Times* as "the émigré synthesis."[19] This paradigm, Sorkin argues, transformed cultural experience and memory into historical scholarship by adjusting allegedly existential categories into analytical ones—"disinterested" categories, in Sorkin's usage. Thus, "assimilation" became "acculturation" and "contribution" became "participation." I have two objections to Sorkin's rubric. First, his generational paradigm casts too big a net; it falsely identifies, in my view, an émigré generation and an émigré culture with the much more particular paradigm, i.e. what I am calling the world according to the Leo Baeck Institute. Second, the boundaries of that discourse notwithstanding, Sorkin exaggerates the paradigmatic shifts he correctly identifies. German Jewish historiography did indeed adjust its vocabulary from assimilation to acculturation and from contribution to participation. But the distance traveled by these moves was not great. It remained circumscribed by the assumption and ideology of the German nation of 1870, within whose pull "contribution to" and "participation in" are not really so different. Thus the history of German Jewish historiography in the two or so émigré generations would appear to me more continuous but less universalizable.

The shape of Libeskind's building may have coerced the curators into articulating moments of historical transition where the building required them to do so. At times the shared ruptures, jags, and discontinuities of the narrative combine powerfully with the building's jagged topography. Hannah Arendt's assertion, displayed on videotape, that the death camps could and cannot be rationalized emanates—as I have already mentioned, hopeful now that my own repetition will express how affected I was by this installation—from a tight, sharp corner of the building itself. Other coincidences of the narrative and its spaces are less felicitous. Thus the gains of the Enlightenment are followed, as the building turns, by a static panorama of Jewish family life, with objects inconsistently collected implying an ahistorical inner private sanctum. Here the museology pays homage (perhaps unintentionally) to a tired binary in German Jewish historiography: that of identity, authenticity, and historicity on the one side, "assimilation," integration, and cultural loss on the other.

The museological and the historiographical thus combine in their obedience to a linear panorama, to a parabolic narrative of rise and fall, to a depiction of internal choice in terms of identity preservation or identity loss. A corrective to this historiographic and indeed museological predicament would involve first of all the willingness to question synthesis, to offer viewers and readers the chance to participate in the search for history as fellow analysts rather than as consumers. Specifically, such an initiative would involve an analytical elaboration of the position that George Mosse began to sketch in his *German Jews Beyond Judaism* and in his exchanges with Gershom Scholem.[20] Scholem famously argued that the "German-Jewish dialogue" had been a delusion; Mosse wittily replied that Scholem was the best example of what he claimed never existed. German Jewish culture, subjectivity, and history involve neither a dialogue nor a symbiosis, as both of these assume a polarity of essentially different positions whose interchange may be more or less successful. For his own storytelling purposes, Amos Elon endorses Sartre's definition of Jews as "those considered by others as Jews."[21] Although the political realities of anti-Semitism made this the legitimate criterion for the identification and indeed self-identification of Jews, it is not historically satisfying as an indicator of experience or subjectivity. Anti-semitism, National Socialism, and Zionism endorsed this same polarity by insisting, with radically divergent purposes and results, that Germanness and Jewishness (*Deutschtum* and *Judentum*) were both national identities and as such not combinable. German Jewish experience includes an awareness and indeed an experience of these pressures but for better or ill cannot assume to have been fully absorbed by any of them. To be sure, individual historians, who carry less of a burden of collective and official representation, need to advance such an agenda before institutions such as the Jewish Museum Berlin can be expected to do the same.

Rethinking German Jewish modernity—the Enlightenment through Weimar and into the émigré period—is thus an agenda repeatedly required and unsatisfied by both historians and curators. It continues to require two basic shifts with regard to existing scholarship: the disavowal of linearity, and the insistence on internal Jewish debate and multiplicity. Both moves refuse an internal coherence which would in turn make separation from "mainstream" society possible, whether from "within" or from "without." The epistemological and indeed ethical necessity to reinterpret European Jewish history in the light of the Holocaust should not be conflated with the retroactive understanding of this history as a prologue to it. Rather than search for identities, or the correct way to talk about identities, cultural history and cultural analysis should, in my view, move beyond identity and toward the understanding of multiplicity. A focus on internal multiplicity and debate seeks to rethink methods of cultural history in general, German Jewish cultural history in particular, in way that directly addressed the role of historical knowledge in the present.

The life and later symbolic role of Moses Mendelssohn provides a strong foundation for such a correction. In the museum and in the historians' world at large, Mendelssohn requires defetishization. He must first be liberated from a tired symbolism facilitated by his own body and countenance: the bespectacled hunchback who thereby already heralds his own destruction, a trope that instills a bizarre pleasure in representations ranging from those of Mendelssohn to those of Walter Benjamin. In fact, with an urgency that parallels Benjamin's but with much more clarity, Mendelssohn composed a body of thought that in the rhetoric of Straussian political philosophy would be called intransigent. Mendelssohn refused synthesis. He refused the synthesis of tradition and modernity, of religion and politics, of sacred and secular. The work most central to these positions, to their intricacy but clarity, remains *Jerusalem*, a close reading of which might productively redirect German Jewish historiography and museology. The refusal of synthesis that Mendelssohn bequeathed to his readers and of course to his children proved too difficult for most of them.

Rather than working with an opposition of "identity or assimilation" or with a sequence of "emancipation and acculturation," Mendelssohn proposed, I would argue, a radical move that involved the emancipation of *religion* (rather than of the Jews or of Jewish religion alone). Mendelssohn's position signifies an engagement with secularization that engages parallel discussions among non-Jewish thinkers and at the same time demands internal, Jewish cultural change. Here one need engage and develop an ongoing debate, associated most recently with David Sorkin and Allan Arkush, about Moses Mendelssohn's Judaism and its relation to secular modernity.[22] For Sorkin, Mendelssohn achieves an inner synthesis of the German and the Jewish, performed linguistically by his mastery of German and Hebrew as languages of argument and interpretation, and even more by his careful choice of preferred language with regard to subject matter and targeted readership. Sorkin incisively asserts that the "myth of the German Mendelssohn" was sustained by readers who read only his German writings. But Sorkin asserts as well that a reconsideration of the Hebrew writings will support a general interpretation of Mendelssohn as a traditionally pious Jew, whose Judaism is unhistorical and certainly historically uncontingent. Arkush, on the other hand, questions Mendelssohn's religious belief, arguing that the inconsistent and unsatisfying endorsement of Sinaitic law as divinely revealed is insincere, born of the fear of antagonizing his fellow Jews. This is a Straussian argument, and I confess to liking it quite a lot. There is much tacit Spinozism in Mendelssohn's writing, in *Jerusalem* especially, and though Mendelssohn was not afraid of excommunication and could therefore write with open contempt about the legitimacy of any form of it, he was, it seems to me, concerned about espousing a position that would undermine his mediating role between Jews and Christians. Without question, Mendelssohn supplies, in *Jerusalem,* a critique of religion, not unlike "Spinoza's Critique of Religion"—the title of Leo Strauss's Weimar-period dissertation (1925–28). Controversially, Mendelssohn's critique of religion seeks, in my view, to negotiate both internal and external forms of patriarchy (the transmission of culture and cultural authority from the father or father figure). Like Socrates, the figure to whom he was glibly compared, Mendelssohn intentionally offers a consciously problematic patriarchal presence, a legacy intended to disconcert the framers of German Jewish modernity. We might call German Jewish modernism that tendency to endorse the Mendelssohnian destablization of claims of harmony between tradition and modernity, among which we might include the *Wissenschaft des Judentums,* as well as the modernisms of—here I am deliberately citing someone else's list, in this case Elon's—Heine, Börne, Kafka, Werfel, Zweig, Wolfskehl, Broch, Kraus, Willstätter, Haber, Ehrlich, Einstein, Freud, Felix Mendelssohn, Mahler, Schoenberg.

The discursive context of the JMB exceeds the debates within German and German Jewish historiography. The building and its contents both engage and symptomatize the boundaries between secular and sacred speech that informs, in my view, recent concerns in historiography as well as in much recent critical writing. Among historians the relation of history to memory has juxtaposed not only debates about the relations between professional and public historical interest and practice but about secular and sacred investments in the past. In the context of recent trends in critical theory, the wake of deconstruction and the subsequent dissatisfaction with its successor paradigms, including cultural studies and identity politics, have generated a certain academic melancholy that also seems to be flirting with the sacred, flirting, indeed, with a posture that wants to call itself theological. This sacralization of historical practice has itself a recent history. One place to find it is in the widespread revalorization of the trope of memory (an endeavor of mixed benefit), I would argue, and most specifically (and more unfortunately) in the accompanying, relative devalorization of history itself.

2

The relation of history to memory became an issue of increasing debate through the 1990s. Its venues included the historical profession, the world of "trade" books and journals, and the sites of public history, including museums. In the first phase of the encounter, the authenticity of memory proved an appealing and productive check on the potentially dehumanizing reaches of history. History classifies and objectifies. The induction of a criterion of memory into the practice of history served, in Walter Benjamin's much cited formulation, to give voice to the unvoiced and to displace historiographic and political emphasis from the exclusivity of the narratives of victors. The debate's second phase, however, questioned the so-called "memory industry" as a symptom of intellectual and political malaise.

If "history," left alone, objectifies, then "memory" unbound shows the converse flaw of losing analytical distance. Memory has taken on the claim of self-authentication, in contradiction not only to the conventional historical principle of analytical objectivity but also in contradiction to the principle of the psychoanalytic construction of a self-questioning subject for whom the past is always, to a degree, a stranger. Moreover, memory as a mode of either individual or collective self-authentication slips easily into ideologies of melancholy, commemoration, and even trauma itself (if we can define trauma in terms of a radical evacuation of the ego)—the very condition it wants most to redeem. Thus the self-authenticating claims of memory paradoxically enable the compromise of the very critical subjectivity in whose name they operate. Memory slips inevitably into ideology unless it disciplines itself with those same principles of historical reasoning that form the foundation of psychoanalytic models, namely, the recognition and analysis of the multiplicity, alterity, and historicity of the subject recollected and the subject recollecting.

The authority of memory rests in its replacement of the claim "I know" with the claim "I remember." This is the replacement of a subject-object relationship, or a subject-other subject relationship, with a relationship of the subject to itself. In short, it is the replacement of historical veracity with historical authenticity. Thus, the postmodern (or indeed post-postmodern) longing for the return of the subject reacts by inserting a mirror image of itself into the past and then tracing, from that mirage, a line of subjective continuity.

History as a critique of memory is similar to memory's critique of itself. In criticizing itself, memory separates the remembering agent from the remembered experience. Memory thus invokes, potentially, the rules of history. This is an interpretive, hermeneutic relationship; a past experience is not an object; therefore the code of objectivity is not really helpful here. In this way, a self-critical memoir may prove able to qualify as the best kind of historical analysis.

Memory's contingency on history is a cornerstone of psychoanalysis as an interpretive enterprise. For Freud, memory is raw and unmanageable and cannot therefore be theorized on its own terms. Freud characterizes memory as an archive of the unconscious with infinite capacity. The memory-trace (*Erinnerungsspur*) that resides in the unconscious has "nothing to do," Freud asserts, "with the fact of becoming conscious."[23] Memory, like dream, is disruptive in its agitation of consciousness, but a memory is immediately and always subject to revision. That revision may arise through the two very differing processes of revision and interpretation. Revision is an unconscious process that obeys the censoring apparatus of the mind, the work of distortion in dreams and repression in general. Interpretation involves the unearthing of previously hidden material, following both the practices and the metaphors of archaeology and history. A memoir title such as Saul Friedländer's *When Memory Comes* pays attention to this multiplicity; memory is recognized as a disruption of history and an incitement to historical work. If the phrase is to be taken seriously, memory "comes" from a different recess of the subject from the one that takes up its narrative or analysis.[24] Memory is staged as raw evidence, to be examined according to rules of historical reasoning.

In Freud's 1910 discussion of *Leonardo da Vinci and a Memory of His Childhood*, memory is connected to dream, fantasy, and history. Memories of childhood, Freud argues, "are not fixed at the moment of being experienced and afterwards repeated, but are only elicited at a later age when childhood is already past."[25] In this instance, philogeny recapitulates ontogeny, as this pattern of memory is compared to "the way in which the writing of history originated among the peoples of antiquity. . . . A man's conscious memory of the events of his maturity is in every way comparable to the first kind of historical writing [which was a chronicle of current events]; while the memories that he has of his childhood correspond, as far as their origins and reliability are concerned, to the history of a nation's earliest days, which was compiled later and for tendentious reasons."[26]

If the tendency to sublate history into memory involves the longing for the return of a continuous subjectivity, then the rise of memory is to be understood at least partially as a symptom of contemporary desire. Memory, in this vein, has become the master trope of truthfulness in the aftermath of trauma, with the recovery of memory posited as the foundation for the working through of trauma and its aftereffects. At the level of personal trauma and also that of collective, historical trauma, specific and urgent reference is made to the Holocaust as modernity's defining trauma.[27] In the process of working through, the recovery of truth and the truthfulness of recovery are not only simultaneous but also held to be identical. In the discourse of Holocaust testimony, memory comes to signify an authenticated history.

In polemical articles of 1993 and 2000, respectively, Charles Maier and Kerwin Klein both refer to the "memory industry."[28] For Maier, memory is a symptom of contemporary discursive melancholy, the attendant breakdown of a viable transformative politics, the "loss of a future orientation," and the rise of identity politics and the politics of recognition.[29] Klein is interested in criticizing the "analogical leap from individual memories to Memory—social, cultural, collective, public, or whatever."[30] Maier and Klein's essays share a certain impatience. Neither distinguishes between memory and commemoration; neither proposes a way out what each identifies as postmodern ennui, thereby sharing symptomatically in the very symptomatology that each wants to expose.[31]

The conflation of memory and commemoration involves the ideological union of opposing tendencies: experienced memory and ritualized memory. Commemoration involves the structuring for collective use of the subtle formation that Maurice Halbwachs referred to as collective memory. Halbwachs, I would argue, was a more scrupulous thinker than many who invoke his categories would suggest. His concept of collective memory, which he laid out in *Les cadres sociaux de la mémoire* (published posthumously in 1952), was strictly contingent on the kinds of social bonds such as those developed by his principal mentor, Emile Durkheim. The only collective unit that Halbwachs ratified was the group, not society or the nation. What many who invoke his example ignore is the artificiality of—to employ his term, now overused—the social construction of collective forms. "Every collective memory," he wrote, "requires the support of a group delimited in space and time."[32] Halbwachs's argument that memory requires a collective context is crucial to any idea of subjectivity that presupposes cultural information and experience. Halbwachs is not empowering nationhood, cultural myths, or, most importantly, national myth.

The interpellation of memory into ideology has occurred most consistently at the level of the subject's interpellation into national identity. An intellectual history of the European fixation on memory will find its explosion at the moment of the triumph of the nation after 1870. At this level, memory, as an experience contingent on subjectivity, is co-opted into commemoration, into the official glossing of memory for hegemonic purposes. The very purpose of national, commemorative narratives is to absorb individuality into the national mold. Nationalism's point is to exclude alterity: both the difference between subject and nation as well as the difference between past and present.

Commemoration disciplines memory in the service of a collective identity—a religious community in the most common premodern context, the nation in the most classical modern one. The classic example of this tendency in recent historiography—"classic" meaning more cited than read—is probably the monumental four-volume sequence called *Les lieux de mémoire*, edited by Pierre Nora (né Aron!). This collected work of sixty historians was published between 1984 and 1986, motivated, in the words of Nora's introduction, by the "rapid disappearance of our national memory." The work was inspired by the wish to recover the French national memory lost, by implication, to socialist victory in 1981. Moreover, a recovered national patrimony would provide the ballast necessary for the commemorations of the Revolution, which were due in 1989. The organization of the four volumes represented a newly inscribed national teleology from republic to nation. (Part I is entitled "The Republic"; Part II, in three volumes, "The Nation.") Whose memory is in play? The memory of the nation, in other words a fictional memory that is systematically cultivated by national symbols, monuments, and narratives. National memory is cultivated to meet national ideology: the greatness of France is to be reconstituted through mystification rather than deconstructed through analysis. Half a century after Halbwachs, Nora might have been more suspicious of his own national *jouissance*.

Nora's national agenda has explicit sacralizing intentions. In his introduction to the books, reprinted as an autonomous essay called "Between Memory and History," Nora equates modernity with the "acceleration of history," resulting in the violation, conquest, and eradication (his terms) of memory and the equation of memory and history. Now history, which is secular and intellectual (again, Nora's terms), stands opposed to memory, which is "affective," "magical," and "absolute."[33] Of these three adjectives, "absolute" may be the most frightening, but I would suggest that "magical" is the most telling. Magic, as Max Weber asserted, is the disavowal of distance: the temporal distance between past and present; the existential distance between humanity and divinity. Finally, Nora asserts that the "last *incarnation*" [emphasis mine] of the "unification of memory and history" was "the memory-nation," according to whose authority "no more discontinuity existed between our Greco-Roman cradle and the colonies of the

Third Republic. . . . Through the nation our memory continued to rest upon a sacred foundation."[34]

Pierre Nora's national narrative of restored commemoration, systematically conflated with memory—sacred memory—is successful on an ideological level largely because of an American model, often referred to as American exceptionalism. France and the United States can engage in narrative triumphalism—in the *jouissance* of Abraham Lincoln's "mystic chords of memory"—without immediate protest, even if the legacies of Vichy and Vietnam have taken some of the wind out of these triumphalist narratives. As the above citations show, Nora appears unperturbed by France's collaborationist or colonialist legacies. This is not an option, however, for postwar Germany, Austria, or Italy, where there have been no easy recourses to postures of national identity, collective memory, or their harmonization.

The German "politics of memory," to borrow Jane Kramer's phrase—and with it the recognition that memory in German public discourse is necessarily a political question—has taken a different tack, which I would describe as the splitting of memory and commemoration. Commemoration has involved the delicate economy of responsibility and blame, thereby following lines of political opportunism: the Social Democrats against the Christian Democrats in the Brandt and Schmitt years; the DDR against the BRD; the "*Preussen-ist-wieder-chic*" neo-nationalism of the new, reunified, Berlinocentric and economically stressed Federal Republic.[35] Occasionally, statist commemorations have strayed into the perverse and the grotesque, such as the Bitburg affair in May 1985, in which the German Chancellor attempted to "normalize" the past by honoring German war dead in the company of an American president. Aside from the scandalous inclusion of Waffen-SS men among the honored dead, this commemorative gesture revealed an instrumental motive. It conflated the nation with the political party in power. The Bitburg affair, as the pollster Elisabeth Noelle-Neumann guilelessly argued, was good for the party.[36]

Distinct from the rhetoric and gestures of official commemoration, "memory" has tended to signify a realm outside of state narratives. As a result, its referent is also a world allegedly beyond the reach of the totalitarian state; I am referring to the mode of popular memory called *Alltagsgeschichte*, or the history of everyday life. The flaw in this mode of alleged historiographic memory has been its self-serving revisionism; *Alltagsgeschichte* has been deployed most heavily in histories focusing on the years between 1933 and 1940, thereby insufficiently avoiding a tacit argument for normalization. The everyday life that is "remembered" in such a framework, replete with work, leisure, and home, appears untouched by Nazism, and even replicates

the same image of a *Volksgemeinschaft* that was sought by National Socialism. To put the matter crudely: there are no Jews in *Alltagsgeschichte*. What
passes as memory is in fact a product of massive and tendentious secondary
revision in the form of ideological work.

Clearly, no German analogue to Nora's project of sacred national memory exists, despite the sporadic calls for a "normalization" of the German
past. Nevertheless, there are placeholders for such a German project. Perhaps the most interesting and the most prominent is the work of Jan Assmann, a leading Egyptologist who has fashioned the discussion of Egypt into
a sustained treatment of what he calls the history of memory or "mnemohis-
tory": *Gedächtnisgeschichte*. In general, the accumulation of memory over
long periods of time produces what Assmann calls "cultural memory."[37]
More specifically: the memory of Egypt becomes an allegory of German
"memory."

Jan Assmann has himself explained lucidly the allegorical assignment
taken on by German Egyptologists after the Second World War. These scholars, says Assmann, "all of whom had witnessed the catastrophic events of
World War II and the horrors of German fascism . . . looked to Egypt not only
as a territory for archaeological, historical, and philological discoveries and
problem-solving but also with the—more or less unconscious—hope of gaining insight into the fundamentals of moral and religious orientation."[38]

The Egyptological project that Assmann inherits from his teachers has a
dual purpose. The first is positivistic, archaeological, historical in the conventional sense. The second involves that so-called "memory of Egypt" in
the form of a normative assignment with the task of rebuilding a style for
German cultural memory. This is the goal of enlightened *Bildung*, education, self-formation, as instantiated in the example that Assmann repeatedly
holds up as the German Enlightenment's outstanding example of Egyptomania: Mozart's opera *The Magic Flute*.[39] Here, good Egyptians speak—or
rather sing—in German.

But when pressure is applied, the model begins to show cracks. There
are two structural options for the cultural memory of Egypt. The first is the
biblical, so-called Judeo-Christian memory of Egypt as a place of idolatry and
slavery. This is "bad Egypt." It is the Egypt that returns, for example, in the
symbolic world of African-American slavery. "Good Egypt," on the other
hand, finds in the assertion of an indigenous Egyptian monotheism—the so-
called Amarna revolution associated with the pharoah Akhnaten—the origins
of everything held dear not only by the same Judeo-Christian tradition but
the origin of a cult of light that literalizes the essential metaphor of, precisely, the Western Enlightenment. The "memory" of this "good Egypt"

can be traced—and Assmann does so—through John Spencer in the seventeenth century, William Warburton in the eighteenth, Sigmund Freud in the twentieth. Assmann provides additional references to the same project in the thinking of Marsilio Ficino, Giordano Bruno, Robert Fludd, Athanasius Kircher, Mozart, Schiller, and Thomas Mann, among others.

The problem is that the cultural memory of "good Egypt" carries a return of the repressed memory of a religious antagonism between Egypt and Israel. Thus in one strand of the early memory of Egypt, found in Manetho and Tacitus, among other accounts, the Akhnaten revolution and its follower Moses are associated with a population of 250,000 lepers who abscond with sacred objects when they are expelled from Egypt.

The question that remains to be put to Jan Assmann involves the nature of the investment in the "good Egypt," i.e. the extent to which his own work follows in the path of his postwar teachers. For them, the embrace of Egypt was the embrace of Sarastro. Assmann's much more nuanced and in multiple ways post-Freudian account poses more of a problem. Here, "Good Egypt" is also at the source of the history of anti-Semitism, the source of a "religious antagonism" that posits sacred Egypt against profane Israel. Assmann states one of his motives as the "hope to contribute to a historical analysis of anti-Semitism."[40] The question is whether "good Egypt" can be separated, indeed redeemed from its co-notion of "bad Israel," i.e. Western anti-Judaism. To put the question another way, can Assmann's nuanced account of the competing Egypt-narratives withstand his promotion of a general theory of cultural memory—ideology—in which anti-Semitic currents repeatedly enter into the narrative flow?

Assmann understands the figure of Moses as a traumatic repetition of the episode of "the forgotten pharaoh" Ahknaten, whom Egyptian records, history, and memory had obliterated from all conscious reference. He argues that "the recollections of Akhnaten's revolution, which were banned from official and historical memory, survived in the form of traumatic memory."[41] "Memory" here is what Assmann elsewhere typologizes as "cultural memory," i.e. an inherited sense of the mythic and foundational past. The question emerges whether this property should not be called memory at all, but rather, ideology. I think, moreover, that the complications and indeed confusions in Assmann's story of Egypt make that argument by themselves.

One way of taking the anti-Semitic sting out of the ideology of cultural memory is to identify the Jews as the people of memory. But the tendency to honor the Jews as the people of memory can also take on a tendentious effort to restore a cultural, indeed primitive, authenticity to a culture that had been scapegoated, in modern anti-Semitism, precisely for the alleged lack of

cultural authenticity. I addressed this issue briefly in my exposition above
of the Jewish Museum Berlin, specifically in its architectural transition from
sacred memory to secular history and the attendant danger of representing
the Jews as the people of memory and the Germans as the people of history.
The JMB, I suggested, successfully avoided that pitfall.[42]

The philo-Semitic alternative of the fixation on Jewish memory is, then,
not so different as it may appear from the residually anti-Semitic aura of
Alltagsgeschichte. In the introduction to his recent book on the culture of
memory in fin-de-siècle France, Matt Matsuda cites Yosef Yerushalmi's position that the Jews are the "the people of memory." "One could make similar arguments for almost any group, ethnicity, heritage," warns Matsuda.[43]
Matsuda's remark may be a bit overreaching, but I think he is basically
right. There exists a unique Jewish textual tradition exalting memory, but
that textual legacy is one vessel for the culture of memory. Memory is not
Jewish, any more than, say, self-hatred is Jewish. Fin-de-siècle Jews participated in discourses of memory as they participated in those of self-hatred,
both of which were historically determined and available to everyone. Moreover, Yerushalmi's overall argument stresses the Jewish paradigm shift from
memory to history as the mark of modernization.

Insofar as subjectivity is itself vulnerable to, indeed desirous of incorporation into, ideology, then collective memory can exist as a form of collective subjectivity. But such usage erodes the boundary between true memory
and false memory, making possible, for example, precisely such patriotic
instances as Ronald Reagan evincing war memories which were in fact
memories of movie sets. The disciplining of memory as a category of subjectivity reflects one dimension of Yosef Yerushalmi's argument in his book
Zakhor: Jewish History and Jewish Memory. Yerushalmi opens with an epigraph from the Book of Job (8:8) containing the command "For inquire . . .
of the former generation, And apply thyself to that which their fathers have
searched out. . . ."[44] At stake here is the command to interrogate ancestors,
not to sentimentalize them or submit to them—on other words, not simply
to retell their stories. The modernizing passage from memory to history has
a melancholic aspect, but also a developmental one.

3

In 1962, as mentioned in chapter 1, Leo Strauss recalled his intellectual
youth in the Weimar Republic as having developed under the sway of the
"theologico-political predicament." Schmitt and Rosenzweig were key players here, as was Heidegger, without doubt. In recent years, the state of both

politics and theory in the United States has become increasingly redolent of and often deliberately focused on a reconstitution of a theologico-political predicament. The revival of Carl Schmitt (and his *Political Theology*) as a legitimate theorist in the 1980s and the simultaneous debate over the relationship of Heidegger's philosophy to his Nazi sympathies formed perhaps the first step in the theologico-political predicament of the new theory.

The politics of Jewish identity, history, and memory form a part of this agenda of resacralization. This does not mean a retreat into religiosity but rather its inversion: an inflation of the claims of religiosity as a language and legitimator of political interests. The trend is of course not a Jewish trend alone; the point is that its Jewish variant joins agendas of resacralization and desecularization in other religious contexts, including Christianity and Islam. Moreover, this agenda appears to pervade the Tower of Babel that usually separates scholarship in the humanities from the political sphere at large.

A scholarly context (largely American) that may offer a surprisingly analogous example is the recent and increasing revival of interest in the work of Franz Rosenzweig. Rosenzweig's major work, *The Star of Redemption*, was hailed by Walter Benjamin as one of the most important works of the 1920s. It now begins to earn the kind of academic cathexis most recently reserved for Benjamin himself. Rosenzweig as man and text may in fact be understood to inspire the same cathexis that Benjamin did and does outside the sobering politicization that informs his work and the agenda of one side of his reception. Benjamin the Marxist (Adorno's Benjamin) has long been at odds with Benjamin the Messianist (Scholem's Benjamin). Rosenzweig seems appropriable as a religious thinker alone. As is the case with Benjamin, personal tragedy offers a certain aura; Rosenzweig succumbed slowly and painfully to amyotrophic lateral sclerosis (ALS or Lou Gehrig's disease) in 1929 at the age of forty.

The Star of Redemption attracts devotion more because of the work's renowned difficulty and esotericism than despite of these qualities. The work can be described, I would hazard, as an existential argument for the resacralization of Jewish life. In this respect, it parallels Rosenzweig's own biographical trajectory from his near conversion to Protestantism in 1913 through a rigorously deliberate agenda of reinvestiture in Jewish practice and ritual. It parallels also the desire for resacralization among present-day readers.

The absence of explicit politics in and around Rosenzweig does not imply that his reception is not multifaceted. Two recent studies offer important similarities and differences. I refer to Eric L. Santner's *On the Psychotheol-*

ogy of Everyday Life: Reflections on Freud and Rosenzweig and to Peter Eli Gordon's *Rosenzweig and Heidegger: Between Judaism and German Philosophy.*[45] Both studies read Rosenzweig in refraction with another, more canonic modernist thinker. The differences between Freud and Heidegger are obvious enough. The differences between Santner and Gordon, however, involve their positions with regard to the agenda of resacralization that informs both Rosenzweig and the current Rosenzweig revival.

Peter Gordon's study clearly attempts to place Rosenzweig in the mainstream of twentieth-century philosophy. But philosophy is also a moving variable in the equation, as Rosenzweig and Heidegger both insisted. As Gordon emphasizes, Rosenzweig sided with Heidegger in the key 1929 disputation in Davos with Ernst Cassirer. Rosenzweig's rejection of Cassirer, a secular Jew who, like his teacher Hermann Cohen, argued the contemporary validity of Kantian principles, carries implicitly a rejection of a secular direction and definition of Judaism. Through Heidegger's "victory," philosophy joined the now classically understood desire for modernism to recapture the stance of the archaic and the primitive: the power of myth, the communion with origin, the language of God.

Santner's *On the Psychotheology of Everyday Life: Reflections on Freud and Rosenzweig,* provides one of the most compelling and rigorous contemporary reconsiderations of German Jewish modernism while at the same time steering both contemporary historical discourse and the traditions it explores onto a new ground of resacralization. Santner reads Rosenzweig not as philosophy but as theology, or rather according to the deliberate and controversial neologism "psychotheology." His book thus takes a place, to my ear, as a Jewish counterpart to the neo-sacred discourse developed on the Christian side by Slavoj Žižek.[46] But whereas Žižek's recent work argues with increasing urgency for the validity and contemporary presence of Christianity *tout court,* Santner argues from a Jewish foundation for a communitarian politics based the embrace of plurality, difference, and the Other. Žižek provides Santner's book with the following blurb:

> I wonder how many people will be aware, when taking this book into their hands, that they are holding one of the key texts of the last hundred years—that a new classic is being born, on a par with Heidegger and Wittgenstein. This book is much more than an intervention into current psychoanalytic-religious debates; Santner opens up a new way to *reactualize* [emphasis mine—MS] the Judeo-Christian legacy against the oncoming offensive of Western Buddhism, New Age wisdoms, and fake fundamentalisms.

This is wild prose, deliberately so. Žižek's beatification of his Jewish colleague has no limits, as his careful buildup of images shows. First, readers are imagined to take Santner's book "into their hands," as if in contact with a material relic or other sacred object. The invocation of reliquary magic or sacred objects itself causes the disintegration of the "Judeo-Christian" cluster, or at least the colonization of the Jewish by the Christian. The book is then described not only as a classic but a classic being born—a messianic metaphor possibly implying a textual Moses emerging from the reeds but more likely a paper version of a child in a manger. Then, the third and most effective strike: the reactualization of the Judeo-Christian legacy itself, in other words a robust vote of confidence in the book's performative and indeed transformative powers. Santner's text carries no responsibility for Žižek's overbearing embrace. The question relevant to my discussion is the extent to which Santner's text sets the stage for such treatment.

Santner's analysis introduces and sustains itself primarily as a political engagement. His most aggressive move, however, involves the reconciliation of politics, theology, and psychoanalysis as compatible forms of therapy. The triumph of the therapeutic involves the reconciliation of law and love. Santner's discussion of Freud focuses on *Moses and Monotheism*, applying to its portrayal of the religion of law and the superego a Rosenzweigian balm which softens these elements in favor of a "commandment to love." Santner follows Rosenzweig's distinction between law *(Gesetz)* and commandment *(Gebot)*, the distinction between a third party imperative (law) and an imperative which, in Rosenzweig's words, "can proceed only from the mouth of the lover." The result, in Santner's summary:

> Rather than being the ultimate religion of the superego as Freud argues in *Moses and Monotheism*, it turns out to be, if we take Rosenzweig's analysis of revelation seriously, just the opposite: Judaism, this first religion of revelation, can rather be understood as a kind of therapy directed precisely against the fantasmatic pressures of the superego and its tendency to keep the subject at a distance from his or her answerability within the world.[47]

The "dialogue" between Freud and Rosenzweig, like the "reconciliation" of law and love, becomes more proleptic than performative: staged, but not enacted. This aggressive gesture reminds me of an installation in the "Berlin/Moscow" exhibition in Berlin in late 2003, in which the juxtaposition of an abstract expressionist work with an example of socialist realism was heralded as a first in the history of museology. Not until 2003, claimed the curators, "could" such works be placed next to one another. Like the curators of Berlin/Moscow, Santner seems to me to remain a third party in his wish to reconcile Rosenzweig and Freud, to make Rosenzweig make Freud safe for love, indeed to make law loveable. Similarly, he is not able to withstand Karl Kraus's indictment that a civilization based on love is a recipe for barbarism. The danger here is for resacralization to become indistinguishable from ideology.

Prefacing his study *Rosenzweig and Heidegger: Between Judaism and German Philosophy*, Peter Gordon offers the following precise account of the sacralizing turn among Weimar thinkers:

> The turn to religion seemed to promise a new breakthrough, a reinvigoration of the philosophical discipline. But the new attraction to theology did not spell a return to religious tradition. Paradoxically, the new philosophy articulated theological questions in a modernist, post-Nietzschean frame. The fruit of this paradox was a distinctive intellectual orientation, poised between the religious nostalgia for origin and the modernist struggle to move beyond metaphysics. Like an expressionist woodcut, the new philosophy thus represented a poignant combination of archaism and modernism.[48]

Significantly and, perhaps, unexpectedly, Gordon's own juxtaposition of Rosenzweig and Heidegger does not apparently share the sacralizing agenda he correctly attributes to them both, to their Weimar context. Neither does Gordon share the similar resacralizing motives of some of his contemporaries as I have portrayed them above. Gordon's central chapter offers a conventionally structured "explication de texte" of *The Star of Redemption*, while at the same time taking analytical distance from Rosenzweig's auratic style—his "touch of wizardry"—by inviting the neophyte to take his or her skepticism seriously. Gordon ups the ante on wizardry by comparing the post-idealist system in Rosenzweig's work to a "system of slanted walls and twisted corridors, like something sprung from the imagination of Caligari." Gordon states that he "will not offer a strong conclusion" as to whether Rosenzweig's *Star* should in fact "be rescued from the skeptics."[49] Note that *The Star of Redemption* and *The Cabinet of Caligari* appeared within a year of each other.

Note also that Gordon says "rescue" and not "redeem." There is a world of difference between these two terms, I would assert: the difference between political action and magical apotheosis. When he launches his explication de texte, bracketing the issue of his own sympathies and implicitly asking the reader to do the same—an authorial request he has by now thoroughly earned—Gordon is clear that the category of redemption is primary and is not to be sidestepped. Italicizing his own sentence for emphasis (a gesture I will not repeat here), Gordon summarizes: "Rosenzweig's chief aim is to expound a new concept of redemption that accords with the post-metaphysical human desire to remain in the world."[50] This post-metaphysical stance, like Rosenzweig's thinking (and Heidegger's) in general, is post-Nietzschean. The problem is that Nietzsche refuses all postures of redemption: its desire, its availability, most of all the arrogation of the claim to dispense it. Recall (among many other such moments) Nietzsche's savage attack on the Munich Wagner Society, who one year after the composer's death dedicated a wreath with the inscription (lifted from the end of *Parsifal*) "Erlösung dem Erlöser": Redemption to the Redeemer. Nietzsche muses that what they really expressed was the relief of their own "Erlösung von dem Erlöser": redemption from the redeemer.

To be sure, Rosenzweig distinguishes between two kinds of redemption, as Gordon lucidly points out. Conventional redemption involves "a kind of metaphysical departure from the world." Rosenzweig's variant, argued, for Gordon, in "a post-Nietzschean vein," insists on "the fundamental premise that to be human is to remain in the world." Ultimately, Rosenzweig redeems redemption as well as metaphysics, and I wonder if it may not be too vulgar to suggest that he, like Heidegger, performs these redemptive gestures by affixing to pre-Nietzschean metaphysical baggage the tag "-in-the-world." Thus metaphysics made safe for the world is also the world made safe for metaphysics; the "worldly" values of Mendelssohn, Lessing, and Arendt are located somewhere else.

The aspect of Rosenzweig's argumentation that Gordon, following Margarete Susman, calls a "hermeneutic of life" appears compatible enough with the disourse of worldliness. Here Gordon separates Rosenzweig from Hermann Cohen and Leo Baeck and the understanding of Judaism as law or ethics, highlighting Rosenzweig's term *Jude-sein*. Infelicitously, to my ear, Gordon's translation of the term maintains the syllabic order and effects a Heideggerian tone: "Jewish-being." I would favor the more ordinary choice "being a Jew."[51] I flag the term "ordinary" for all its political connotations, as developed most thoroughly perhaps by Stanley Cavell, with abiding reference to Wittgenstein and Emerson.[52] I would also place the ordinary into the same orbit as the secular. But this is an orbit that Rosenzweig does not seem to want to sustain. Again, redemption.

Gordon's gamble here is to capture Rosenzweig's argument with the attractive phrase "redemption-in-the-world" and to posit this concept alongside Heidegger's concept of authenticity. Judaism and Jews emerge from *The Star* with a unique claim to redemption and authenticity, a claim based on the "self-grounding" of Judaism in history. The first aspect of this self-grounding is statelessness, a move that is both anti-Hegelian (or, rather, post-Hegelian in the context of Rosenzweig's intellectual biography) and anti-Zionist. Indeed, it fits with notions of diasporic modernism. The second principle is blood and blood-community, an assertion shared by Jewish thinkers (such as Buber) and by racialist ideologies, including Nazism. Here Gordon does seem to apologize for Rosenzweig, asserting that blood might be understood symbolically, "as a name for the Jews' special temporality as against the normal temporality of the world." "The crucial idea," Gordon summarizes, "is that the Jewish people does not look to the world to provide the anchors for its understanding of authentic being." This claim of collective subjectivity, of *völkisch* identity, is breathtaking.[53] Like Santner and Santner's Rosenzweig, Gordon (despite his sobriety and disclaimers) and his Rosenzweig seem vulnerable to the question as to whether all communitarianisms depend on a politics of exclusion. For the Heidegger of *Being and Time*, Gordon is careful to point out, authenticity is open to individuals and to everyone, whereas Rosenzweig's redemption is a Jewish option only.

One paradoxical possibility which may in fact inform the Rosenzweig revival is the chance that Rosenzweig's redemption-in-the-world carries a certain auratic desire: the flagging of a worldly reenchantment via a restoration of magical presence. This normativity can be understood to be coded as Catholic in the central European culture most relevant here. Indeed, Gershom Scholem referred to Rosenzweig as a "mute saint" in his eulogy at the Hebrew University in 1930.[54] To be sure, the immediate or most obvious contexts do not add up. Rosenzweig's German world outside his German Jewish world was decisively Protestant. It was to Protestantism that he nearly converted in 1913. It was for his sympathy for "the heights of German Protestant culture" that his *Doktorvater* Friedrich Meinecke praised his dissertation on *Hegel and the State* while lamenting (in a tribute for the *Historische Zeitschrift*) his alleged retreat "into the world of his blood."[55]

The Catholic presence in Rosenzweig's life would likely be understood to be Heidegger himself. In his argument for their dialogicity, Gordon does not pursue this possibility. He flags Heidegger's Catholicism in the standard manner, citing his personal background, his early work on scholasticism, and his considering of a career in the Jesuit priesthood. Like most commentators, he identifies Heidegger's mature view of religion as "ancillary" and "irrelevant" to philosophical inquiry.[56]

4

The Jewish Museum Berlin opened to an unexpectedly agitated world. The news of the attacks of September 11 arrived on the afternoon of its open-ing day to the general public. The building was evacuated and temporarily closed. Equally relevant if less uncannily timed, the return of the so-called "new anti-Semitism" to Europe at once raised the stakes and compromised the efficacy of the museum's narrative. Spurred by the second Intifada of September 2000, contemporary European anti-Semitism took on varied na-tional valences. In Germany, its relation to the Holocaust and to the Holo-caust debates of the 1980s and 1990s has been clear. Among its principal elaborations has been the *Historikerstreit* of the late 1980s and its aftermath, specifically the calls for the "normalization" of German history and na-tional identity in general and of the Nazi past in particular. Martin Walser's 1998 speech in Frankfurt's Paulskirche—a shrine to the failed liberals of 1848—renewed that call, questioning in particular the various projects of commemoration under discussion and construction in Germany, especially in the new Berlin.

Perhaps most simultaneous and most symptomatic to the moment of the Jewish Museum Berlin's opening was the controversy surrounding the publi-cation, in early 2002, of Walser's novel *Tod eines Kritikers* (Death of a Critic). Notwithstanding its title's echo of Arthur Miller's *Death of a Salesman*, this novel carried an anti-Millerian allegory. Walser's protagonist was not an Everyman but an anti-Everyman, not a German but a Polish-born Jew, not a creator but a critic, and indeed not a man who dies but a man who feigns death. The critic was also an explicit take-off on Marcel Reich-Ranicki, the survivor of the Warsaw ghetto who became a principal arbiter of German literary taste. Walser clearly traffics here in deep German anti-Semitic tropes that go back to Wagner; whether he serves them or undermines them is most unclear. That is the problem. In their uncertainty, the *Frankfurter Allgeme-ine Zeitung* broke an agreement to publish the book in serial form. Beyond the possible personal targeting of Riech-Ranicki, the novel's most aggressive aspect (as cited by *FAZ* co-editor Frank Schirrmacher) involved the issue of the feigning of death for instrumental purposes. At risk, therefore, is a poten-tially new anti-Semitic trope targeting the survival of Jewish culture beyond the Holocaust. According to this monstrous conceit—what the editors of the *FAZ* might conceivably have been afraid of, or afraid of being understood to endorse—the Holocaust would have provided world historical Jewry with an opportunity, a cover, through which to perpetuate its conspiracies while cloaked in the disguise of historical extinction.

For several months prior to the announced selection of Daniel Libeskind as the "master architect" of the new World Trade Center site, Libeskind was locked in a final, public competition with a dramatically different proposal by the Think Group, e.g. the architects Frederic Schwartz, Rafael Viñoly, Ken Smith, and Shigeru Ban. They proposed twin towers constructed of open, latticed structures, reminiscent of the Eiffel Tower, parts of which would contain enclosures devoted to civic and learning centers as well as a museum devoted to 9/11. In a polemical comparison of the two proposals, the *New York Times* architectural critic Herbert Muschamp opposed the two in stark and, in my view, largely convincing ways.[57] Muschamp described Libeskind's design as "a war memorial to a conflict that has scarcely begun," "an emotionally manipulative exercise in visual codes." ("A skyscraper tops off at 1776 feet"—Muschamp winks, or perhaps winces; we can infer a repetition of the numerological kitsch that built the 49 columns of the Garden of Exile in Berlin, filled forty-eight of these with earth from Berlin and one with earth from Jerusalem and then asserted that these stand for 1948 and the establishment of the state of Israel.) Muschamp summarizes the Think team's proposal as "an occasion for civic self-regard." Muschamp's preference is clear. His bifurcation proceeds in telling ways. It exudes a painful historical and conceptual sloppiness, but its polemic remains robust:

> Mr. Libeskind's plan is nostalgic for the world of pre-Enlightenment Europe, before religion was exiled from the public realm. . . . The seductive spirituality of premodern society goes far toward explaining the emergence of memorial architecture as a leading genre in the public realm today. An examination of this phenomenon is overdue. Inadvertently, perhaps, Mr. Libeskind has forced the issue into the foreground.
>
> The secular public space is a modern invention. Like the United States, it is a child of 18th-century Enlightenment thought. Before then . . . public space was religious space.
>
> Today's disputes over the display of crosses, manger scenes, menorahs and other icons are throwbacks to a time before religion had been separated from civil society. This separation comes with a cost. It has left a void in public space that has not been completely filled in by reason, recreation, art, nature or the other secular alternatives placed there over the last few centuries.
>
> That is the void that overtook ground zero on 9/11. We can use words like sacred or spiritual to describe this emptiness, but what we are really referring to is the absence of organized religion from the modern

civil sphere. Memorial architecture has long been one way to fill the void. . . .

Like other institutions in civil society, memorialization is vulnerable to political pressure. What and how we remember are not neutral, self-evident propositions. They are debates. Their outcome is often susceptible to manipulation by those in power.

This should be a reminder of why the religious and civil spheres were separated in the first place by Enlightenment thinkers. . . .

This is why the Think team's proposal is the correct one for us. The spaces it proposes for memorial observance could be as eloquent as a cathedral's. But they would be enclosed with the Enlightenment framework that has stabilized this country since birth. From mourning, it would build towers of learning.

Secularity and anxiety: paradigm of cultural loss or of cultural recovery? How to translate this subject position, if at all, into public history, specifically the public history appropriate to museology?

If museums sell narratives as if they were consumer products, then self-assurance is key. The museum-goer, according to this model, can only be expected to invest time and money if a reliable product is offered in return. In museology as in pedagogy, however, the disavowal of the consumerist model may the necessary, if risky, alternative. What would happen if the JMB questioned its own content and mode of representation by saying to its visitors—to its schoolgroups—we don't know who we are in Berlin in 2008; the Jews of 1780, 1840, 1870, and 1920 had a similar anxiety. This was Moses Mendelssohn's position, one for which he was castigated, as Lessing predicted, by his Jewish readers.

The politics of commemoration continues to entrap. In late October 2003 a new controversy erupted around the unfinished Memorial to the Murdered Jews of Europe, designed by Peter Eisenman and under construction in the center of the city, between Pariser and Potsdamer Platz. The memorial takes the form of multiple concrete steles. On Eisenman's request, the chemical firm Degussa was contracted to provide the protective film for the steles. Degussa's product is unique, according to Eisenman, both for the invisibility and the quality of its sealant capacity against dirt, weather damage, and especially against graffiti. It now emerged (at least to the public) that a subsidiary of Degussa had been the supplier of the poison gas Zyklon-B to the Nazi death camps. The governing board in charge of the monument subsequently voted to withdraw the contract from Degussa. Among the voices commenting on this controversy was Michael Naumann, co-editor of the Hamburg weekly *Die Zeit*. "Germany," he wrote in a front-page column, "together with its corporations, is no longer identical to that state whose Jewish victims the monument commemorates." He called on the monument's board to reverse its decision.[58]

There was an urgency in Naumann's tone that seemed exceptional to his readers, and which produced some vehement objections.[59] Beyond his argument, Naumann may have been reacting symptomatically, sharing in a reaction that might be termed commemoration saturation, what Charles Maier called the surfeit of memory in 1993. Has Germany's zeal to commemorate overtaken its drive to historical work? Naumann argued his position at a level of rational secularity and historical differentiation. But in this case these values are trumped, derailed by the symbolic universe of the monument and its commemorative logic. The issue parallels the controversy surrounding the de facto ban on the playing of Wagner in Israel, for example.[60] For Naumann, the Degussa Corporation in 2003 was as far removed from its analogues in 1942 as the Federal Republic is removed from the Nazi state. Daniel Barenboim and Zubin Mehta have pointed out that Wagner predated Nazism by close to a century and that the association of the two only serves to fan the stuff of legend. Their motives are, no doubt, doubly honorable: they want to play great music and they want to relieve one public sphere of a burdensome taboo. But these arguments may falter, in Jerusalem as well as in Berlin, because they tread too confidently over the fissures that open between memory and history, between sacred and secular thinking and their adherent temporalities.

The temporality of the sacred remains a- and antihistorical. Thus it partakes in the repetitive dynamics of trauma itself. The movement out of trauma into historicizing rationality is the work of both individuals and cultures. But individuals (or, indeed, generations) who refuse or delay such restorative trajectories have the right, I would argue, to question other people's assertions that a collective working through of the past has been achieved. If the city of Berlin and the Federal Republic choose to play by the rules of the culture of memory, they must unavoidably respect as well the accompanying rules of trauma. It would then follow that those voices who cannot abide a symbolic return of the makers of Zyklon-B should be respected. The danger here is clear. "Memory" is fodder for fetishization and appropriation as a guarantor of ideological strength and legitimacy. Once the dynamics of "memory" are activated, they cannot be followed selectively. In the paradigmatic context of the Jewish Museum Berlin, it would then follow that

FIG. 8.3. Micha Ullmann, Monument Commemorating the
Bookburning, Bebelplatz

the more the secular historiography of the evolving exhibition outpaces the
sacralizing rhetoric of the surrounding structure, the more public discourse
and historical responsibility will thrive in Germany. So much may prove a
reasonable if high expectation from a society comfortable with the secularity of its public sphere.

On May 10, 1933 the infamous burning of Jewish books took place on the
Bebelplatz, directly in front of the Royal Library of the Humboldt University. On this spot today stands an unusually effective memorial, designed by
Micha Ullman (fig. 8.3). At the site of the burning is placed, almost invis-
ibly, a glass panel through which the spectator is invited to look down into

an emptied white space, walled by empty white bookshelves. This monument employs the same trope of the "void" that Libeskind does, but with no monumentality and therefore with no self-monumentality.

A similar understatement informs the memorial to the Jewish textile merchants of the Hausvogteiplatz, as designed by Renate Stih and Frieder Schnock (figs. 8.4, 8.5, 8.6). The U-Bahn passenger emerging from the station at Hausvogteiplatz encounters commercial names engraved into the treads of the stairway, uncannily similar to the advertisements placed in the same spot in other stations. But these are the names of the Jewish merchants, and their addresses, whose livelihoods were cut off by the Nazi regime. At the top of the stairs we find a triangle of mirrors, inside of which is offered a short Jewish business history of the square. Only one person at a time fits within this little structure. I read the short history of the Jewish merchants of the Hausvogteiplatz as my peripheral gaze unavoidably looks at my own image in the mirror. The effect and its capacity for instruction are gentle, moving, and even a bit humorous. The vanished merchants of the Hausvogteiplatz might have designed my own clothes, I think to myself: who am I, what do I look like, how do I look different in the absence and through the loss of the Jewish merchants of Berlin? I find myself somehow implicated in this story but not accused; rather I feel invited to ponder a history that has affected my own life and for whose knowledge I am therefore responsible.

The principal site of deportation to the east from Berlin was the train station at Grunewald. Today the station is a fairly quiet one. Here a very different commemorative site has been established. The so-called Track 17—Gleis 17—commemorates individually each deportation train (figs. 8.7, 8.8, 8.9). The barren space and unused track appear first to be completely empty. But a closer inspection reveals a sequence of information almost unbearable in its literalness and sheer quantitative accumulation. Running along the edges of the track, at the edge of the platform on both of its sides, 186 steel bars are imprinted with information of every train that deported Jews from Berlin. Information includes the date of the train's departure, the numbers of victims (mostly, but not always, identified as Jews) it carried, and its destination. The first trains headed to the Polish ghettoes, reconstructed as urban prisons for Jews; later trains headed directly to Auschwitz and Theresienstadt.[61]

In the Berlin neighborhood known as the Bayerisches Viertel (Bavarian Quarter), in the Schöneberg district, most streets carry the names of Bavarian towns. To commemorate the presence and absence of the area's high numbers of Jewish citizens, eighty signs have been placed at random spots

FIGS. 8.4, 8.5, and 8.6.
Renate Stih and Frieder
Schnock, Monument on the
Hausvogteiplatz

13.10.1941 / 1251 JUDEN / BERLIN - LODZ

GLEIS 17

Zum Gedenken an die 1941 - 1945
durch Züge der Deutschen Reichsbahn
in die Todeslager Deportierten

27. Januar 1998

Errichtet durch die Deutsche Bahn AG

FIGS. 8.7, 8.8, and 8.9.
Hirsch, Lorch, and
Wandel, Memorial
at "Gleis 17"

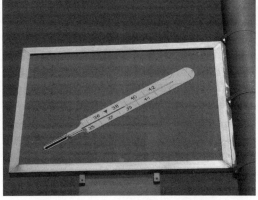

FIG. 8.10 and 8.11 (top). Renate Stih and Frieder Schnock, Schöneberg Memorial. "Berlin bathing and swimming facilities are off limits to Jews."

FIG. 8.12 (middle). Renate Stih and Frieder Schnock, Schöneberg Memorial. "Jewish physicians are no longer permitted to practice."

FIG. 8.13 (bottom). Renate Stih and Frieder Schnock, Schöneberg Memorial. Thermometer appears on back of the sign in Fig. 8.12.

FIGS. 8.14. Renate Stih and Frieder Schnock, Schöneberg Memorial. "Jewish children may no longer attend public schools."

FIG. 8.15. Renate Stih and Frieder Schnock, Schöneberg Memorial

throughout the neighborhood. These are simple white rectangular panels, each of which contains the text of one of the more than four hundred anti-Semitic laws and decrees proclaimed by the Nazi state between 1933 and 1945. Along the Barbarossastraße, for example, one can spot the following signs:

1. Berliner Badeanstalten und Schwimmbäder dürfen von Juden nicht betreten werden.
Berlin bathing and swimming facilities are off limits to Jews (figs. 8.10 and 8.11).

2. Jüdische Ärzte dürfen nicht mehr praktizieren.
Jewish physicians are no longer permitted to practice (figs. 8.12 and 8.13).

3. Jüdische Kinder dürfen keine öffentlichen Schulen mehr besuchen.
Jewish children may no longer attend public schools (fig. 8.14).

4. Verbot jeglichen Schulbesuchs.
All school attendance is forbidden (fig. 8.14).

5. Juden benötigen zum Verlassen des Wohnorts einen polizeilichen Er-laubnisschein.
Jews leaving their place of habitation require a police permit.

This "decentralized" memorial was installed in 1993. The first signs went up several weeks before the official dedication, to the consternation and objections of many confused local residents. The white signs had—by intention of their designers—a disarmingly "normal," presentist, and indeed normative presence. They matched the local street signs. Such disorientation was intended by the memorial artists, the team of Renate Stih and Frieder Schnock, the same artists responsible for the Hausvogteiplatz memorial, who specialize in what they call "social sculptures."[62]

But there are coincidences at work here that are beyond the control, and obviously beyond the intentions, of the memorial's creators. The mirror effect of the Hausvogteiplatz inspires its viewer into multiple, unpredictable, and generous trains of thought which the memorial does not claim to inhibit. Though the same rhythm may be intended for the Bayerisches Viertel, the effect fails, in my judgment, overcome by confusing political valences. The name Barbarossa refers of course to the Hohenstaufen emperor but also, ineluctably, to the invasion of the Soviet Union and thereby the initiation of the mass murder of Jews by the Einsatzgruppen that accompanied the Wehrmacht. Street signs all over Berlin carry the same black on white lettering as the memorial signs of Schöneberg, and the result is discomforting. My fourth example above, "Jews leaving their place of habitation require a police permit," is located at the corner of Barbarossastraße and Berchtesgadenerstraße (fig. 8.15), Berchtesgaden referring unavoidably to the Bavarian town that was the site of Hitler's Alpine retreat. These are problems of function and not of intention. But they exemplify and validate what in literary theory is called the intentional fallacy. In other words, the political and commemorative intentions of the memorial notwithstanding, the memorial founders at the level of the functional.

Most problematically, however, is the tacit assumption that the present-day neighborhood is relatively empty of Jews, and that there is therefore no potential problem of address, no chance that a Jewish resident will feel confused or indeed addressed—hailed, interpellated—by the unembodied but strangely powerful and Kafkaesque utterances of these statements. Through its surprising functional reenactment of the very persecutory voice it wants to disavow, this unfortunate monument often offends exactly those people whose persecution it claims to atone for, and with reason.

Like the Garden of Exile in the Jewish Museum Berlin, the Schöneberg memorial does not place its interlocutor in a position where education and indeed thinking can take place. Here the confusion is cognitive rather than corporal. Both sites violate a principle of the public sphere whereby the dignity of the interpreter and the potential for free and clear thinking is protected. Like a classroom, a memorial site educates its interlocutor first by according and protecting his or her subjectivity, her ability to think openly. On these values rests the enormous success of the memorials on the Bebelplatz and Hausvogteiplatz, and the failures of the Garden of Exile and the Schöneberg memorial.

The rhetorics of public history and public memory combine successfully when they negotiate carefully the dynamics of distance from the past. The past is by definition temporally distant. Understanding the past requires a connection from another point in time. It is the reality of both points that the category of history recognizes. If memory brings the past into the emotional life of the present, history and its modes of distance enable the perceiving subject to grasp that past reality. This kind of historicizing, reasoning subject has at least a chance, as Hegel and Freud argued, of grasping a promise of freedom.

Peter Eisenman's Memorial to the Murdered Jews of Europe (Gedenkstätte für die ermordeten Juden Europas) opened to the public on May 10, 2005. Its 2,711 grey steles of irregular heights accumulate into a five-and-a-half-acre maze of cobbled passages at the center of Berlin. Its blocks and grids create a ghost city on a spot that the bombing of Berlin and the Berlin Wall had rendered an empty space for fifty years. Vaguely but powerfully, the facelessness of the structures captures the violent disappearance of the victimized. The memorialized victims are the Jews of Europe, murdered by a centralized authority that ran its regime from this same spot. But the memorial structures possess an inherent generosity in their abstraction; they are symbolically capable of referring as well to the civilian victims of the bombing of German cities, a concern that has entered legitimate public discourse in recent years, and not without controversy.

The site offers an open metaphor of construction and destruction, maintaining an abstraction both of signification and emotion. By declining to signify, the memorial takes hold of the surfeit of both meaning and meaningless that informs its object of commemoration. Its modernism engages the dialectic that the art theorist Wilhelm Worringer in 1908 called "abstraction and empathy."[63] But, rather than positing these values as irreconcilable opposites, as Worringer did, Eisenman's structures apparently assume an aesthetic and emotional reception that will know how to combine them. This is a modernism that Worringer rejected, as did well-known followers, among them the expressionists Emil Ludwig Kirchner and Emil Nolde. For them, empathy accompanied a cultural solidarity and the communicativity and realism of recognizable, sensual forms. (Nolde coveted acceptance by the National Socialist regime on the basis of these principles but was rejected.) The international modernism that defined twentieth-century aesthetics was, rather, a modernism of distance bordering on one of alienation from styles and forms whose particularity might motivate targeted exclusions. A century after Mondrian, Mies, and Schoenberg, this austere modernist message and its forms have been tamed to the point where an installation like Eisenman's is assumed comprehensible or at least engageable by a general, global public. A strong nominalism is required, however, for Eisenman's gamble to work; we have to *know* that the site is a Holocaust memorial in order to connect its abstraction to our empathy, its nonreferentiality to a referential world of history and memory.[64]

An editorial in *Berliner Zeitung* on May 11 offered a cautious reaction to the memorial and its opening, expressing the hope that this aesthetic construction, with its immanent appeal to emotion and its agnostic silence as a scene of instruction, information, enlightenment, would encourage people to think. It would be most unfortunate, Arno Widmann suggested, if the new memory site fanned the momentum of mystification with regard to the Holocaust.[65] Several weeks later, a short feature on German "export television," the *Deutsche Welle* network, tracked a day in the life of the memorial and its varied visitors. It first caught children and adults jumping across the steles and interviewed a young adult man saying that the invitation to lightness encouraged him to think productively about the Holocaust. An elderly survivor, interviewed later the same day, offered a similar and equally positive evaluation. The artist Renate Stih, co-creator of the Hausvogteiplatz and Bayerischer Viertel memorials, discussed above, was more skeptical. The experience is pleasant, she said, but not relevant to the Holocaust.[66]

The danger, one might extrapolate, would be for the site to enable a vacuous and even a self-righteous gesture in which an alleged act, ritual, or performance of memory is in fact only about itself and not about history or trauma or injustice at all, for the Holocaust to become the "Holocaust," for each stele to become a concrete quotation mark around all imagined aspects of the Holocaust. If the Holocaust becomes the "Holocaust," then the work of history and memory become performances of "history" and "memory," consumer pieties disguised as civic and moral duties. Such a nightmare of obliviousness was in fact once caught by a founding moment of musical modernism: the last moments of Alban Berg's opera *Wozzeck*, in which Marie's son hops on his hobby horse, having just been told that his mother is dead but having no sense of what that might mean.

Of Jews, Music, and Scholarship

The American Academy in Berlin overlooks the lake and river system known as the Wannsee and sits opposite the neoclassical villa that housed the Wannsee Conference, where in January 1942 the Nazi genocide of the European Jews was set into motion. The "Haus der Wannsee Konferenz" itself sits a few houses away from the Jewish modernist painter Max Liebermann's villa and workshop, and just around the bend in the water from the point where Heinrich von Kleist took his life. Welcome to Germany. Since 1998 the American Academy hosts American scholars for a semester's research, well-being, and hobnobbing in Berlin.

Each new semester a new cohort of scholars is inaugurated with a ritual that Kleist may have unwittingly prophesied in his essay *Über das Marionettentheater:* namely, the presentation of the scholars to an invited crowd of Berlin's elite, all hosted by the most snaggable super-elite icon of the season. In my fellowship season, Fall 2003, the ritual was hosted by the Federal Republic's current minister of the interior, the one-time sixty-eighter Otto Schily. Welcome to the new Germany. The occasion's main rule of behavior is what the Germans call *Salonfähigkeit,* or, suitability to the salon. The noun, like many aspects of German good behavior and dissimulation, is imported from France. We scholars all had different ways of negotiating this performance, especially when our turn came to mount the podium for no more than three minutes to offer an autobiographical specimen and disclose the reason and purpose of our sojourn in Berlin. The academy's director, Gary Smith, presided, first introducing Minister Schily and then offering a preview of the center's fall program, its fifth anniversary program with a gala dinner to be graced by the presence of United States Senator Chuck Hagel (H-A-G-E-L). He then introduced the first scholar, political theorist Dana Villa, and his project on Tocqueville and Hegel (H-E-G-E-L). I believe my turn was next, and I began my three minutes by alerting the distinguished guests that they had already heard the name Hagel/Hegel twice, that both Hagel/Hegel's in question were indubitably distinguished in their own fields, but that I was an expert on neither of them and tended to be suspicious of both. My own interest, I then confessed, to the rising panic of Executive Director Smith, was a set of topics that I presumed the first Hagel knew nothing about and the second Hegel had decisively excluded from his world-historical system: namely, music and Jews.

I have told this story semipublicly once before, in Berlin, some two months after the event itself, in the company, among others, of Daniel Barenboim. However, after repeating my disclosure "I am interested in the two phenomena that Hegel left out of his system: music and Jews," I recklessly sailed into the additional claim: "Of course what I also believe is that the two categories are in fact the same." My face was still flushed when, to my abiding pleasure, Maestro Barenboim responded, "Of course." This Parnassian benediction gives me the courage to stick with the assertion and to turn it into a question. Why, then, are Jews and music the same?

At stake in the cases of both music and Jews are non-essentializable products of history, temporally, culturally, politically contingent beings, whose own subjectivities and subject-positions are aesthetically constituted and therefore require an aesthetic dimension from the discourses that attempt to understand them. Music is inanimate and therefore possesses no subjectivity. The rise of the cultural and intellectual importance of music in nineteenth-century Europe was, however, rooted in the fiction that music could be heard as if possessing subjectivity, as if it itself were listening to the world and the past and finding its own position within the multiple contexts of space and time. The inverse proposition is also valid. Just as an aesthetic form can be understood as possessing attributes of subjectivity, so can subjectivities be understood as aesthetically constituted, and understood so without trivialization or irresponsibility. The discourses which engage these subjectivities analytically, a key one of which I understand to be intellectual history, do their objects of study and their own discursive dignities no good by exorcising the aesthetic, namely, the presence of sensation, style, affect, and humor, from their own discursive subjectivities and practices. An aesthetic constitution recognizes depth of feeling and depth of conviction. It also recognizes the outward manifestation, enactment, or performance of feeling which I would and do classify as style. I understand and deploy the category of style, including the term cultural style, to signify the aesthetic resolution of contradiction, a process that can be governed by repression or by reconciliation.

By admitting, or readmitting, the aesthetic into scholarly/scientific discourse, in other words by reaestheticizing our own analytic practices, we
can enter into a more respectful and generous dialogue with our historical
subjects and objects, allowing also for the analytical capacities of their own
aesthetic constitutions. We are speaking here of the reaestheticization of
subjects and not objects, and certainly not of subjects *as* objects, which is the
practice of politically pernicious aestheticisms such as racism and fascism.
We are speaking about Isabel Archer and not the Golden Bowl, about the instinctively wise Brünnhilde and not the beautiful and idiotic Siegfried.

"The intelligence of art," to invoke once again Thomas Crow's title, inhabits the world, historical subjects, and potentially the analytical practices
of historians and other cultural analysts.[1] For Crow, the muteness of visual
art immediately challenges the viewer to build an interpretive world that
paradoxically compensates for the work's grammars of communication and
non-communication. Music is not mute. But it also declines articulation. It
is not a language in this most conventional sense. Music, as it moves into
and through the nineteenth century and as musical discourse includes the
ancillary dimension of musical aesthetics and criticism, remains uncannily
close and at the same time uncannily separated from a capacity for and practice of articulation. Its relation to articulation can be called anxious. It is
completely of the world and about the world but never knows its own place,
and never feels at home. Its energy is epistemological and not ontological,
powered by knowing and not by being. Perhaps the austerity of a music of
knowing (as distinct from a music of being) is what ultimately characterizes
so-called "classical" or "art" music.

Can the aesthetic dimension or constitution of subjectivity itself be analytically and politically responsible? We might understand political responsibility according to Hannah Arendt's jargon of worldliness, as developed in
her 1959 essay on Lessing.

Worldliness implies a distance from both spatial and temporal stasis. It
implies also a distance from language as a provider of *Heimat*. Distance has
nothing to do with alienation; indeed it functions as the contrary of alienation in its enablement of subjectivity. Lessing's principle of *Selbstdenken*,
which Arendt cites, is absorbed as a key tenet of the Kantian universe and
recaptured a century later by Aby Warburg as the principle of *Denkraum*. At
the same time, worldliness functions with a high level of anxiety through its
very disavowal of stasis or *Heimat*. We are getting close here to a working
definition of secularity in the aspects of distance, worldliness, and anxiety.

To stay with language for a moment, we can speak here as well of the
anxiety of articulation, where articulation functions as a determination or

fixation of meaning. This anxiety inhabits both the relevant subjectivities and experiences as well as the discursive and analytical practices which attempt to make sense of them. Thus alongside musical works and their listeners we have the evolution of music criticism and the philosophy or philosophical aesthetics of music; alongside cultural experience we have the analysis of culture in its older incarnations (exegesis, history) and its newer ones (newer historiographic practices and related disciplines). Meaning, value, and identity are the main categories of articulation and its anxieties in both categories.

As an experiment, we might highlight some basic trends in the modern, i.e. post-Enlightenment history of writing about Jews and music. Both surveys exhibit the ongoing anxiety of articulation, the positing of meaning, value, and identity.

The history of the philosophical aesthetics of music makes a big leap in the early nineteenth century, largely in response to the music of Beethoven. The leap proceeds from the general assumption and assertion of the meaninglessness of music to the assertion of the abundant meaning of music, indeed the superabundant or meta-meaning of music. In German idealism, music is not worth taking seriously. In the discourse reasonably associable with Romanticism, music is the status to which language should aspire. The philosophical and rhetorical culmination of this shift comes with Nietzsche and the many variations of his call "Learn to sing, o my soul."

The alleged passage of music into meta-meaning is often associated with the valorization of music as a universal language. But this largely sentimental claim does not hold a historical place in the history of musical aesthetics. It is a claim that has in fact derailed discussion in historical as well as normative discursive contexts. The Romantic valorization of music and of its desire for articulation stays close to literary models, from Beethoven to Schumann. Writers from this period, from E. T. A. Hoffmann to A. B. Marx, describe music's unique precision in the embodiment and articulation of moods, *Stimmungen,* of largely conscious and often political energies in the world of Beethoven, of secret, erotic ones by the time one gets to Schumann. This referential world returns in the early twentieth century, where in the German tradition the music of Richard Strauss plays a key role. Strauss exults in his capacity of material description through music, of objects (a silver rose), or of erotic or sexual states (including intercourse and ejaculation). As of about 1850, in other words for musical generations and taste between Schumann and Strauss, this musical capacity and indeed culture is nationalized through the overwhelming presence of Wagner.

Wagner nationalized German myth, music, and musical aesthetics, monopolizing not only the orchestra and the stage but the writing about them as well. It remains, after a century and a half of commentary, whether one should be more surprised by the fact of his attempt at monopolization and nationalization or by the extent of his success. The myths he recycled were largely non-German.[2] The musical tradition he largely relied on was, but he redefined German music not as a kind of music, a particularity, but as a principle of music itself. In Wagner's proclaimed aesthetic, German myth and music were realized through the German body and the German voice, all of which were fully realized only by his music dramas and were in turn necessary for their realization in performance. Only a Siegfried could sing Siegfried, although Jewish conductors were useful.[3] Unlike Siegfried, the conductor was to be invisible in Wagner's aesthetic and in his architecture for the Bayreuth theater, present only in his labor and not in his body. In other words, Wagner nationalized music by claiming to achieve its total articulation as national content and form, body and mind. The young Nietzsche bought the formula of a national mythology as the rebirth of tragedy; when he changed his position, the most devastating reproach was that Wagner was in the end unmusical.

Musical aesthetics has always had difficulty taming, processing, including Wagner. None of its professional patriarchs, from Eduard Hanslick to Heinrich Schenker, Curt Sachs, Guido Adler, and Paul Bekker, proved helpful on Wagner. All of them retained Beethoven as the measure of greatness. Hanslick famously opposed himself and the musical tradition to Wagner and attached himself and the trajectory of music history to Brahms. Adler and Bekker did the same with Mahler, half a century later. All of them, Sachs most productively, regrounded music history in the baroque period and in J. S. Bach specifically.

The names I have mentioned worked before 1933. After 1933, as is well known, German and eventually European music scholarship accommodated Nazi aesthetic and racist norms or emigrated. In its Anglo-American exile, music scholarship *(Musikwissenschaft)* called itself musicology, drawing from the French term *musicologie* and its allegedly more scientific aura. The result is the well-known story of musicological positivism, as practiced in the United States in both method and choice of repertoire, an academic culture unbroken until the 1980s.

American musicology's main guide into contextual scholarship was Theodor Adorno. Adorno had studied composition briefly with Alban Berg in Vienna in the 1920s. As a scion of Berg and a spokesperson and advocate of Schoenberg (especially during their overlapping years in American exile in southern California), and a founder of the critical social theory that still carries the name "Frankfurt School," Adorno called on music to speak an ascetic truth to the world. It is not often enough remembered in his musical context that Adorno's *Habilitationsschrift* and first book had been a study of Kierkegaard, the most exciting philosophical voice on music prior to Nietzsche. Music and its powers of seduction play a central role in *Either/Or*, written in Berlin in the 1840s, and its opposition of the aesthetic life to the ascetic. Adorno now wanted an ascetic aesthetic. Writing in the shadow of the 1940s and the Nazi regime, Adorno's drive to reconstitute music and music criticism as a political and moral discourse tended to neglect this enormous Kierkegaardian complication, which brought music as well as the discursive world around back into the maelstrom of the sensual.

So long as American musicology remained safely positivist, it stayed away from the nineteenth century, and did so on at least manifestly musical grounds. It thus avoided both good music and bad nationalism (Wagner), and what it judged to be good nationalism and bad music (Verdi). It avoided both politics and the pleasure of the text.

We historians who engage works of art assume that we are in some way combining intellectual and cultural history, in other words interpreting texts and fields that are both driven by intellection and at the same time redolent of inarticulate meaning. Inarticulate meaning may be understood as the common denominator in the history of musical analysis. The argument in favor of inarticulation produces formalism; the will to articulation produces allegory. The issue encompasses the language we chose to use in our scholarly practice as well. This is one obvious way to preserve a border between intellectual and cultural history. This border, if recognized at all, tends to relate intellectual history to philosophy and cultural history to anthropology and to art, and thereby to spheres of under-articulation, from early anthropology's assumption of voiceless agents to the more evolved discussions of alternate articulations through ritual, performance, and artifact. When Thomas Crow speaks of the mute work of art in the contexts of Meyer Schapiro's study of the portal sculpture on the Romanesque abbey of Souillac, of Claude Lévi-Strauss's art-historical legitimation of the masks of the Pacific Northwest, and of Michael Baxandall's depiction of cosmological crisis in pre-Reformation German limewood sculpture, he invokes the muteness, the anxiety, yet at the same time the communicative capacities of artifacts and practices in fused aesthetic and anthropological contexts. In an interesting opening gambit that receives no subsequent development, Crow introduces both Schapiro and Lévi-Strauss in a specific context: New York intellectual life in the 1930s and 1940s, part leftist, part Jewish, part exilic. Schapiro and Lévi-Strauss are both identified as Jews, Schapiro as a left-wing Jew, Lévi-Strauss as a Jewish exile from Nazi Europe. And in an insertion of cartilage that Crow apparently cannot resist, he highlights the fact that Schapiro and his wife encountered Walter Benjamin in Paris in 1939, at which time he had tried vainly to persuade Benjamin to come to New York. We might call this a presentation of a weak contextualism, short of contingency, short of allegory, both of which seem to be important tropes in the text/context dialectics of intellectual and cultural history.

If the aesthetic is contingent on the sensory and the subjective, then we clearly lose something if we drive sense and affect from our sense of the music as we hear it ourselves or as we mediate the music and our own take on it for our readers. At the same time, we are not in business to be seduced or to be seducers. The combination of pleasure and analytical integrity has been elusive in an academic culture that remains completely tied, no matter how much it may protest, to liberal education's principle of analytical autonomy, to the professional standard of "original work." There is no scholarship without distance. What I hope for is a scholarship that distinguishes distance from alienation on the one hand, from what might be termed aestheticism or ecstasy on the other. In other words a practice that refuses the choice between the assertion of identity (the alleged blending of subject and object, individual and collectivity, scholar and world), and an alienation that desubjectivizes both scholars and their objects of study.

∞

Identity. So now we can get back to the Jews. More precisely, we can get back to the Jews by considering the categories of identity and articulation together. The categories are in fact very close. Both involve a projection of self and utterance into a finite world in which in turn a place exists into which they can be received. If we take language as the most obvious sphere of articulation, we can assert the most obvious fact that the Jews have never known what language to speak. Neither Hebrew, Yiddish, nor German provided identity or articulation, although all have been candidates in both political and existential terms. A current project at the University of Leipzig under Dan Diner's direction attempts to establish German as the historical Jewish language, the language of European Jewish culture and cosmopolitanism. The claim has historical validity but is of course also provocative and peraps even perverse, though to my taste in an unusually delightful way.

Theodor Adorno is a preeminent critic of the ideology of identity with respect to politics, philosophy, music, and Jewishness. He rarely took on— rarely articulated—these spheres at the same time. He did so in what I understand as one of his most wide-ranging utterances, his stunning book on Gustav Mahler, which contains the following three passages:

> Mahler's symphonies plead anew against the world's course. They imitate it in order to accuse; the moments when they breach it are also moments of protest. Nowhere do they patch over the rift between subject and object; they would rather be shattered themselves than counterfeit an achieved reconciliation.

> What is Jewish in Mahler does not participate directly in the folk element, but speaks through all its mediations as an intellectual voice, something non-sensuous yet perceptible in the totality. This, admittedly, abolishes the distinction between the recognition of this aspect of Mahler and the philosophical interpretation of music in general.

> Mahler's vigilant music is unromantically aware that mediation is universal.[4]

Mahler's music is thus at once musical and unmusical, Jewish and un-Jewish, and is these things in a way that blends together the blurred contradictions. There is no such thing as Jewish music, in Mahler's case or anywhere else, just as there is no such thing as Jewish modernism. But there are significant convergences of Jewishness and musicality, convergences that are to be understood in the context of highly specific cultural mediations and overdeterminations. Here too, what I am attempting to describe as the anxiety of articulation is in play, in play in both history and (my own) historiography. This anxiety is coincident with the critique of identity. This austere example and practice has, in my view, been insufficiently heeded in what one might call Jewish intellectual history. By Jewish intellectual history I mean to highlight the study of Jewish thinkers, who may or may not focus their thought on Jewish issues, and indeed where the very marking of such thinkers as Jews and the decision to address their own engagement with Jewish issues form a significant aspect of scholarly practice. These questions have produced radically different tendencies in Europe and the United States.

American scholarship has sought to preserve, strengthen, and indeed often refine identity in general and Jewish identity in particular. Most American scholars of Jewish history—certainly not all—have been Jews. Most are '48-ers—1948-ers—not necessarily Zionists and by no means defenders of Ariel Sharon but usually of the conviction that Zionism and Israel have

legitimately recuperated Hebrew as the language of the Jews. The tendency
here is to teach Jewish history as a coherent process compatible with the
category "the Jewish people." This tendency has been strengthened by the
growing institutional availability of teaching positions and chairs in Jewish
history.

As a critic of ideologies of identity, Adorno resembles Hannah Arendt,
with whom he did not get on. As a thinker about music and as an advocate
of musical truth within the constraints of inarticulateness, Adorno is succeeded most decisively by Edward Said. In this context I cite a passage from
Daniel Barenboim's "In Memoriam" to his friend Edward Said, from October 2003:

> Edward saw in music not just a combination of sounds, but he understood
> the fact that every musical masterpiece is, as it were, a conception of the
> world. And the difficulty lies in the fact that this conception of the world
> cannot be described in words—because were it possible to describe it in
> words, the music would be unnecessary. But he recognized that the fact
> that it is indescribable doesn't mean it has no meaning.[5]

The association of music with a conception of the world approximates
Hannah Arendt's central rhetorical and political insistence on the category
of the world as the place of politics, secularity, and non-exlusion. One could
analyze Barenboim's passage musically, with its strong, instinctive repetitions of words and phrases and the apparently accidental ironies in those
repetitions—"doesn't mean it has no meaning"—a very Mozartean gesture.
But at a more basic level, the challenge is clear: how to understand a conception of the world that cannot be articulated, by its bearer or by its analyst,
including by us, its historians, who would embrace secularity and refuse
mystification, but who would still like to feel strongly about the world.

The question remains: can one sing and tell the truth at the same time,
i.e. tell the truth through song, musically? The possibility never loses an
element of anxiety, the anxiety of articulation that I mentioned earlier. The
anxiety of articulation combines with the anxiety about identity. Music
hesitates, hesitates reflectively and reflexively. To be musical, then, is to
hold onto an element of stubborn unmusicality—not like Nietzsche's Wagner but like Schoenberg's Moses. Modern Judaism requires, according to
the same logic, a dose of un-Jewishness. Moses and Aaron need each other
to stake out their positions; each is unthinkable without the other, but the
two never reconcile or converge. Schoenberg and Spinoza, on the other hand:
now there is a match.

NOTES

INTRODUCTION

1. Saul Bellow, *Ravelstein* (New York: Viking, 2000), 171.

2. Theodor Adorno, *Mahler: A Musical Physiognomy,* trans. E. Jephcott (Chicago: University of Chicago Press, 1992), 149.

3. For the recent turn to a paradigm of multiple Judaisms, see David Biale, *Cultures of Judaism* (New York: Schocken Books, 2002) as well as Michael Satlow, "Defining Judaism," cited below in note 13 of the Introduction. For the now classic study of the emergence of secular history and historiography in Jewish culture see Yosef Haim Yerushalmi, *Zakhor: Jewish History and Jewish Memory* (Seattle: University of Washington Press, 1984).

4. Lionel Trilling, *Sincerity and Authenticity* (London: Oxford University Press, 1972), 99.

5. Arnaldo Momigliano, "The Rhetoric of History and the History of Rhetoric: On Hayden White's Tropes," *Comparative Criticism: A Yearbook,* vol. 3, ed. E. S. Shafer (Cambridge: Cambridge University Press, 1981), 263–64.

6. See George L. Mosse, *German Jews Beyond Judaism* (Bloomington: Indiana University Press, 1984) and David Sorkin, *The Transformation of German Jewry, 1780–1840* (Oxford: Oxford University Press, 1992). See more recently Wolf Lepenies, *The Seduction of Culture in German History* (Princeton: Princeton University Press, 2004), for a critical reappraisal of the German valorization of culture over politics, a diagnosis that applies strongly to German Jewish history. Thus the principle of *Bildung* and the general identification of German Jews with German culture, in itself completely legitimate, enabled as well a delusion of protection against anti-Semitic politics.

7. See Nicholas Capaldi, *John Stuart Mill: A Biography* (Cambridge: Cambridge University Press, 2004), 87–88.

8. In this usage, *Mitteleuropa* signifies German Europe as distinct from *Zentraleuropa,* which retains a multinational profile. *Mitteleuropa* is most often associated with a book of that title by Friedrich Naumann (Berlin, 1915). Its genealogy travels through the various stages of the history of nineteenth-century German liberalism. As the program of

National Liberalism matures in the period of the Second Empire and Bismarck, the idea of *Mitteleuropa* as inherited from Constantin Frantz and Friedrich List and brought forward by Heinrich von Gagern signifies a German Europe "from Hamburg to Trieste."

9. See Doris Sommer, ed., *Bilingual Games: Some Literary Investigations* (New York: Palgrave Macmillan, 2003).

10. I take the notion of deterritorialization from Gilles Deleuze and Felix Guattari's 1975 study *Kafka: Toward a Minor Literature*, trans. D. Polan (Minneapolis: University of Minnesota Press, 1986), esp. 16 and 18, in which the authors argue that "a minor literature doesn't come from a minor language; it is rather that which a minority constructs within a major language." Deleuze and Guattari propose the three categories of minor literature as "the deterritorialization of language, the connection of the individual to a political immediacy, and the collective assemblage of enunciation."

11. See Steven M. Lowenstein, *Frankfurt on the Hudson* (Detroit: Wayne State University Press, 1991). See also Mosse, *German Jews Beyond Judaism*, especially the concluding speculation that the German Jews took the best of German culture with them into emigration after 1933.

12. Shaye J. D. Cohen, *The Beginnings of Jewishness: Boundaries, Varieties, Uncertainties* (Berkeley and Los Angeles: University of California Press, 1999). As with the work of many critics, the term "Beginnings" should be understood as importantly distinct from the more default term "origins." Beginnings are made rather than found, a function of epistemology rather than ontology. See Edward Said's argument in the book called, precisely, *Beginnings*. Also Michael Wood's comment in his introduction to the posthumous collection *On Late Style: Music and Literature Against the Grain* (New York: Pantheon Books, 2006): "the whole point about beginnings, as distinct from origins, is that they are chosen" (xvii).

13. Michael L. Satlow, "Defining Judaism: Accounting for 'Religions' in the Study of Religion," *Journal of the American Academy of Religion* 74, no. 4 (2006): 837–60. Satlow provides a concise genealogy of the term "Judaism," which first occurs in 2 Maccabees, which understands the Greek *ioudaismos* as the antonym to another new word, *hellenismos*. Judaism is thus a indicator of a cultural advocacy and opposition—first to the Greeks and then, with Paul, to the Christians. The Church Fathers use the term to characterize non-Christian others; the entry of the term Judaism into Hebrew occurs only in the Middle Ages, most prominently in Abraham Abulafia's *Book of the Testimony*. "Only in modernity," Satlow writes, "did Jews begin to reify their religion as 'Judaism.'"

14. Arnaldo Momigliano, *Pagine Ebraiche* (Torino: Giulio Einaudi, 1987); *Essays on Ancient and Modern Judaism*, ed. Silvia Berti (Berkeley and Los Angeles: University of California Press, 1994).

15. See Isaac Kramnick and R. Laurence Moore, "Politics and Piety," *Dissent* (Spring 2001): 5–12.

16. See Charles Krauthammer, "Demystifying Judaism: Joseph Lieberman's Rise May Change How America Thinks of Jewish Practice," *Time* 156, no. 8, August 21, 2000.

17. See Thomas Crow, *The Intelligence of Art* (Chapel Hill: University of North Carolina Press, 1999).

18. Michael p. Steinberg, *Listening to Reason: Culture, Subjectivity, and Nineteenth-Century Music* (Princeton: Princeton University Press, 2004).

19. I refer to the opening section of *Civilization and its Discontents*.

20. See Aby Warburg, *Images from the Region of the Pueblo Indians of North America*, trans. Michael P. Steinberg (Ithaca: Cornell University Press, 1995).

21. See Darian Leader, "Freud, Music, and Working Through," in *Freud's Footnotes* (London: Faber and Faber, 2000), 88–119. See also Michelle Duncan, "Listening After Freud," dissertation in progress, Cornell University.

22. See Max Weber, *The Rational and Social Foundations of Music*, trans. D. Martindale, J. Riedel, and G. Neuwirth (Carbondale: Southern Illinois University Press, 1957).

23. See G. W. Bowersock, "Momigliano's Quest for the Person," as well as Karl Christ, "Arnaldo Momigliano and the History of Historiography," in *History and Theory*, Beiheft 30 (1991), 27–36 (cited at 30 and 32) and 5–12.

24. The term itself carries a basic ambiguity. *Bewältigen/Bewältigung* means to master/mastery. Does the mastery connote a relationship of work, and even love, as in the mastery of a difficult piece of music? Or does it connote a master/slave relationship? In psychoanalytic terms, is the relationship with the past one of working through or of acting out?

CHAPTER ONE

1. Edward Said, "Freud, Zionism, and Vienna," *Counterpunch*, March 16, 2001.

2. For example in the *New York Times* on March 10, 2001.

3. See Edward W. Said, *Freud and the Non-European*, introduction by Christopher Bollas, response by Jacqueline Rose (London: Verso and the Freud Museum, 2003).

4. I am grateful to Allan Arkush for pointing out this usage in a recent lecture, "Heinrich Graetz on the Enlightenment and the Haskalah," Cornell University, April 27, 2003.

5. Johann Wolfgang von Goethe, *Faust: Der Tragödie, Erster Teil*, lines 682–3.

6. Gotthold Ephraim Lessing, *Laocoön: An Essay on the Limits of Painting and Poetry*, trans. E. A. McCormick (Baltimore: Johns Hopkins University Press, 1984).

7. This is a question I pursue, along with more sustained readings of figures addressed in this chapter, in a forthcoming study called *The Cultural Style of the German Jews*.

8. E. H. Gombrich has criticized both the historiography of fin-de-siècle Vienna and the focus on the Viennese Jews in numerous publications. See in particular *Kokoschka and His Time* (London: The Tate Gallery, 1986). Steven Beller, *Vienna and the Jews, 1867–1938: A Cultural History* (Cambridge: Cambridge University Press, 1989).

9. See Hannah Arendt, "What Remains? The Language Remains: An Interview With Günter Gaus," in *The Portable Hannah Arendt*, ed. P. Baehr (New York: Penguin Books, 2000), 3–24.

10. Hannah Arendt, "Portrait of a Period," in *The Jew as Pariah: Jewish Identity and Politics in the Modern Age*, ed. Ron Feldman, 112–21 (New York: Grove Press, 1978), 117.

11. Hannah Arendt, "Zionism Reconsidered," in *The Jew as Pariah*, 131–63, at 131.

12. Gershom Scholem, Letter of January 28, 1946, in *Gershom Scholem: A Life in Letters*, ed. A. D. Skinner (Cambridge: Harvard University Press, 2002), 330.

13. Leo Strauss, *Spinoza's Critique of Religion* (Chicago: University of Chicago Press, 1962), Preface to the English Translation, 1.

14. Spinoza's profession was lensmaking, which in itself becomes a potent metaphor

for the mediation between vision and (non-)transparency, a key metaphor in the return to Spinoza in the late or post-Enlightenment. The metaphor also guides George Eliot's invocation of Spinoza via the character of Mordecai in *Daniel Deronda;* see chapter 3.

15. Strauss, *Spinoza's Critique of Religion,* 14.

16. Ibid., 24.

17. Elisabeth Young-Bruehl, *Hannah Arendt: For Love of the World* (New Haven: Yale University Press, 1982), 392.

18. Ibid., 3. For an English translation of the interview, see Arendt, "What Remains? The Language Remains: A Conversation with Günter Gaus," cited above.

19. Hannah Arendt, "On Humanity in Dark Times: Thoughts on Lessing," trans. C. and R. Winston, in Arendt, *Men in Dark Times* (New York: Harcourt Brace Jovanovitch, 1968), 3–31, at 4.

20. Ibid., 30.

21. Ibid., 5.

22. Ibid., 11–12. Arendt's discussion of respect in *The Human Condition* provides a close corollary: "Respect, not unlike the Aristotelian *philia politike,* is a kind of 'friendship' without intimacy and without closeness; it is a regard for the person from the distance which the space of the world puts between us, and this regard is independent of qualities which we may admire or of achievements which we may highly esteem." Hannah Arendt, *The Human Condition* (New York: Doubleday Anchor Books, 1959), 218.

23. Arendt, "On Humanity in Dark Times," 13.

24. Ibid., 25, 30.

25. Ibid., 8–9.

26. Horst Bredekamp, "'Du lebst und thust mir nichts': Anmerkungen zur Aktualität Aby Warburgs," in *Aby Warburg: Akten,* ed. Bredekamp, Diers, and Schoell-Glass (Weinheim, 1991), 2. Cited in Louis Rose, *The Survival of Images: Art Historians, Psychoanalysts, and the Ancients* (Detroit: Wayne State University Press, 2001), 26–27.

27. See Aby Warburg, *Images from the Region of the Pueblo Indians of North America,* translated with an interpretive essay by Michael P. Steinberg (Ithaca: Cornell University Press, 1995).

28. Cited in Warburg, *Images,* 80–81.

29. Ibid.

30. Edward Said and Daniel Barenboim, *Parallels and Paradoxes: Explorations in Music and Society* (New York: Random House, 2002).

31. Ibid., 181.

32. Ibid., 41.

33. Said, "Barenboim and the Wagner Taboo," *Al Hayat,* August 15, 2001, reprinted in *Parallels and Paradoxes,* 175–84, at 181.

34. Edward Said, *Power, Politics, and Culture: Interviews with Edward Said,* ed. Gauri Viswanathan (New York: Pantheon Books, 2001), 458.

35. Walter Laqueur, audience intervention at the conference "At the Cutting Edge: German and Jewish Cultural and Intellectual History," Schloss Elmau, Bavaria, July 12–14, 2004.

36. For Barenboim's filmed account of his encounter with Furtwängler, see Tony Palmer's film *The Salzburg Festival* (2006).

37. Barenboim, *Parallels and Paradoxes*, 4, 6.

38. Akeel Bilgrami, Foreword to Edward W. Said, *Humanism and Democratic Criticism* (New York: Columbia University Press, 2004), ix.

CHAPTER TWO

1. See Carl E. Schorske, "Politics in a New Key," in *Fin-de-siècle Vienna: Politics and Culture* (New York: Alfred A. Knopf, 1980), 160–61, and my chapter, "The Catholic Culture of the Austrian Jews," in *Austria as Theater and Ideology: The Meaning of the Salzburg Festival* (Ithaca: Cornell University Press, 2000), 179–81.

2. For an abidingly robust attribution of *The Dissolution of the Habsburg Empire* to the pull of centrifugal force, nationalism in particular, see Oscar Jaszi's book of that title (Chicago: University of Chicago Press, 1929).

3. See Peter Gay, *Freud: A Life For Our Time* (New York: W. W. Norton and Co., 1988).

4. See Carl E. Schorske, "Politics and Patricide in Freud's *Interpretation of Dreams*," in *Fin-de-siècle Vienna: Politics and Culture*, 181–207.

5. Darian Leader, "Freud, Music, and Working Through," in *Freud's Footnotes* (London: Faber and Faber, 2000), 88.

6. See my *Listening to Reason: Culture, Subjectivity, and Nineteenth-Century Music* (Princeton: Princeton University Press, 2004), introduction and passim.

7. William J. McGrath, *Freud's Discovery of Psychoanalysis: The Politics of Hysteria* (Ithaca: Cornell University Press, 1986), 61–63.

8. Nicholas Capaldi, *John Stuart Mill: A Biography* (Cambridge: Cambridge University Press, 2004), 268. (External) liberty and (internal) freedom can be understood as synonymous with the ideas of "negative freedom" and "positive freedom," as developed by Isaiah Berlin in his essay "Two Ideas of Liberty."

9. Capaldi, *John Stuart Mill*, 240.

10. Letter of John Stuart Mill to Theodor Gomperz (1832–1912), October 5, 1857, cited in Mill, *On Liberty*, ed. Edward Alexander (Peterborough, 1999), 178.

11. Nicholas Capaldi makes this error in the generally excellent and lucid biography cited in this chapter and elsewhere.

12. Freud's translations of Mill comprise volume 12 of Theodor Gomperz's edition, *John Stuart Mills Gesammelte Werke* (12 volumes, Leipzig, 1869–80), volume title: *Vermischte Schriften*. They include "Über Frauenemanzipation," "Plato," "Die Arbeiterfrage," and "Sozialismus." See Philip Merlan, "Brentano and Freud," *Journal of the History of Ideas* 6, no. 3 (June 1945): 375–77. Gomperz published a biography of Mill in 1889. Among his early writings, it is interesting to note, is *Traumdeutung und Zauberei* (Magic and the Interpretation of Dreams, 1866).

13. Gay, *Freud*, 36.

14. Ernest Jones, *The Life and Work of Sigmund Freud* (New York, 1953), 1:55–56, 175–76.

15. Sigmund Freud, *Briefe 1873–1939*, ed. Ernst and Lucie Freud (Frankfurt: S. Fischer Verlag, 1968), 81–83: ". . . die Stellung der Frau wird keine andere sein können, als sie ist, in jungen Jahren ein angebetetes Liebchen, und in reiferen ein geliebtes Weib."

16. McGrath, *Freud's Discovery of Psychoanalysis.*

17. Sigmund Freud, *Civilization and Its Discontents*, trans. J. Strachey (New York: W. W. Norton and Co., 1961), 25.

18. Ibid., 40.

19. This short piece was first published as a note to Otto Rank's book *Der Mythus von der Geburt des Helden* (1909). See Freud, "Family Romances," in *Collected Papers*, ed. James Strachey (London, 1950), 5:74–78.

20. Freud, *Civilization*, 15. I have altered the Standard Edition in one place, changing "ego-feeling" to "sense of self" *(Selbstgefühl).*

21. For an account of the myth of *Tsimtsum*, see Gershom Scholem, "Isaac Luria and His School," in *Major Trends in Jewish Mysticism* (New York: Schocken Books, 1946).

22. Freud, *Civilization*, 91.

23. Ibid., 84, 86.

24. Eric Santner, *My Own Private Germany: Daniel Paul Schreber's Secret History of Modernity* (Princeton, 1996), 120.

25. Ibid., 122.

26. Freud, "The Moses of Michelangelo," in Peter Gay, ed., *The Freud Reader* (New York, 1989), 529–30.

27. Ibid., 536.

28. Freud invoked the example of Lucius Junius Brutus with reference to his judgment of his daughter Anna and a presentation of hers to the Vienna Society for Psychoanalysis in 1922. Freud wrote to Max Eitingon that "I will feel like Junius Brutus the elder when he had to judge his own son." Letter of May 19, 1922, cited in Elisabeth Young-Bruehl, *Anna Freud: A Biography* (New York, 1988), 108.

29. Freud, "The Moses of Michelangelo," 539.

30. See Ritchie Robertson, "Freud's Testament: *Moses and Monotheism*," in *Freud in Exile: Psychoanalysis and its Vicissitudes*, ed. E. Timms and N. Segal (New Haven: Yale University Press, 1988), 82.

31. Freud, *Moses and Monotheism*, trans. K. Jones (New York: Vintage Books, 1939), 125.

32. Santner, *My Own Private Germany*, 123.

33. Freud, *Beyond the Pleasure Principle*, trans. J. Strachey (New York: W. W. Norton and Co., 1961), 12–13.

34. See chapter 6 for a discussion of this dynamic with regard to Arnaldo Momigliano and the meeting of Italian Jewish life and culture, Italian Hegelianism, and British liberalism in historiography and politics.

CHAPTER THREE

1. Edith Wharton, *The House of Mirth* (1904), in *Wharton: Novels* (New York: Library of America, 1985), 5.

2. This is the predominant move in James scholarship, including that written from the perspective of moral philosophy. See, for example, Robert B. Pippin, *Henry James and Modern Moral Life* (Cambridge: Cambridge University Press, 2000). Pippin understands modernity, and James's view of it, in terms of "the great social change" and "new

intricacy" defined by money and social mobility, generating "psychological suspicions," "new, much more extensive and deeper forms of social dependencies," as well as "very new ways of understanding the fluid, relatively unfixed, quite variously interpretable dimensions of psychological life" (11–12). Baudelairean fluidity is flagged here but not with approval, and the generally hostile view to the modern seems either to remove or delegitimate its emancipatory potential.

3. See Daniel H. Borus, *Writing Realism: Howells, James, and Norris in the Mass Market* (Chapel Hill: University of North Carolina Press, 1989), 154, and Leon Edel, *Henry James*, 5 vols. (New York, 1972), 4:274.

4. Henry James, "Emile Zola," *Atlantic Monthly*, August 1903.

5. Edel, *Henry James*, 5:167.

6. Lyall Powers, ed. *Henry James and Edith Wharton, Letters: 1900–1915* (New York: 1990).

7. Martha C. Nussbaum, "Flawed Crystals: James's *The Golden Bowl* and Literature as Moral Philosophy," *Love's Knowledge: Essays on Philosophy and Literature* (Oxford: Oxford University Press, 1990), 133.

8. Ibid., 131.

9. Henry James, *The Golden Bowl* (1904), 20–21. Citations, hereafter placed parenthetically in the text, refer to the Penguin Classics ed. (Harmondsworth, 1987).

10. See Pippin, *Henry James and Modern Moral Life*, 76.

11. See Nussbaum, "'Finely Aware and Richly Responsible': Literature and the Moral Imagination," *Love's Knowledge*, 157.

12. See Pippin, *Henry James and Modern Moral Life*, 71.

13. Martha Nussbaum, letter to me of March 21, 1991.

14. See Nussbaum, "Flawed Crystals," 137.

15. Pippin, *Henry James and Modern Moral Life*, 77–79.

16. Edel, *Henry James*, 2:371.

17. See Barbara Hardy, Introduction to George Eliot, *Daniel Deronda* (Harmondsworth: Penguin, 1967), 17–18.

18. Edel, *Henry James*, 2:371.

19. Nussbaum, "'Finely Aware,'" 155.

20. Wayne Booth, *The Company We Keep* (Berkeley and Los Angeles: University of California Press, 1988), 288.

21. Nussbaum, "Flawed Crystals," 125.

22. Harold Bloom, *Kabbalah and Criticism* (New York: Continuum, 1975), 52. The translation of the term *Sefirot* is from Gershom Scholem, *Major Trends in Jewish Mysticism* (New York: Schocken Books, 1946), 13.

23. Gershom Scholem, "Isaac Luria and His School," *Major Trends*, 261.

24. Ibid., 267.

25. Ibid., 287.

26. The quotation is from Gershom Scholem, "Toward an Understanding of the Messianic Idea," in Scholem, *The Messianic Idea in Judaism* (New York: Schocken Books, 1971), 13.

27. Gershom Scholem, *Sabbatai Sevi*, trans. R. J. Zwi Werblowsky (Princeton: Princeton University Press, 1957).

28. Walter Benjamin, *Gesammelte Schriften*, ed. Rolf Tiedemann and Hermann Schweppenhauser (Frankfurt: Surhkamp Verlag, 1977), 4.1:18. Translations will be mine unless otherwise indicated.

29. Gershom Scholem, *Walter Benjamin: The Story of a Friendship*, trans. H. Zohn (New York: Jewish Publication Society of America, 1981), 14, 28, 43, 32, 38.

30. Walter Benjamin, "On Language as Such and on the Language of Man," *Reflections*, trans. E. Jephcott (New York: Schocken Books, 1979), 326–27.

31. Anson Rabinbach, "Between Enlightenment and Apocalypse: Benjamin, Bloch and Modern German Jewish Messianism," *New German Critique* 34 (Winter 1985): 105n.

32. Scholem, *Walter Benjamin: The Story of a Friendship*, 83.

33. Ibid., 88–89.

34. Walter Benjamin, *Briefe*, ed. G. Scholem and T. Adorno (Frankfurt: Suhrkamp Verlag, 1966), 1:234. This chapter dated from 1912. It was included in the 1918 edition of Ernst Bloch, *Geist der Utopie*, but deleted in the edition of 1923. See Rabinbach, "Between Enlightenment," 89n.

35. Scholem, *Walter Benjamin: The Story of a Friendship*, 91.

36. Benajmin, *Briefe*, 1:248.

37. Scholem, *Walter Benjamin: The Story of a Friendship*, 100–1.

38. Ibid., 95–98. I refer to a work in progress by Gary Smith, and several personal conversations about it.

39. See Rabinbach, "Between Enlightenment," 98.

40. See Benjamin, *Reflections*, 312.

41. Walter Benjamin, "Critique of Violence," *Reflections*, 279.

42. See E. M. Butler, *The Tyranny of Greece Over Germany* (Cambridge: Cambridge University Press, 1936).

43. The path of Greek-inspired German aestheticism ends in Heidegger (and his use of Hölderlin), specifically in Martin Heidegger, "The Origin of the Work of Art" of 1936. Translated in Heidegger, *Basic Writings*, ed. D. F. Krell (New York: HarperCollins, 1967), 149–87.

44. Walter Benjamin, "The Task of the Translator," *Illuminations*, trans. Harry Zohn (New York: Schocken Books, 1968), 70.

45. Ibid., 72; translation altered.

46. My translation of "So ist die Übersetzung zuletzt zweckmässig für den Ausdrück des innersten Verhältnisses der Sprachen zueinander. Sie kann dieses verborgene Verhältnis selbst unmöglich offenbaren, unmöglich herstellen; aber darstellen, indem sie es keimhaft oder intensive verwirklicht, kann sie es." Benjamin, *Gesammelte Schriften*, 4.1:12.

47. In German: "Sehnsucht nach Sprachergänzung," in ibid., 18.

48. Ibid., 21.

49. See Paul de Man, "Conclusions: Walter Benjamin's 'The Task of the Translator,'" *The Resistance to Theory* (Minneapolis: University of Minnesota Press, 1986), 80. At the same time I want to add that de Man's discussion of Benjamin's invocation of the broken vessels—de Man, 89–90—is faulty. In insisting, correctly, that Benjamin resists the implication the lost totality can be restored, de Man insists, incorrectly, that Benjamin is not discussing a synechdochical relationship of fragments to a vessel. Of course he is

discussing such a relationship, but insisting at the same that it cannot be restored by human agency.

50. James, *The Golden Bowl*, 27.

51. See Martha Nussbaum, "Perception and Revolution: *The Princess Casamassima* and the Political Imagination," *Love's Knowledge*, 195–219.

52. Henry James, Preface (1909) to *The Princess Casamassima* (Harmondsworth: Penguin, 1987), 33, 34, 35.

CHAPTER FOUR

1. "Eduard Fuchs, der Sammler und der Historiker," first published in the *Zeitschrift für Sozialforschung* 6 (1937); an English translation appears in *The Essential Frankfurt School Reader*, ed. Andrew Arato and E. Gebhardt (New York: Continuum, 1982), 225–53. The translators use the title "Eduard Fuchs, Collector and Historian." I have restored the definite articles, to echo the German more closely, but also to affirm the sense of separation of the two categories "collector" and "historian" from the actual person of Eduard Fuchs. For Benjamin, "the collector" and "the historian" are two types that coincide with, but are not delimited by, the person of Eduard Fuchs. I do this despite the fact that Benjamin wrote a French abstract of the piece called "Edouard Fuchs, collectionneur et historien"; Walter Benjamin, *Gesammelte Schriften*, 7 vols., ed. Rolf Tiedemann and Hermann Schweppenhäuser (Frankfurt, 1972–), 2:1361 (hereafter *GS*). Citations and quotations from Benjamin are from this edition, in my translations—unless otherwise indicated.

2. For accounts of the rejection of Benjamin's habilitation, see Martin Jay, *The Dialectical Imagination* (New York: Little, Brown and Co., 1973), Susan Buck-Morss, *The Origin of Negative Dialectics* (New York: The Free Press, 1977), and Rolf Tiedemann's notes in *GS* 1:895–902. Horkheimer's role is omitted from these discussions.

3. See *GS* 2:1316. Horkheimer's report appeared as an addendum in Fuchs's book, *Die Meister der Erotik* (Munich, 1930). The history of eroticism formed a part of Fuchs's overall project of the history of caricature. See Benjamin's footnote in Arato and Gebhardt, eds., *The Essential Frankfurt School Reader*, 356.

4. Letter of September 18, 1937, cited in *GS* 2:1324. All translations, unless indicated otherwise, are mine.

5. Letter of March 16, 1937: *GS* 2:1331.

6. Hermann Broch, letter of September 1947 to Erich Kahler, quoted in Ernestine Schlant, *Hermann Broch* (Chicago: University of Chicago Press, 1986), 149–50.

7. Benjamin, "Eduard Fuchs, Collector and Historian," ed. Arato and Gebhardt, 227.

8. Benjamin's critique of the ideology of progress—whether in a capitalist or Marxist mode—has been analyzed in Michael Löwy, "Fire Alarm: Walter Benjamin's Critique of Technology," in *Democratic Theory and Technological Society*, ed. Richard Day, Ronald Beiner, and Joseph Masciulli (Armonk, N.Y.: M. E. Sharpe, 1987), 271–79. Löwy's principal image is drawn from the preparatory notes for the "Theses on the Philosophy of History" (*GS* 1:1232), in which Benjamin suggests that "Marx said that revolutions are the locomotives of world history. But perhaps they are something quite different. Perhaps

revolutions are the hand of the human species traveling in this train pulling the alarm brakes."

9. The two opposing terms in Benjamin's usage are *Kulturgeschichte* and [*die*] *Geschichte der Kultur*. I am translating these, respectively, as "the history of culture" and "cultural history." This may be confusing, as the reverse would seem more immediately logical, but the ideological connotations are most important, and "the history of culture," which in its implications of linearity and totality, carries, within the term itself as well as in the academic programs operating in its name, the weight of the German *Kulturgeschichte*. "Cultural history," in contrast, is currently used widely in the historical profession to denote a historical, critical practice in many ways compatible with the practice Benjamin advocates. See, for example, Roger Chartier's book of essays, *Cultural History* (Ithaca: Cornell University Press, 1988). Note that my translations of the two terms are the reverse of the translations used in the Arato and Gebhardt translation of the Fuchs essay!

10. Alfred Weber, "Der soziologische Begriff," in *Verhandlungen des Zweiten Deutschen Soziologentages: Schriften der Deutschen Gesellschaft für Soziologie*, vol. 1 (2) (Tübingen, 1913), 11–12.

11. "Das Kunstwerk im Zeitalter seiner technischen Reproduzierbarkeit," *Zeitschrift für Sozialforschung* 5 (1936). As with the title of the Fuchs essay, the most accurate English translation of the title follows on the German original and must ignore the French title provided by Benjamin. His own "L'oeuvre d'art à l'époque de sa reproduction mécanisée" apparently generated the common "Work of Art in the Age of Mechanical Reproduction," which does justice neither to the words nor to the meaning of the German title. See Walter Benjamin, "The Work of Art in the Age of Its Technological Reproducibility," in *Walter Benjamin: Selected Writings, 1935–1938*, ed. Michael W. Jennings, 4 vols. (Cambridge, Mass.: Harvard University Press, 2003), vol. 3.

12. Benjamin was not interested in considering the auratic power of the movie star. Ironically, the circulation of his essay in film studies has places the word *aura* into the vocabulary of Hollywood and the movie star. For example, the Parisian restaurateur Natacha, speaking of Mickey Rourke in the *New York Times Magazine*, October 21, 1990, p. 43: "When he came in the first time, I saw this young guy, surrounded by people, and I thought, that is a star. He had an aura. For me it was like seeing James Dean all over again." One might argue that the physical presence of the movie star—in a restaurant, not on the screen—returns the aura to a cult object that, precisely for the reasons of Benjamin's argument, cannot be available within the confines of a reproduced film.

13. Heidegger, "Der Ursprung des Kunstwerkes," first version (lecture) November 1935; second version (three lectures) November–December 1936. Quoted here is the English translation by Albert Hofstadter, "The Origin of the Work of Art," in Heidegger, *Poetry, Language, Thought* (New York: Harper Colophon Books, 1971), 15–87. Hereafer cited parenthetically in the text.

14. "*Art is then the becoming and happening of truth*" (71; Heidegger's emphasis).

15. *Gestell* is defined on p. 64: "The strife that is brought into the rift and thus set back into the earth and thus fixed in place is *figure, shape, Gestalt*. Createdness of the work means: truth's being fixed in place in the figure. Figure is the structure in whose shape the rift composes and submits itself. This composed rift is the fitting or joining of

the thing of truth. What is here called figure, *Gestalt*, is always to be thought in terms of the particular placing [*Stellen*] and framing or framework [*Gestell*] as which the work occurs when it sets itself up and sets itself forth."

16. In an unpublished paper, Stephen Hastings-King places the rejection of the social that goes on in the "Origin" within the turn in Heidegger's thinking, in the early fascist period, against the historicizing endeavor that had guided his critique of Husserlian phenomenology through *Being and Time* (1927). For a thorough account of Heidegger's post-1927 ahistorical turn, see Jeffrey Barash, *Martin Heidegger and the Problem of Historical Meaning*, 2d ed. (New York: Fordham University Press, 2003).

17. Meyer Schapiro, "The Still Life as Personal Object," in *The Reach of Mind: Essays in Memory of Kurt Goldstein* (New York: Springer Publishing, 1968). Reprinted in Schapiro, *Theory and Philosophy of Art: Style, Artist, and Society* (New York: George Braziller, 1994), 135–42.

18. On Van Gogh's evangelicalism, see Debora Silverman, "Weaving Paintings: Religious and Social Origins of Vincent Van Gogh's Pictorial Labor," in *Rediscovering History: Culture, Politics, and the Psyche*, ed. Michael S. Roth (Stanford: Stanford University Press, 1994), 137–68.

19. Jacques Derrida, *The Truth in Painting*, trans. Geoff Bennington and Ian McLeod (Chicago: University of Chicago Press, 1987), 10.

20. The "(a)" is the English indefinite article, suggesting the different "me's" involved in the different levels of appropriation being addressed.

21. Meyer Schapiro, "Further Notes on Heidegger and Van Gogh," in *Theory and Philosophy of Art: Style, Artist, and Society*, 147.

22. "Wenn aber Fuchs gegen ihn geltend macht: 'Gerade diese formalen Momente ... sind es, dies sich nirgends anders hier erklären lassen als aus der veränderten Stimmung der Zeit' [*Erotische Kunst* 2:20], so weist das doch in erster Linie auf die erwähnte Bedenklichkeit von kulturhistorischen Kategorien hin" (*GS* 2:481). ("But when Fuchs argues against [Wölfflin]: 'These very formal elements can only be explained according to the changing mood of the time,' this is a function of the impoverished categories in the history of culture to which I have already referred.")

23. Thomas Y. Levin, "Walter Benjamin and the Theory of Art History," *October* 47 (Winter 1988): 77–78. My only caveat here has to do with how swiftly Levin turns a practice (of art history) into a "theoretical concern." My focus is clearly on Benjamin as a practician.

24. Letter of Benjamin quoted in ibid., 79–80.

25. Michael Podro, *The Critical Historians of Art* (New Haven: Yale University Press, 1982), 89.

26. Walter Benjamin, "Rigorous Study of Art," trans. Thomas Y. Levin, *October* 47 (Winter 1988): 87.

27. The "flat, universalizing" history of art to which Benjamin refers is analogous to the history of culture (*Kulturgeschichte*) he attacks in the Fuchs essay.

28. "Creativity" is *Schöpfertum*, the same word used in the "Work of Art" essay.

29. Françoise Meltzer, "Acedia and Melancholia," in *Walter Benjamin and the Demands of History*, ed. M. P. Steinberg (Ithaca: Cornell University Press, 1996).

30. Walter Benjamin, *Das Passagenwerk: Aufzeichnungen und Materialen*, ed. Rolf

Tiedemann (Frankfurt: Suhrkamp Verlag, 1983), *Konvolut* H: 1:268–80. Translations are mine.

31. John Forrester, "'Mille e tre': Freud and Collecting," in *Cultures of Collecting*, ed. John Elsner and Roger Cardinal (Cambridge, Mass.: Harvard University Press, 1994), 224.

32. See Carl E. Schorske, "Freud's Egyptian Dig," *The New York Review of Books* 41, no. 10 (May 27, 1993): 35.

33. See Forrester, "'Mille e Tre,'" 227–28, 234.

34. H.D. [Hilda Doolittle], *Tribute to Freud: Writing on the Wall, Advent* (London, 1985), 96–98; quoted by Forrester, 237–38.

35. For very different recent readings of the Heidegger-Benjamin juxtaposition, see, e.g., Rebecca Comay, "Redeeming Revenge: Nietzsche, Benjamin, Heidegger, and the Politics of Memory," in *Nietzsche as Postmodernist*, ed. Clayton Koelb (Albany: SUNY Press, 1990); Christopher Fynsk, "The Claim of History," in a special issue of *Diacritics* 22 (Fall-Winter 1992); and various essays in Andrew Benjamin and Peter Osborne, eds., *Walter Benjamin's Philosophy* (London: Clinamen Press, 1994), esp. the editors' introduction, and Howard Caygill, "Benjamin, Heidegger, and the Destruction of Tradition," Alexander Garcia Düttmann, "Tradition and Destruction: Walter Benjamin's Politics of Language," and Andrew Benjamin, "Time and Task: Benjamin and Heidegger Showing the Present."

36. When the Metropolitcan Museum built a wing for the Temple of Dendur, the goods-gods question emerged in its full referentiality. Was this a new site of the sacred or a new commodity; the alliance of art and religion, or of art and Disney? When, about the same time, the Met's board of trustees proposed to appoint its first Jewish members, one of its stalwart members warned, "You will have bar mitzvahs taking place in the Temple of Dendur." The insistence on the godly over the goodly is of course wrapped up in anti-Semitic tropes. The Jew without spirituality, which means without Christian spirituality, is reduced to materiality, to trading in goods or money. For Heidegger, goods become gods; for Freud and Benjamin, gods become goods. Their agenda is precisely to turn an anti-Semitic trope on its head. By flirting so closely with that anti-Semitic stereotype, the collector's inflecton of materiality, rather than being symptomatic of the gods-to-goods degradation, shows the ideology of the goods-to-gods exaltation. Everyday life rejects the sublime.

37. Heidegger, "The Origin of the Work of Art," 43.

CHAPTER FIVE

1. Franz Kafka, "In the Penal Colony," *The Penal Colony, Stories, and Short Pieces*, trans. Willa and Edwin Muir (New York: Schocken Books, 1948), 204.

2. Francis Barker, *The Tremulous Private Body: Essays on Subjection* (Cambridge: Cambridge University Press, 1984), 3.

3. Griselda Pollock, "Theatre of Memory: Trauma and Cure in Charlotte Salomon's Modernist Fairy Tale *Leben? Oder Theater?*," in *Reading Charlotte Salomon*, ed. Michael P. Steinberg and Monica Bohm-Duchen (Ithaca: Cornell University Press, 2006), 34–72.

4. See chapter 8. For the contemporary *locus classicus* of the advocacy of a return to memory, precisely for its capacity for immediacy and identification with a lost past, see

Pierre Nora, "Between Memory and History: *Les lieux de mémoire*," *Representations* 26 (Spring 1989): 7–25.

5. Though not so articulated, this principle of "modernist authenticity" stands close to George Mosse's central argument in his *German Jews Beyond Judaism* (Bloomington: Indiana University Press, 1985). "Beyond Judaism" may imply that a disavowal of religious practice be understood as a necessary component of the stance, an attitude that was widespread but is not necessary for the validity of the general argument. Much more typical of the historiography of modern German Jewry is Michael Brenner's *Renaissance of Jewish Culture in Weimar Germany* (New Haven: Yale University Press, 1996). Brenner relies heavily on "the search for authenticity" (the title of the book's third part) as an organizing historiographic principle. Though he does not provide a conceptual or theoretical discussion of the term as he uses it, his usage makes no distinction among authenticity, essentialism, or the search for origin. The book's title recalls Martin Buber's phrase "Jewish renaissance," and the book itself evinces a Buberian attitude about the recovery of Jewish authenticity, essence, and origins, through the Jewish culture of Eastern Europe. Brenner thus follows Buber in universalizing and normativizing one among many Weimar attitudes. Consequently, he fails to mark clear disagreements between figures such as Buber and figures such as Gershom Scholem, whose work did indeed constitute, as Brenner writes, a "search for a lost Judaism" (3), but who disagreed fundamentally with Buber's discourse of return. See also chapter 8, note 13.

6. These two arguments (the advocacy of a highly qualified and differentiated principle of authenticity and the thesis of dual [internal/external] patriarchy) form the crux of my study in progress *The Cultural Style of the German Jews*.

7. Darcy Buerkle, "Historical Effacements: Facing Charlotte Salomon," in *Reading Charlotte Salomon*, 87.

8. Alfred Wolfsohn survived the Second World War and settled in England, where he taught voice, until his death in 1962. He wrote several manuscripts, including *Orpheus, oder der Weg zu einer Maske* (Berlin, 1938); *Die Brücke* (London, 1947); *The Problems of Limitations* (London, 1958). The Alfred Wolfsohn Archives are in the care of Marita Guenther, Malerargues, Ansuze, France. The Jewish Historical Museum in Amsterdam holds copies of *Orpheus* and *Die Bruecke*. See Noah Pikes, *Dark Voices: The Genesis of Roy Hart Theatre* (Woodstock, Conn.: Spring Journal Books, 1999), 31n as well as 29–65 for a portrait of Wolfsohn and his postwar career. See also Paul Newham, *The Prophet of Song: The Life and Work of Alfred Wolfsohn* (London and Boston: Tiger's Eye Press, 1997).

9. In this context it is worth returning to the texts engaged in chapter 3, specifically James's *Golden Bowl* and Eliot's *Daniel Deronda*. In the latter, the character Mirah Lapidoth clearly suffers from a trauma in relation to her father and his abuses. Whether or not Maggie Verver does so as well with regard to her father, Adam Verver, is a possibility not to be ruled out. Robert Pippin comments insightfully on this issue in the general context of Henry James's fiction and psychological-moral concerns: "Some element of the basic Jamesean human drama (especially in its specifically modern framework) makes self-exposure, the risks of love or even moral acknowledgment, difficult, potentially painful, even frightening. For example, when the tyrannical father is added to the mix (when the triangle is 'squared' as in *Washington Square* or *The Golden Bowl*), the suggestion of some original trauma or fear as source of future resistance—that frequent hint of incest or

'unspeakable' desire as source of repression—is not negligible." See Robert Pippin, *Henry James and Modern Moral Life*, 81.

10. Alois Riegl's essay on *The Cabinet of Dr. Tulp*, referred to in the previous chapter, made this work a standard referent, theoretically and visually, for students of the history of art. Charlotte Salomon, twenty-five years younger than Walter Benjamin, grew up in a similar referential world. Berlin is the most obvious common referent, but the canons of art history figure as well.

11. In 1924 the Frankfurt Kulturbund organized a concert in honor of the sixtieth birthday of Arnold Schoenberg, and the Cologne chapter staged a performance of Paul Hindemith's children's opera *Wir bauen eine Stadt*, locating it in Palestine. See Saul Friedländer, *Nazi Germany and the Jews* (New York: Harper-Collins, 1997), 67.

12. The connections among the personality, music, and politics of Richard Strauss, the first and short-termed president of the *Reichsmusikkammer* in 1933–34, have been commented on without consensus. See my essay "Richard Strauss and the Question," in *Richard Strauss and His World*, ed. Bryan Gilliam (Princeton: Princeton Univeristy Press, 1992).

13. Friedländer, *Nazi Germany and the Jews*, 65, 66.

14. Ibid., 136–37.

15. Archive of the Akademie der Künste, Berlin.

16. Friedländer, 36–37.

17. Anneliese Landau, "Gustav Mahler: Der 'Unzeitgemässe,'" in *Almanach der Jüdischen Kulturbund* (1935?), 53–56, at 56.

18. See Friedländer, 283–84.

19. I am grateful to Barbara Hahn and Philip V. Bohlman for some of these suggestions.

20. Nanette Salomon, "The Impossibility of Charlotte Salomon in the Classroom," in *Reading Charlotte Salomon*, 212–22.

21. Peter Gradenwitz, *The Music of Israel From Biblical Times to the Present* (New York: Amadeus Press, 1996), 210–11. See also Bernd Sponheuer, "Musik im Jüdischen Kulturbund," in *Musik in der Emigration*, ed. Horst Weber (Stuttgart, 1994), 108–35.

22. Theodor Adorno, *Mahler: A Musical Physiognomy*, trans. E. Jephcott (Chicago: University of Chicago Press, 1992), 166–67.

23. I refer to *1951, No. 6 (Violet, Green, and Red)*, Catalogue no. 454 in David Anfam, *Mark Rothko: The Works on Canvas* (New Haven: Yale University Press, 1998).

24. By invoking images from Caspar David Friedrich and Mark Rothko, I am opening all sorts of problems in historical genealogy as well as teleology. Charlotte's three years at the Berlin Academy of Arts provided her with a solid foundation in art history. She did not know Rothko and Rothko did not know of her. If, on the other hand, we think of the history of art according to an externalist model of the history of style, then we slip into the artificial terms of canon building. Whether or not Charlotte Salomon can be engaged by, not to say included in, an art-historical question is an important question for the politics of the discipline, but this is not my focus here.

The bridge between Friedrich and Rothko has been made by Robert Rosenblum in *Modern Painting and the Northern Romantic Tradition: Friedrich to Rothko* (New York: Harper and Row, 1975). Rothko's connection is historical and linear, beginning with

Friedrich and continuing with discussions of Van Gogh, Munch, Hodler, Nolde, Marc, Kandinsky, and Mondrian, on the way to Rothko. For Rosenblum, the central, style-defining metaphor of this canonic trajectory is a depiction of transcendence, in keeping with such aspects of Romantic-generation Protestantism as pietism (Schleiermacher) and transcendentalism (Emerson). This stylistic and contextual insight is important. But I would distance myself from Rosenblum's presentation in two ways. First, I find that his analyses of paintings tend to ignore the experiencing subject of/in the images in favor of impersonal assertions of transcendence. This tendency is particularly marked in his discussions of Friedrich's depictions of women. The women themselves are not addressed. Second, I would suggest that an engagement of transcendence may go along with a disavowal of transcendence or of a faith in its possibility, a pessimism and/or reality principle that is key to my reading of Salomon and, indeed, Rothko. On this point my reading jibes with that of Leo Bersani and Ulysse Dutoit in their book *Arts of Impoverishment: Beckett, Rothko, Resnais* (Cambridge, Mass.: Harvard University Press, 1991). The notions of impoverishment, "blocked vision," the "immobilization of perception," and "unreadability" capture Rothko's apparently deliberate convergence of vision and image with blindness and invisibility. The consistent association of seeing with the prohibition on seeing acts as a disavowal of transcendence, while at the same time transcendence is referred to as a forbidden object of desire.

CHAPTER SIX

1. Arnaldo Momigliano, *On Pagans, Jews, and Christians* (Middletown: Wesleyan University Press, 1987), ix. I am very grateful to my new colleagues in History and Judaic Studies at Brown University for their extremely generous comments on this chapter, in particular Deborah Cohen, David Jacobson, David Kertzer, Maud Mandel, Kenneth Sacks, and Michael Satlow.

2. Karl Christ, "Arnaldo Momigliano and the History of Historiography," *History and Theory*, Beiheft 30 (1991), "The Presence of the Historian: Essays in Memory of Arnaldo Momigliano," ed. M. P. Steinberg, 5–12, at 5.

3. "Arnaldo Dante Momigliano, 1908–1987," bearing only the name of the University of Chicago, and containing an unsigned introductory note by Edward Shils; the texts of three eulogies delivered at the memorial service on October 22, 1987 by Peter Brown, James Whitman, and Shils; a comprehensive bibliography of Momigliano's published work between 1928 and 1987, consisting of 724 entries.

4. Arnaldo Momigliano, *The Classical Foundations of Modern Historiography* (Berkeley and Los Angeles: University of California Press, 1990), viii.

5. Ibid., 54.

6. Kenneth Sacks, personal communication, May 8, 2006.

7. Arnaldo Momigliano, *Alien Wisdom: The Limits of Hellenization* (Cambridge: Cambridge University Press, 1975), 12.

8. See Carlo Ginzburg, "Momigliano and De Martino," *History and Theory* 30, no. 4:46.

9. Karl Christ, "Arnaldo Momigliano and the History of Historiography," *History and Theory* 30, no. 4:8.

10. Ibid, 7.

11. Arnaldo Momigliano, "The Rhetoric of History and the History of Rhetoric: On Hayden White's Tropes," *Comparative Criticism: A Yearbook*, vol. 3, ed. E. S. Shafer (Cambridge: Cambridge University Press, 1981), 259–68, at 263–64. The "other" research of the quotation's opening line refers to non-archaic Roman history.

12. Momigliano, *Alien Wisdom*, 2, 10, 1–2.

13. Ibid., 10.

14. Ibid., 6.

15. Ibid., 11.

16. Ibid., 16–17, 38, 21.

17. Ibid., 30.

18. Ibid., 36.

19. Ibid., 40. Momigliano refers to Peretti's *La Sibilla Babilonese* (1943).

20. Arnaldo Momigliano, *Filippo Il Macedone: Saggio sulla storia greca del IV secolo a.C.* (Firenze: Felice Le Monnier, 1934); 2d ed., with a new preface (Milano: Guerini e Associati, 1987).

21. Momigliano, *L'opera dell'Imperatore Claudio* (Firenze: Vallecchi Editore, 1932). Translated by W. D. Hogarth as *Claudius: The Emperor and his Achievement* (Cambridge: Heffer, 1961).

22. "Tanto più ci pare di vista da cui crediamo debbe essere studiato—il quale si distacca forse da quello dei nostri predecessori, Rostovtzeff compreso—ci permetterà di scendere nella viva coscienza dell'imperatore e di cogliere nelle sue stesse contraddizioni il faticoso processo per cui lo spirito di Roma repubblicana, vagheggiato e perseguito in apparenza, si dissolve nella costituzione monarchica e cosmopolitica a cui l'Impero tende." *L'opera dell'Imperatore Claudio*, 9.

23. In a speech of November 1919, Filippo Tommaso Marinetti defined Futurism as a doctrine of blood, race, and cosmopolitanism: "Futurism carries within it a moral foundation more cosmopolitan than nationalist, despite its nationalist appeal, its calls to the Italian race, its willful amorality, and remains difficult to categorize within strict and coherent racist parameters of the classical type." Quoted in Renzo De Felice, *The Jews in Fascist Italy*, trans. R. Miller (New York: Enigma Books, 2001), 24. For a discussion of cosmopolitanism *(Weltbürgertum)* in its German discussions in and after Kant, see my chapter "Nationalist Cosmopolitanism," in *Austria as Theater and Ideology: The Meaning of the Salzburg Festival* (Ithaca: Cornell University Press, 2000).

24. *L'opera dell'Imperatore Claudio*, 83.

25. Ibid., 55.

26. Ibid., 59.

27. Ibid., 61. "Gli Ebrei erano una religione e un popolo; e Claudio, coerente alla sua politica favorevole ai provinciali, voleva rimanere in pace con il secondo, ma reprimere l'attivo proselitismo che la prima veniva facendo, alimentato ormai anche dai nuovi fermenti della predicasione cristiana, ancore indistinta dalla sinagoga."

28. Ibid., 65. The sources are contradictory on this matter, as Momigliano recounts. Suetonius stresses the expulsions of the Jews from Claudius's Rome.

29. J. G. Droyen, *Geschichte Alexanders des Grossen* (Leipzig, 1931). Momigliano, *Filippo Il Macedone* (1934), xi: "Quando il Droysen, cent'anni or sono, nel 1833, pub-

blicava la sua *Storia di Alessandro Magno*, le correnti panelleniche del pensiero del IV secolo a. C. erano trascurate. Il Droysen, nello 'scoprire' che Filippo de Macedonia non concluse la storia greca, ma distrusse l'autonomia delle singole città per effettuare l'unità dell'Ellade e riunire in un fascio solo le forze logorantisi nelle contese fraterne, non partiva dalle aspirazioni dei Greci, dalla loro volontà, cioè, di riunirsi in uno Stato solo, ma, come è noto, era guidato dalle esigenze di trovare una mediazione tra Classicismo e Cristianesimo nel mondo ellenistico."

30. Momigliano, *Filippo Il Macedone*, xv–xvi: ". . . la storia successiva in antitesi al particularismo greco è venuta creando non già in senso nazionale, ma in senso cosmopolitico. Scopo del nostro lavoro sarà appunto in definitiva di dimostrare che è già in Filippo chiaramente la base dello Stato supernazionale di Alessandro."

31. Ibid., 135, 183.

32. Ibid., 138, 139.

33. Ibid., 199.

34. Archival document ACS SPD CR B.1 F.2 SF, Gentile Giovanni, courtesy of Federico Finchelstein.

35. Momigliano, Review of Meir Michaelis, *Mussolini and the Jews: German Italian Relations and the Jewish Question in Italy* (Oxford, 1978), in the *Journal of Modern History* 52 (1980): 282–84.

36. Christ, "Arnaldo Momigliano and the History of Historiography," 8.

37. Ibid., 5–6.

38. Momigliano, *Filippo Il Macedone* (1987): "Questo è un libro chiaramente dettato dalla situazione politico-culturale degli anni 1929–1934, anni in cui fu pensato e composto e tanto più significativi per un Ebreo come me, che già allora era molto preoccupato per le sue libertà non solo politiche ma religiose" (n.p.).

39. Aldo Ferrabino, *La dissoluzione della libertà nella Grecia antica* (Padova, 1929).

40. G. Turi, *Giovanni Gentile: Una biografia* (Firenze: Guinti, 1995), 426.

41. See Michaelis, *Mussolini and the Jews*, 67–70 and De Felice, *The Jews in Fascist Italy*, 609–21. Cited in Alexander Stille, *Benevolence and Betrayal: Five Italian Jewish Families Under Fascism* (New York: Summit Books, 1991), 354.

42. De Felice provides the official census figure of 47,252 for 1938 but affirms the unreliability of such information. The census did not account for Italian Jews abroad, for non-Italian Jews in Italy, or for the various ways Jews might or might not identify themselves. Thus in 1938 the Fascists used divergent aggregate figures, occasionally claiming a number as high as 180,000 (De Felice, *The Jews in Fascist Italy*, 2). In David Kertzer's summary: "No serious scholar has ever put the number much higher than 50,000 for 1938 and [the correct estimate] was more likely 40,000 (personal communication, April 18, 2006).

43. Stille, *Benevolence and Betrayal*, 44, 21.

44. Ibid., 73.

45. See the issue of *Quaderni di storia*, 2001; Simonetta Fiori, "Scoperta una lettera a Bottai di Momigliano," *La Repubblica*, March 22, 2001, p. 26; Alexander Stille, "Il Caso Momigliano: Attenti a come si parla di storia," *La Repubbblica*, April 5, 2001, pp. 26–27.

46. See Nicholas Capaldi, *John Stuart Mill: A Biography* (Cambridge: Cambridge University Press, 2004), 306.

47. Momigliano, "George Grote and the Study of Greek History," cited by Christ, "Arnaldo Momigliano and the History of Historiography," 8.

48. Emilio Gabba, "Arnaldo Momigliano: Pace e Libertà nel Mondo Antico," *Rivista Storica Italiana* 111, no. 1 (1999): 146–54.

49. Ibid., 150: ". . . appariva implicita la valorizzazione del suo interiorizzarsi come libertà morale."

50. Carl E. Schorske, *Fin-de-siècle Vienna: Politics and Culture* (New York: Alfred A. Knopf, 1980), xviii–xxii.

51. G. W. Bowersock, "Momigliano's Quest for the Person," *History and Theory* 30, no. 4 (1991): 27–36, at 36.

52. To cite a series of examples from the graduate program in which I was involved for many years, a colleague whose focus was the history of the French *ancien régime* made his career in the history of the material and symbolic economies of bread; in the past decade he has supervised a dissertation on meat, one on corsets, and one on hair. One task of these projects has been for its practitioners to distance themselves from antiquarianism but not to do so too decisively, in the end not to protest too much, lest the symbolic investment and hence the dispensability of their symbolic objects of analysis threaten to render their macro-analyses virtually interchangeable.

53. Momigliano, "A Piedmontese View of the History of Ideas," *Essays in Ancient and Modern Historiography* (Middletown, Conn.: Wesleyan University Press, 1975), 5.

54. Momigliano, "Historicism Revisited," *Essays in Ancient and Modern Historiography*, 371. Momigliano cites the work of Hans Ulrich Wehler and Bruce Mazlish.

55. Momigliano, "Reconsidering Croce," *Essays in Ancient and Modern Historiography*, 350.

56. Ibid., 356, 357

57. The relevant essays were collected in *Pagine ebraiche* (1987), translated as *Essays on Ancient and Modern Judaism* (1994), cited above.

58. Momigliano, "Gershom Scholem's Autobiography," *Essays on Ancient and Modern Judaism*, 191.

59. Ibid., 195.

60. Momigliano, "Walter Benjamin," in ibid., 201.

61. Karl Christ, "Arnaldo Momigliano and the History of Historiography," 5

62. Hannah Arendt, "Truth and Politics, "*Between Past and Future* (New York: Penguin Books, 1968), 238.

63. Arnaldo Momigliano, "Vico's *Scienza Nuova:* Roman 'Bestioni' and Roman 'Eroi,'" *History and Theory* 5:1 (1966): 3–23; reprinted in Momigliano, *Essays in Ancient and Modern Historiography* (Middletown: Wesleyan University Press, 1977), 253–76.

64. See Donald R. Kelley, "Mythistory in the Age of Ranke," in G. Iggers and J. Powell, eds., *Leopold von Ranke and the Shaping of the Historical Discipline* (Syracuse: Syracuse University Press, 1990), 3–20, as well as Kelley's chapter "Mythistory" in his *Faces of History: Historical Inquiry from Herodotus to Herder* (New Haven: Yale University Press, 1998); see also Joseph Mali, *Mythistory: The Making of a Modern Historiography* (Chicago: University of Chicago Press, 2003), a study that attempts, both descriptively and normatively, to graft this Vichian paradigm onto a tradition of historiographic modernism which includes Burckhardt, Warburg, Benjamin, and Kantorowicz.

65. Momigliano, "How Roman Emperors Became Gods," *American Scholar* 55 (Spring 1986); reprinted in the *Ottavio Contributo alla Storia degli Studi Classici e del Mondo Antico* (Rome, 1987), 297; also in *On Pagans, Jews, and Christians*, 92.

CHAPTER SEVEN

1. Peter Weiser, *Wien Stark Bewölkt: Ein humorvoller Wetterbericht der letzten fünfzig Jahre* (Munich: Molden Verlag, 1979). Weiser is also the German translator of Leonard Bernstein's prose works, including his Charles Eliot Norton Lectures *The Unanswered Question* (*Musik: Die offene Frage* [1983]).

2. The phrase gained currency by way of Hugo Bettauer's novel *Die Stadt Ohne Juden: Ein Roman von Übermorgen*, published in 1922 and set in post-1918 Vienna.

3. Marcel Prawy, *Marcel Prawy erzählt aus seinem Leben* (Munich: Wilhelm Heyne Verlag, 2000), 53.

4. See Krips's memoir, *Ohne Liebe kann man keine Musik machen* (Wien: Böhlau, 1994).

5. Prawy, 131.

6. Ibid., 316.

7. Humphrey Burton, *Leonard Bernstein* (New York: Doubleday, 1994), chap. 32, pp. 352–62.

8. Ibid., 353.

9. Ibid.

10. Letter from Leonard Bernstein to Helen Coates, The Leonard Bernstein Collection, The Library of Congress, Washington, D.C. N.B.: Correspondence written by Leonard Bernstein used by permission from Paul Epstein, Executor of the Estate of Leonard Bernstein, Proskauer, Rose LLP, 1585 Broadway, New York, NY 10036.

11. Cited in Joan Peyser, *Bernstein: A Biography* (New York: William Morrow, 1987), 370.

12. Burton, *Leonard Bernstein*, 354.

13. Ibid.

14. Otto Strasser, *Und dafür wird man noch bezahlt: Mein Leben mit den Wiener Philarmonikern* (Vienna: Paul Neff Verlag, 1974). I am grateful to Werner Hanak for this reference.

15. Gerhard Scheit and Wilhelm Svoboda, *Das Feindbild Gustav Mahler: Zur antisemitischen Abwehr der Moderne in Österreich* (Wien: Sonderzahl, 2002).

16. Ibid., 258.

17. Michael Freedland, *Leonard Bernstein* (London: Harrap, 1987). Freedland does not always present his evidence reliably. In his account of Bernstein's first encounter with the Vienna Philharmonic members, he offers an account similar to Burton's and indeed cites Bernstein's BBC-TV interview with Burton. But he adds: "[Bernstein] could detect murmuring in the orchestra—they were too disciplined to behave like Israelis and make their concert hall resemble a market-place" (211). The source of the simile—of clear importance to the story and its resonance—is not named.

18. Weiser, *Wien Stark Bewölkt*; recounted in Burton, 355.

19. See Prawy, 148.

20. Burton, 403.

21. Cited in Burton, 407.

22. See Nietzsche, *Jenseits von Gut und Böse,* aphorism 256.

23. Prawy, 247.

24. Burton ignores it entirely. Joan Peyser misleads with the statement: "Important secular organizations registered disapproval [of the work]. The Vienna State Opera, which had scheduled *Mass* for production, canceled its plans" (421).

25. Prawy, 192. For a very respectful account of *Mass*'s ecumenical hybridity, see Alexandra Scheibler, *'Ich glaube an den Menschen': Leonard Bernsteins Religiöse Haltung im Spiegel seiner Werke* (Hildesheim: Georg Olms Verlag, 2001), 195–236 and *passim.*

26. *High Fidelity Magazine,* February 1972, p. 68; cited by Scheibler, 229, 230, 232.

CHAPTER EIGHT

1. The reference here is to Benjamin's early essay "On Language as Such and the Language of Man" as well as his better-known essay "The Task of the Translator." See Benjamin, *Illuminations,* trans. H. Zohn (New York: Harcourt Brace Jovanovitch, 1968), 69–82.

2. Daniel Libeskind, "Trauma," in Shelly Hornstein and Florence Jakobowitz, eds., *Image and Remembrance: Representation and the Holocaust* (Bloomington: University of Indiana Press, 2003), 43–58, at 43. The assumption of the validity and clarity of the term "posthistorical" is itself problematic, as will be discussed below.

3. See James Young, "Memory and the End of the Monument," in Hornstein and Jakobowitz, *Image and Remembrance,* 61–78. Hoheisel's proposal left apparently unaddressed the ramifications of the act of violence that such an act of destruction—whether undertaken literally or not—would invoke or repeat. In subsequent years, this issue moved to the center of the Berlin and German debate about the possible "restoration" of the Berliner Schloss on the site of the Palast der Republik of the former German Democratic Republic. This debate centered not only on the desirability of a neo-neo-baroque replica of the palace, but on the ramifications of another act of destruction in the city center. The Palace of the Republic was built on the site of the palace that had been razed by the GDR; those who would raze the current structure argue for the symbolic razing of a remnant of the GDR itself. Those in opposition cite the questionable sanctioning of the act itself as well as the obliteration of the one public building whose associations are happy ones for the citizens of the former GDR, as this was the place where weddings and other important personal milestones were celebrated. On the politics of the Berliner Schloss and its reconstruction, see Svetlana Boym, *The Future of Nostalgia* (New York: Basic Books, 2001), 173–218.

4. I am deploying the concept of kitsch as theorized by Hermann Broch. "Not for nothing," he writes, "was the word *kitsch* coined in Munich" in the mid-nineteenth-century cultural context of "the humorless comic rag" *Die Fliegenden Blätter.* He defines *kitsch* as "the confusion of the ethical with the aesthetic, and therein lies its relation to the radically evil." At stake are false claims about the world which appear to be false through aesthetic errors but are false as ethical positions or claims. See Broch, *Hugo von Hofmannsthal and his Time: The European Imagination, 1860–1920* (Chicago: University of Chicago Press, 1984), 60, 170. In the context of Nazism and its representations

see Saul Friedländer, *Reflections of Nazism: An Essay on Kitsch and Death* (New York: Harper and Row, 1984).

5. This dichotomy became especially sensitive during the *Historikerstreit* of the 1980s as Nicolas Berg analyzes in *Der Holocaust und die westdeutschen Historiker: Erforschung und Erinnerung* (Göttingen: Wallstein Verlag, 2003). The key discussion of the memory/history split within Jewish thinking remains Yosef Hayim Yerushalmi, *Zakhor: Jewish History and Jewish Memory* (Seattle: University of Washington Press, [1982] 1996).

6. This sequence is duplicated in the museum publication that serves as a de facto catalogue of the permanent exhibition: *Stories of an Exhibition: Two Millennia of German Jewish History* (Berlin: Stiftung Jüdisches Museum Berlin, 2001). The publication's acknowledgment page states that "a scholarly catalogue is in preparation."

7. Amos Elon, "A German Requiem: Two Millennia of German Jewish History," *New York Review of Books*, November 15, 2001, pp. 40–43, at 43.

8. Sander Gilman and Jack Zipes, eds., *The Yale Companion to Jewish Writing and Thought in German Culture, 1096–1996* (New Haven: Yale University Press, 1997).

9. Michael A. Meyer, ed., *German Jewish History in Modern Times* (New York: Columbia University Press, 1996–98).

10. Paul Mendes-Flohr, *German Jews: A Dual Identity* (New Haven: Yale University Press, 1999).

11. Amos Elon, *The Pity of It All: A History of Jews in Germany 1743–1933* (New York: Metropolitan Books, 2002).

12. Ibid., 1, 403.

13. Michael Brenner, *The Renaissance of Jewish Culture in Weimar Germany* (New Haven: Yale University Press, 1996). Brenner is careful to point out that "[w]hat might have appeared as authenticity was in fact a modern innovation" (52). He invokes "modern composers" and writes: "The term *authenticity* represented for them the creation of art products that would be received not as modern inventions but as modern interpretations of long-established 'genuine' religious or fold traditions" (154). Brenner is consistently careful to cite exceptions to such formulations; here he cautions: "Any attempt to define the creativity of Max Liebermann and Kurt Weill as 'Jewish art' or 'Jewish music,' for example, would do them injustice." But the problem, I would suggest, is less the allowance for exceptions than the awkwardness of the authenticity model itself. Recent work on Jewish and non-Jewish composers alike—Bartok comes most explicitly to mind—has called into question precisely the desire for folk-music authenticity that had been the founding assumption of earlier scholarly as well as popular reception. See my chapter "The Voice of the People at the Moment of the Nation" in *Listening to Reason: Culture, Subjectivity, and Nineteenth-Century Music* (Princeton: Princeton University Press, 2004).

14. See Elon, *The Pity of It All*, 9–10.

15. Mordechai Breuer, "The Early Modern Period," in Michael Meyer, ed., *German Jewish History in Modern Times* (New York: Columbia University Press, 1996), 1:115–16.

16. Brenner, *Renaissance of Jewish Culture in Weimar Germany*, 131.

17. Berlin's new Film Museum at Potsdamer Platz addresses this issue by juxtaposing two radically different cinematic treatments of the Jud Süß story. The final moments

of the Nazi film, culminating in Jud Süß's hanging to the cheers of the crowds (to be doubled, the film presumably intends, by the film audiences) is juxtaposed against the conclusion of the British and émigré film, also from 1934, which focuses on its protagonist's final moments of lament and integrity, and which does not allow its camera to witness his death.

18. W. Michael Blumenthal, *The Invisible Wall: Germans and Jews, A Personal Exploration* (Washington, D.C.: Counterpoint, 1998). In German, with an interesting alteration in the subtitle, as *Die unsichtbare Mauer: Die dreihundertjährige Geschichte einer deutsch-jüdischen Familie* (Munich: Hanser Verlag, 1999).

19. David Sorkin, "The Émigré Synthesis: *German Jewish History in Modern Times*," in *Central European History* 34, no. 4: 531–59.

20. George Mosse, *German Jews Beyond Judaism* (Bloomington: Indiana University Press, 1985).

21. Elon, *The Pity of It All*, 5.

22. See the debate in *New German Critique* 77 (Spring/Summer 1999).

23. Sigmund Freud, *Beyond the Pleasure Principle*, trans. J. Strachey (New York: W. W. Norton, 1961), 18–19.

24. Saul Friedländer, *When Memory Comes*, trans. H. Lane (Noonday Press, 1991).

25. Sigmund Freud, *Leonardo da Vinci and a Memory of His Childhood*, trans. A. Tyson (New York: W. W. Norton, 1961), 33.

26. Ibid., 34.

27. This move should not, in my view, be conflated with the tendency to characterize modernity in general as traumatic. This latter inclination often results from the desire to participate in trauma at little cost, a symptom of the difficulty of grounding contemporary selfhood.

28. Charles Maier, "A Surfeit of Memory?," *History and Memory* 5, no. 2 (1993) and Kerwin Lee Klein, "On the Emergence of *Memory* in Historical Discourse," *Representations* 69 (Winter 2000).

29. Maier, 150. This is, I think, a reliable summary of the strong critical points Maier makes; his argument's pitfalls are numerous but less relevant to my concerns here. These include a confused attack on history after the linguistic turn (my summary), an uncritical call for the return of causal analysis, alleged to have been "replaced by representation" (141).

30. Klein, 135. The "whatever"—marking a node of ressentiment and carelessness—seems the rhetorical operative here.

31. I would agree with Dominick LaCapra's assessment that Maier's indictment of memory does not impugn the integrity of memory-work in the Freudian sense. I am more sympathetic than LaCapra to Maier's portrayal of the memory discourse as a symptom, although I see ways, as indicated above, in which Maier gets caught in his own symptomatology. See LaCapra, "History and Memory: In the Shadow of the Holocaust," chap. 1 of *History and Memory After Auschwitz* (Ithaca, N.Y.: Cornell University Press, 1998), 15–16.

32. Lewis A. Coser, Introduction to Maurice Halbwachs, *On Collective Memory*, trans. Lewis A. Coser (Chicago: University of Chicago Press, 1992), 22.

33. Pierre Nora, "Between Memory and History: *Les lieux de mémoire*," *Representations* 26 (Spring 1989): 7–25, at 8.

34. Ibid., 11.

35. See Hans-Ulrich Wehler, *Preussen ist wieder chic. . . : Politik und Polemik* (Frankfurt: Suhrkamp, 1983).

36. Elisabeth Noelle-Neumann, public lecture, University of Chicago, October 1985. In May 1985, Chancellor Helmut Kohl invited President Ronald Reagan to honor German war dead in the cemetery at Bitburg, to compensate for the commemoration of the fortieth anniversary of the D-Day invasion, held the previous year, to which Kohl had not been invited. On the disclosure that the Bitburg cemetery contained graves of members of the Waffen-SS, Reagan was urged to cancel the visit but in the end went through with it. See the anthology *Bitburg in Moral and Political Perspective*, ed. Geoffrey Hartmann (Bloomington: Indiana University Press, 1986).

37. Geoffrey Winthrop-Young has recently suggested that Jan Assmann's trope of "cultural memory" can be described as "an attempt to extend some of the dynamics of Halbwachs's collective memory across longer stretches of historical time." This may be an accurate description of Assmann's intentions, but it is highly problematic as a comment on Halbwachs's, as my reference above to Halbwachs would argue. See Geoffrey Winthrop-Young, "Memories of the Nile: Jan Assmann, Egyptian Media, and German Theory," unpublished paper presented to the German Studies Colloquium, Cornell University, September 2001.

38. The scholars whom Assmann names are Joachim Spiegel, Eberhard Otto, Hellmut Brunner, Siegfried Morenz, and Walther Wolf. Jan Assmann, *Moses the Egyptian:The Memory of Egypt in Western Monotheism* (Cambridge: Harvard University Press, 1997), 22. The phrase "catastrophic events of Word War II" is vague enough to evoke discomfort. Does it imply events in which Germans were aggressors, as does the subsequent phrase invoking German fascism, or does it imply German victimhood? This is not to say that both did not exist, but rather that the distinction between them needs to be drawn explicitly.

39. Assmann, *Moses the Egyptian*, 16, 21, 134, 135. See also Assmann, *Religion und kulturelles Gedächtnis* (Munich: C. H. Beck, 2000), 219. Notably, Assmann codes *The Magic Flute*'s Egyptomania as German rather as Masonic or "masonic-international."

40. Assmann, *Moses the Egyptian*, 6.

41. Ibid., 25.

42. Let me provide an example, or rather an anecdote, to speak to the problem of identifying the Jews as the people of memory. Early in 1993, the Kulturwissenschaftliches Institut in Essen announced a series of conferences on the theme of memory. The institute's director, Lutz Niethammer, had been meeting in seminar for over a year in which fin-de-siècle sciences of memory had been the theme. After collective investigations of the work of Bergson, Halbwachs, Proust, Freud, Warburg, and Benjamin, the participants had noticed that all six of these innovators in the sciences of memory were Jews. The "Essen Six," as I have come to refer to Bergson, Halbwachs, Proust, Freud, Warburg, and Benjamin, are certainly powerful thinkers about memory. But the Essen scholars—as they came to recognize—had made the same mistaken assumption that has continued

to impair portraits of fin-de-siècle Austria: namely, the derivation of critical modernism from an essential Jewish "identity." A small workshop was convened with the purpose of planning a large-scale conference on "Judaism and Modern Memory." Jan Assmann was in attendance, as was I.

In Essen, the political and historical fallout proved interesting. Several weeks before the initial planning workshop, a list of participants was circulated, including such names as Yerushalmi and Friedländer. To the surprise of most, the name of Hans Robert Jauss was also on the list. Jauss's wartime career in the Waffen-SS had recently been exposed in the American press, and he had had a long correspondence with Gabriel Motzkin, also a participant at Essen, on the question of a possible public discussion of his wartime career, which Motzkin encouraged and Jauss declined.

The meeting was organized into discussions of the six fin-de-siècle figures, and each discussion was opened by a short position piece from one of the participants. Jauss spoke on Proust. In a short presentation, he argued that the modernist autobiographer at work in the *Recherche* was a voice of continual self-renewal, that self-reinvention was in fact the hallmark of modernist narrative. The ironies of this performance were of overwhelming perversity. Was Jauss in fact behaving as transparently as he let on; was he taking the mantle of Proust and self-reinvention to suggest a reading of his own professional trajectory as Franco- and Judeophile as a self-reinvention following his service in the Waffen-SS and his participation in the massacre at Oradour?

Although the agitated discussion of the Jauss performance in the wings and coffee breaks of the workshop proceedings would suggest as much, I am unsure what effect it had on the sense of the meeting as a whole. Without explicit reference to it but with increased nervousness no doubt, several of us argued that the Jews had no claim on memory, and that the place of memory in the construction of modern subjectivity was not a Jewish affair. By the meeting's end, the plans for the large-scale conference were scrapped. The endeavor's fatal problem lay in the ideology of the construction of memory present in the entire project. That ideology involves first the identification of memory as something Jewish, and then the embrace of memory as an embrace of a discourse of stratetic, cleansing self-Judaification.

Here we have an other guise of the ideology of commemoration—commemoration of and identification with a minority or victim rather than a majority or victor. Rather than offer incorporation into the grand narrative—the logic of the *lieu de mémoire*—the ideological tendency here is to validate that grand narrative through a strategic identification with a subaltern component. Such are the potential ideological stakes of Black History Month in the United States, of Germans honoring Jews after 1945, indeed of Israelis after 1948 honoring European Jews before 1948.

43. Matt Matsuda, *The Memory of the Modern* (New York: Oxford University Press, 1996), 15.

44. Yosef Yerushalmi, *Zakhor: Jewish History and Jewish Memory*, xi.

45. Eric L. Santner, *On the Psychotheology of Everyday Life: Reflections on Freud and Rosenzweig* (Chicago: University of Chicago Press, 2001), and Peter Eli Gordon, *Rosenzweig and Heidegger: Between Judaism and German Philosophy* (Berkeley and Los Angeles: University of California Press, 2003).

46. See for example Žižek's *The Fragile Absolute—or, Why Is the Christian Legacy*

Worth Fighting For? (London: Verso, 2000) and *The Puppet and the Dwarf: The Perverse Core of Christianity* (Cambridge: MIT Press, 2003).

47. Santner, *On the Psychotheology of Everyday Life,* 104. See p. 68 for the Gebot/Gesetz distinction and the "commandment to love."

48. Gordon, *Rosenzweig and Heidegger,* xxviii.

49. Ibid., 123, 125, 131.

50. Ibid., 149.

51. Ibid., 184.

52. See for example Cavell, *A Pitch of Philosophy* (Cambridge: Harvard University Press, 1994). Here it is important to keep distinct the ordinary in the political inflections advanced by Emerson, Wittgenstein, and Cavell and the "everyday" as practiced in the kind of "history of everyday life" *(Alltagsgeschichte)* which I take issue with above. My critical point above is in fact that the idealization of the everyday can in fact turn into the very political opposite of the valorization of the ordinary, namely the valorization of an aestheticized or otherwise sanitized world made that way through exclusion or other violence.

53. Gordon, *Rosenzweig and Heidegger,* 212, 213. Gordon addresses Rosenzweig's concept of blood-community in a legitimizing and indeed even defensive tone. He then stands down somewhat with the comment that the concept's apparent justification of "an extreme sort of Jewish chauvinism" causes a "worry [that] is perhaps more accurate than some previous interpreters have cared to admit" (214).

54. Gershom Scholem, "Franz Rosenzeig and His Book *The Star of Redemption,*" in Paul Mendes-Flohr, ed., *The Philosophy of Franz Rosenzweig* (Hanover, N.H.: University Press of New England, 1988), 40–41.

55. Friedrich Meinecke, "Franz Rosenzweig—Nachruf," *Historische Zeitschrift* 142, no. 1 (1930): 219–20, cited in Gordon, 119.

56. Gordon, 12. For an excellent account of Rosenzweig scholarship, see also Gordon's essay, "Rosenzweig Redux: The Reception of German-Jewish Thought," *Jewish Social Studies* 8, no. 1 (Fall 2001): 1–57. Following Scholem's prediction, Gordon suggests that "Time has brought a certain disenchantment to the study of modern Jewish thought." Santner's study, which Gordon acknowledges but which appeared too late for him to address, might have proved an incentive for him to revise this view. See also Leora Batnitzky's study *Idolatry and Representation: The Philosophy of Franz Rosenzweig Reconsidered* (Princeton: Princeton University Press, 2000). As Batniztky strongly implies on her first page references to Marx and Adorno, the term "idolatry" approximates "ideology" in her usage as a mode of false consciousness within a sacred or sacralizing discourse. Notwithstanding the contours of such sacred discourse, Batnizky comes closest to interpreting Rosenzweig as a thinker of political modernity, even secular modernity. In this context, some "idolatries" become politically necessary, chief among these being Zionism, which "makes possible the physical reality of Jewish existence" (190, 195). With this argument, Batnitzky defends Rosenzweig from Gillian Rose's accusation that he "elevate[s] Judaism as 'life' beyond the political history of 'the world'" (189; Rose, *Judaism and Modernity* [Oxford: Blackwell, 1993]).

57. Herbert Muschamp, "Balancing Reason and Emotion in Twin Towers Void," *The New York Times,* February 6, 2003, E1 and E5.

58. Michael Naumann, "Hygiene am Bau: Schuldig für immer? Degussa und das Berliner Holocaust-Mahnmal," *Die Zeit*, October 30, 2003, 1. The decision was reversed by the executive committee of the monument site, with the codicile that account of the controversy would be included in the site's eventual museology.

59. For example, in an interview with Lea Rosh, vice president of the monument commission, in the *Berliner Morgenpost*, November 11, 2003.

60. See most recently the discussion in Daniel Barenboim and Edward W. Said, *Parallels and Paradoxes: Explorations in Music and Society* (New York: Vintage Books, 2004).

61. The Grunewald memorial was commissioned by the German Railroad (Deutsche Bahn) following the relinking of the two systems in 1990. The architects who won the design competition are Hirsch, Lorch, and Wandel of Saarbrücken and Frankfurt am Main.

62. See Caroline Wiedmer, "Designing Memories: Three Berlin Memorials," in *Alphabet City* 4–5 (Toronto, 1995): 6–12, and also Wiedmer, *The Claims of Memory* (Ithaca: Cornell University Press, 1999). The artists also have a website: http://www.stih-schnock.de.

63. Wilhelm Worringer, *Abstraktion und Einfühlung: Ein Beitrag zur Stilpsychologie* (Munich: Piper Verlag, 1908).

64. It would be worth comparing Eisenman's Memorial and its invocations to the series of eight sculptures by Richard Serra unveiled as a permanent exhibition of the Guggenheim Museum, Bilbao, in June 2005. Serra's forms are oversized brown steel curvatures and coils, fully abstract in their presentation, carrying no historic or other referent, but at the same time functionally comparable to Eisenman's steles in their envelopment of the spectator and their apparent encouragement of experiences as well as rhetorics of memory. For one such reading, see Michael Kimmelman's review in *The New York Times*, June 7, 2005, E1 and E6.

65. Arno Widmann, "Schön wär's," *Berliner Zeitung*, May 11, 2005.

66. *Deutsche Welle*, broadcast of May 30, 2005 (Ithaca, New York).

AFTERWORD

1. Thomas Crow, *The Intelligence of Art* (Chapel Hill: University of North Carolina Press, 1999).

2. See Roberta Frank, "Wagner's *Ring*, North-by-Northwest," *University of Toronto Quarterly* 74, no. 2 (Spring 2005): 671–76.

3. See Marc Weiner, *Richard Wagner and the Anti-Semitic Imagination* (Lincoln: University of Nebraska Press, 1995).

4. Theodor Adorno, *Mahler: A Musical Physiognomy*, trans. E. Jephcott (Chicago: University of Chicago Press, 1992), 7, 149, 15.

5. Daniel Barenboim, "In Memoriam: Edward Said (1936–2003)," in Daniel Barenboim and Edward W. Said, *Parallels and Paradoxes: Explorations in Music and Society* (New York: Vintage Books, 2004), x.

INDEX

Page numbers in italics refer to figures.